AOTEAROA NEW ZEALAND & THE PANDEMIC

A VEHICLE FOR REIMAGINING OUR WORKING LIVES, AND REFLECTING ON OUR LIFESTYLES

PHILIP DEWE

Published by Philip Dewe
© Philip Dewe 2024
The moral right of the author has been asserted

Designed and typeset by Imelda Morgan
Cover illustration by Monique Johnson
Produced by Intelligent Ink Press

Printed and bound in Wellington, New Zealand by YourBooks

ISBN 978-0-473-73008-6

As always, for my wife, Linda and to our grandchildren,
if suitably skilled, they will have the opportunity to benefit
from flexibility in their working life.

Contents

Preface

This book is a history of the Covid pandemic in Aotearoa New Zealand from 2020 to 2024. But it is also a book that has, as its overriding theme, a sense of hope.

For this reason, this book is also about how the pandemic was the vehicle for change and transition that ultimately heralded the future shape of our working lives. In 2020, researchers and commentators started speaking about the lenses we are choosing as we look ahead – whether they see us clinging to the old ways and the status quo, or seeing a future of opportunities that reflect whatever we think is possible. The pandemic weaved a path that touched all the corners of society and swept in a future that was not expected to arrive as rapidly as it did. The pandemic was accompanied with animated conversations, discussions, and debate. But it is also important to recognise that change and transition have never been more achievable than they are now. The difference is that now the need for change means we have a real chance to refine the future of work.

Organisational psychology and behaviour have been a staple of my career, and I have written extensively on coping, stress, work, and ethics. I draw upon my years of experience as a professor of Organisational Behaviour, a field I've dedicated much of my academic career to, including at Birkbeck, University of London. Over the years, my research has focused on the complexities of workplace stress and how individuals and organisations interact. So as the Covid pandemic emerged, I was particularly fascinated by how it would reshape our lives and work, and what we might learn from it when it came to building a more balanced future.

Guided by the driving force of *Why do we work in the way that we do?* I have attempted to understand the debates and conversations that have occurred since the pandemic began. Broad changes have been prompted by the pandemic, waiting to shape our working lives. *How will we build our careers, as employment patterns begin to change? How might leadership and management change as it shifts away from the traditional top-down approach to one where the emphasis is on empathy, trust and social connection? Will we accept that learning will become lifelong, as we move through these transitions?* These changes will simply ripple out and raise questions about work-life balances and our lifestyles as time goes by. We will be forced to re-evaluate what we prioritise and value, what we hope for, and how we express them – and in turn, how they express us and who we want to be.

This book begins with a history of the Covid pandemic in Aotearoa New Zealand, setting the context for the debates and discussions that follow. But we don't just log the pandemic's journey in the way that a traditional diary would. Instead, by using keywords and interlinked events, we build a context that captures and expresses the nature of the pandemic's journey. In this way, we are in every sense shadowing the twists and turns of that journey. We explore the way that the pandemic's journey is accompanied by a new vocabulary – one that reflects the (emotional) ups and downs of the pandemic. It prompts us to reflect on what the 'new normal' may look like, what it is that you really value, how you may change the priorities you set, and what possibilities you hope for.

But the pandemic's journey is not just about dates. In its wake, it stirred up a diversity of opinions and views – some of which led to protests. As a result, the government was fighting a battle within a battle – Covid, and then misinformation and conspiracies. When we reflect on the pandemic, we are naturally immediately drawn to think of it as in terms of lockdowns, regulations, mandates, alert levels, trauma, anxieties, worries, uncertainties, protests, disruptions, and restrictions, and of course, death and grief. But the pandemic has many faces, and reflecting on it as containing 'uniquely instructional moments' gives us the chance to explore the opportunities ahead of us and the future person we want to be.[1] This gives us a sense of hope – the key element in building resilience. This sets the context for the chapters that follow. From here, we consider how the pandemic has rippled out and touched different parts of society. We go on to explore how we live, including how the pandemic may yet have a lasting say on the shape of our cities of the future particularly through the ideas of sustainable cities and the potential of the 15-minute city. More widely, we have also been made to reassess our preoccupation with economic growth and GDP, and how we might refine capitalism. Change was – and still is – compellingly relevant for all of us.

Life is filled with experiences that push our repertoire of thinking, feeling, and behaving. The pandemic – and associated restrictions of movement – challenged how we navigated these. The next chapter explores classical mental health strategies and specific coping strategies that fit to the events of the pandemic. These include relationship-building coping, prosocial coping, perceiving benefit coping, benefit-reminding coping and reappraisal coping, and autogenic strategies (self-starting strategies) like exercise and the healing power of walking, the significance of social connections, the power of habits and routines, the necessity of rest, the cult of busyness and downtime, and reflecting on the 'future you.' This chapter doesn't tell you what to do, but gives you a sense of what may fit with the nature of the pandemic and perhaps how you can build your resilience long-term.

Then we turn to the climate crisis, and what significant lessons that can be distilled, and learnt, from the pandemic response and that reflect and can be applied to the climate crisis. So we turn to Cyclone Gabrielle, and explore the science and the relationship between climate crisis and cyclones in terms of their frequency, and their intensity. Gabrielle ravaged provinces, cities, town, settlements, homes, pastures, highways, and livelihoods in February 2023. This chapter explores the resilience of those affected, and how communities came together in the face of the devastation. In a climate crisis, resilience takes on a broader meaning, starting with the response to individual trauma before broadening out to consider cities, communities, land, and infrastructure. The chapter then turns to what are the options and planning for the targets we set, and the immediate challenges being faced – all evidencing that we are already grappling with a climate crisis.

Finally, we acknowledge that Covid lingers, even though the regulations have gone. The science and research on Covid will likely continue, and now, when reflecting on the pandemic, it is the time to begin to think of it as a unique opportunity to reappraise our own lives, lifestyles, values, what we want, what our priorities will be. In this final chapter, we explore why the traditional way of working built around a 9-to-5 structure was simply not working for many. It was the long-felt demand for flexibility at work that was immediately exposed by the pandemic. Will this way of working prevail?

We also in this final chapter explore the 'age of untruth' and the significance of research and science to determine the truth and their role in the battle of misinformation. The chapter ends with several mainstream reflections that offer a broad context to structure readers' further thoughts.

As we reflect on the lessons of the pandemic, it's clear that we are not merely returning to old ways, but stepping into a future of possibilities. We have the chance to reshape how we work, live, and engage with the world around us. The transitions prompted by the pandemic offer a unique opportunity to embrace flexibility, foster connection, and rethink our values. By harnessing these changes, we can build a more resilient, balanced, and hopeful future. Because we are capable of so much more than we thought possible.

CHAPTER 1:

New Zealand and the Pandemic

THE BEGINNING

The early days of 2020 were to unleash a series of events that would have not only serious implications for the world's health, but also unforeseen and far-reaching consequences for the way societies work. It may come as a surprise — although perhaps not to epidemiologists — to learn how it was the trigger that quickly unfolded the sequence of events that were to follow. Across those early days "patients with a mysterious illness were reported to the World Health Organization (WHO) by Chinese authorities". [1] The alarm was raised as events gathered momentum.

By 7 January "a new type of coronavirus was identified and isolated by Chinese authorities". [2] Six days later, "China shares with the world the genetic sequence of the virus for countries to use in developing diagnostic kits." [3] In this period the WHO also set up an Incident Management Support Team (IMST) and "places the organization on an emergency footing for dealing with the outbreak". [4] By 23 January the WHO had also set up an Emergency Committee (EC) "to assess ... the outbreak". [5] By 24 January New Zealand's Ministry of Health had assembled "a team to monitor the situation". [6] A week later, the WHO's EC "advises the Director-General that the outbreak constituted a Public Health Emergency of International Concern". [7] By 11 February the WHO had named the disease "Covid-19"; short for "coronavirus disease 2019" [8] Just a month later, "deeply concerned both by the alarming levels of spread and severity, and by the levels of inaction, [the] WHO made the assessment that COVID 19 can be characterized as a pandemic". [9]

So, we were in a pandemic. New Zealand's government had already acted quickly to protect the country. On 3 February it had placed restrictions on incoming foreign nationals who had travelled from, or transited through, mainland China, with their being required to isolate for 14 days. [10] On 28 February, New Zealand reported its first case of Covid-19. [11] The next day passengers on direct flights from a number of South East Asian countries were being met at the airport by health staff to enforce the quarantining measures. [12] Measures soon moved more widely than the airports. By 15 March a number of large public events had been cancelled, cruise ships were no longer able to dock and disembark, and strict border measures had been put in place, including health assessment requirements. [13] As March progressed, for the first time in New Zealand's history, the government closed the country's borders to all but New Zealand citizens and permanent residents. Prime Minister Jacinda Ardern explained: "I recognise how extraordinary this is [but] I'm not willing to take risks here." [14]

In spite of this rapid response and the precautions taken, the number of Covid cases continued to rise, as did our emotions. It became clear that our response needed to ramp up accordingly. So, on 21 March the prime minister and the Director-General of Health Dr Ashley Bloomfield announced a system of alert levels. After explaining the four levels, they said that New Zealand had moved into threat level 2. "meaning the risk of community transmission is growing". [15] By 23 March, the total number of cases had surpassed 100 and included two cases being treated as community transmission, and health workers were urging the country to enter level 4 alert. [16] The prime minister announced that the country was moving "to alert level 3, then Level 4 in 48 hours". [17] The next day history was again being made, when the prime minister announced Level 4, the headline in *The Dominion Post* shrieking "Capital under lock and key". [18] Ardern explained: "We have a window of opportunity to stay home, break the chain of transmission, and save lives ... It's that simple." [19] The entire country was "now preparing to spend at least four weeks within the confines of their homes to prevent Covid-19 from taking hold". [20] A poll commissioned by *Stuff* showed that New Zealanders "are increasingly backing the government and its actions over the coronavirus pandemic", [21] a "sombre mood" [22] prevailing.

A CONTEXT AROUND THE DATES

Although dates are used here to give a sense of coherence to what being in a pandemic means, this chapter does not log the pandemic's journey in the way that a traditional diary would. Rather, by using keywords that capture and express the nature of the pandemic's journey, we are in every sense shadowing the twists and turns of that journey. In this way a context is given in which we can explore the peaks and troughs of the pandemic's journey, while also providing an opportunity to consider the pandemic as a vehicle for exploring how we may reimagine our working lives and reflect on the question *of why we work in the way that we do.*

Professor Julia Hobsbawm articulates this more eloquently: "The pandemic lifted the lid on a desire to work differently, or less or with more work–life balance ... [T]he pandemic brought workplaces centre-stage in the debate about the future of work ... [It is as if the pandemic] acknowledge[d] [the] changes that have been building up for decades waiting, perhaps, for this extraordinary time ... but no one anticipated ... a global pandemic, let alone prepared for it. Far from it. This made 2019 the last year of modern working life as it had been known since 1945." [23] Professor Lynda Gratton writes: "The pandemic has presented the unique opportunity to 'raise the bar' and 'really lift up' in part because it removed institutional lag, or the delay between institutions and businesses implementing the changes individuals want and need." [24]

Even if unforeseen, the pandemic's consequences were to go to the heart of our social construct: "In the early months of the pandemic, it was possible to think of Covid-19 as an essentially medical and above all *transitory* emergency. Now we can see it for what it was and remains, the trigger for fundamental and in some cases likely permanent changes to our economies, societies and patterns of work and employment ... The question of *where* and *how* we work is central to all of these challenges. Almost no one now believes that we will ever go back to the five-day-a week office life of even a few years ago." [25]

These themes reflect the core arguments that will be developed throughout this book. The book is not so much about the pandemic *per se*, but *how the pandemic is a vehicle for change and transition that ultimately heralds the future shape of our working lives.* When reading the chapters that follow, keep in mind that, while not all workers will have the opportunity to engage in hybrid working or a four-day week, the pandemic's wake will nevertheless move beyond these two "great experiments" and offer other challenges for all workers to reflect on. These are more broader changes that are awaiting to shape our working lives. These include, for example, how we will now build our careers as employment patterns begin to change. Is this the last "hurrah" for hierarchies? For leadership and management models will also change, with a shift away from the traditional top-down approach to one where the emphasis is on empathy, trust and social connection. The need to accept that learning will become lifelong is also crucial as we move through these transitions. These changes will simply ripple out and raise questions about work–life balance, our lifestyles, and what we prioritise, value and hope for. How we express these values and aspirations, and in doing so express who we are.

Let's go back to the pandemic and its journey so far. We have seen that, crucially, there was only around four weeks between the first case of Covid-19 in Aotearoa New Zealand and the nationwide lockdown being announced. The speed and spread of the virus, coupled with the speed of attendant change, have left all of us with a sense of bewilderment, anxiety and uncertainty, and with a loss of familiar routines. There are feelings of what does it mean to be in a pandemic, what is now normal and how sustainable is it? Not forgetting the feeling that we are not in control — and more crucially what can we do to regain control. Remember, for most of us this is the first time we have experienced a pandemic, and so our feelings are raw to the point where our emotions feel on fire. It is also our first experience of a lockdown, and these events have an added extraordinary significance simply because they are something "that was literally not even imaginable" weeks before, [26] and signify "the biggest peacetime intervention the government has ever made in the economy". [27] This must go some way to explain why our emotions are in turmoil. But it feels the right thing to do when Prime minister Ardern says: "It is time for each of us to step up and do our bit, and take our responsibilities seriously." [28]

THE PANDEMIC'S VOCABULARY

Another possible contributor to our worries and anxiety is the language that accompanies the pandemic. we are introduced to a whole new vocabulary, with phrases like "go hard, go early" [29] — the mantra for when the policy is elimination — "being in a bubble", "lockdowns", "physical distancing", "coughing and sneezing etiquette", "elbow nudging", "hand washing protocols", "community transmission", and a relentless focus on monitoring case numbers, along with the idea of "a new normal". [30] As the pandemic progresses other phrases will be added to this list. While many of the phrases are self-explanatory, their power over our emotions may come from the behaviours associated with them. When engaging in these behaviours, we are continually reminded that we are in a pandemic, prompting uncertainties, unease and worries. However, the phrases also deliberately carry a positive message, because they remind us to be vigilant, to keep ourselves safe, and in this way save lives.

WHAT IS A "NEW NORMAL"?

Let's take a look at the phrase "a new normal" in the Covid pandemic context. For nearly 200 years the ways we work have been built on established and customary routines, procedures, structures and traditions, which have all, to some extent, been enshrined in our vernacular as "the good old 9 to 5". But now even this is in a state of flux. Why? Because, as Williams points to in his piece in *The Economist*, the pandemic's "lasting legacy may be a better world of work, as it speeds changes that were already under way and highlights those places where further improvement is needed". [31] As Carroll writes in *The Dominion Post*, being under our alert levels "comes with the request that all businesses which can have staff work from home do so [and] ... so people [begin to] work remotely". [32] A trend that has largely been invisible up to now, hidden away in academic and management journals, emerges with the pandemic's intervention and is raised to a new level, having us asking ourselves why we work in the way that we do. It is a question that we all should be asking: *Why do we work in the way that we do?* This theme will be developed throughout the chapters that follow.

As the country goes into lockdown, organisations respond to the government's call, in the "challenging times ... helping ... [people] get comfortable with re-establishing our 'new normal' whether that be new ways of working or how we prioritise work". [33] This is the beginning of "a new normal" and the re-imagining of the way we work. All hastened by the pandemic, raising questions about the future of workplaces, the design of the centre of cities, and transport systems, leading to a re-imagining of shopping habits, and exploring new financial models for small businesses. More about that in later chapters. For now, the headline of Carroll's column captures the moment: "Today a new normal for at-home employees". [34] This is not of course emotion-free — it is challenging established routines hitherto thought unalterable, and is disturbing the work–life balance generally. Tension points will inevitably emerge when the old collides with the "new normal".

EXISTENTIAL WORRIES ABOUT HEALTH AND THE HEALTH SYSTEM

There may also be an existential component to our worries and anxieties when directed to the issues of health. Will I get the virus? What will happen to me if I do? What are the symptoms like? With the weight of a pandemic, is the health system under threat? These are just some of the universal worries and anxieties swirling. Polling by *Stuff* shows that "58 percent were worried about catching Covid-19 themselves and just 17 percent thought New Zealand's medical system was adequately prepared to deal with a 'large-scale outbreak". [35] All adding to the atmosphere that surrounds the pandemic and leading to a cumulation of anxieties, uncertainties, and worries 'to a threat no one can see or hear.' [36]

And is there something to the fear and worry about how the health system will cope? After all, the underlining reason for the lockdown is to prevent a significant outbreak of the virus, giving hospitals the space and capacity to manage the inevitable increase of highly infectious patients. Maintaining capacity and space in the health system also requires everyone in the wider community to do their bit, by keeping to the lockdown rules and other pandemic regulations, so others are not put at risk. This is just the beginning of the journey for the health system, and worries and concerns about illness and support will linger as the unpredictable path of the virus twists and turns.

THE PANDEMIC IS ABOUT FAMILIES

What "looms large in the minds" of New Zealanders is the idea of "go home, and stay at home", [37] alongside which sits the concept of essential and non-essential workers. With only supermarkets, petrol stations, pharmacies and health clinics being open, and the need to avoid infection transmission, adjustments to how we live and interact will need to be made. The whole idea of shopping will have to be re-imagined, as will buying habits and travel, all underpinned by the idea of physical distancing, with its two-metre rule and the importance of sticking to your bubble. Income support through the wage subsidy will help some to ease the financial worries arising from not being able to work.

The pandemic is also about families, and during the lockdown schools and universities will be closed and studies will be disrupted. Home teaching and online learning will present another challenge that parents, children and young adults will have to cope with. Zhong, in her article about "the young adults of 'generation Covid'", points to "the long-term effects of the disruption to their education may ... take time to show up". She adds that "younger children have also been identified as vulnerable as they lack developed coping strategies and emotional reactions", on top of the growing accumulation of all the other tensions that surround and define the pandemic. [38]

Tensions inevitably develop within families when they are all together over extended periods. So when families are also dealing with a world that is in a state of upheaval, this can only be defined as a significantly difficult time to manage the worries, anxieties and concerns that emerge. Contact between networks, friendships and extended families will be disrupted, and adjustments will be needed to maintain them through Zoom and other remote communication techniques, with again these challenges requiring re-imagining of how friendships and networks may be continued and worked.

WHY BUILD A CONTEXT AROUND THE DATES AND THE PANDEMIC

The idea of placing a context around all of the dates that describe the path of the pandemic is not to get you wondering how on earth you have managed so far. Although, of course, it may be a useful thing to do, since it can be a healing process. In situations where the future is uncertain, there is a tendency to yearn for the past in the face of insecurity. As Karen Mangia suggests, this feeling is not dissimilar to homesickness, where you "wish for the way things were". [39]

Providing a sense of the evolving context is to get you to acknowledge that the pandemic is a time of tremendous change, and with change comes transition. Another major theme that will be developed throughout the book is that the pandemic has offered us an opportunity to think of it in terms of what Jeff Schwartz describes as a "uniquely instructive moment". He argues that the pandemic is inviting us "to reimagine how we work ... and view the future as a broad set of new opportunities that will reflect whatever we think is possible". He encourages us to extend that reimagining to think about "our educational institutions [and how the focus of learning may change], how we build our careers, shape our companies [and manage them and lead them] and our communities", [40] and how we redesign our inner cities, and deal with climate change.

Another theme that will be developed in following chapters as we begin to better understand the twists and turns of the pandemic is *'What has the pandemic taught us?'* We can look to adapt the resilience we have developed in the pandemic experience to answer in a positive way the question "Are you ready to change?" Warzel and Petersen argue "the good news is that we can change, if we commit ourselves to refiguring the place of work in our lives". [41] The same sentiments are echoed by Mangia, as she makes clear "that even in the midst of global upheaval, there's still a chance to move forward". [42] But more of this later, as it is time to once again turn back to the events that define the path of the pandemic.

THE PATH OF THE PANDEMIC

The mood of the pandemic at this time (March-April 2020) is well expressed in the word lockdown. The decision to move to alert level 4 is reflected in the *Dominion Post*'s front-page headline as lockdown began its first full day (25th of March, 2020) 'Capital under lock and key.' The opening paragraph of the column sums up this mood. ... "central city shops thrust into darkness and a palpable desperation to get home to loved ones has become Wellington's new reality." [43]

The lockdowns would become partnered by the phrase "case numbers", with the focus centred on "the seven-day rolling average of cases". We would become obsessed with these phrases while waiting for the daily 1pm briefings, with our emotions rising steadily as the number of new cases rise. On 29 March, New Zealand's first Covid death was reported. By now we were accustomed to terms like "rolling average", "testing stations", and "PPE" (personal protective equipment) to keep us up-to-date with our "pandemic speak". This time and this month were simply described as the country being in a "Quiet War". [44] While people seem to have (mostly) accepted the need to stay local, questions remain about the restriction. The common one is why is lockdown so strict? We know the lockdown is to help stop the spread of Covid-19, but perhaps not everyone realises the extent of what could happen in New Zealand if these measures are not taken. So, the answer to "Why is the lockdown so strict?" is made clear: "Research suggests up to 80,000 Kiwis could die if the virus is not contained." [45]

April is a month where the "Quiet War" continues, but accompanying the feeling that the lockdown is working and freedom is on the horizon is the sad news of more deaths. April is a month that has highs and lows — not just in the number of cases, but in our emotions as well. Our days are still governed, as are our emotions, by the 1pm announcements. On 2 April we learn that the day's "89 new cases are the biggest increase in one day". [46] A week later we celebrate "those people essential to keeping New Zealand going through the Covid-19 crisis." [47] The government rolls out "a raft of distance learning tools, including TV channels, for the new school term" [48], and calls for a "tightening of New Zealand's border is needed to 'turn the tap off' on coronavirus". [49]

Easter passes, but sadly more deaths are recorded. There is a glimmer of hope emerging as the case numbers begin to bottom out and drop to a new low. This could be what prompts a "group of public health experts" to set out a case "calling for a return to near-normal life in two weeks". [50] However, the prime minister demurs, instead urging New Zealanders to "stick to efforts that were showing signs of success, warning there would be no early easing of lockdown rules". [51] The prime minister's firm ruling introduces a phrase that will become familiar as the path of the pandemic winds on. It is that decisions are made with an "abundance of caution", [52] in order to save lives. On 16 April the prime minister responds to a question "whether world leaders are sharing ideas with one another right now — we are!" This week she had a phone call from the Prime Minister of Denmark, indicating "we may be far away but we're all in the same fight against Covid". [53]

That same day, a Thursday, the prime minister outlines what alert level 3 will look like, "should she and her Cabinet decide next Monday that's what they wish to move to when the initial lockdown period expires on Wednesday evening". [54] Monday, 20 April, arrives and *The Dominion Post* captures the significance of the moment with its front-page headline: "Ardern's decision of a lifetime". [55] Again, it proves to be a time calling for an "abundance of caution", with the PM announcing that "New Zealand needs an extra five days of full lockdown to cement the gains made over the last month ... Let's finish what we have started." [56] ANZAC Day arrives and lockdown prevails. "The tradition of remembering and commemorating our veterans and service personnel" [57] is still strong, and we celebrate in our homes and on our balconies, or distanced at the top of our driveways at dawn.

Sadly, another death was reported. The quiet war is not over, and we hear another new phrase that will become a mantra of the pandemic: "keep up the vigilance". The Director-General of Health Dr Ashley Bloomfield says: "Although it was encouraging to have another day with a single-digit increase, vigilance remains crucial. As the country prepare[s] to move to alert level 3 'it was important not to slacken off the effort'." [58] Nevertheless, on Tuesday, 28 April, we emerge into alert level 3. We may well be seeing the 'tail' of the virus, but the PM cautions: "As long as we can keep those numbers down, then our chances of spending less time in [level] three are good but I can't predict it." She continues: "Whilst your work life may be changing, unfortunately your social life can't for now." [59] Keeping vigilant will be the key to our success. This period is expressed in four phrases that tumble against each to get into our pandemic vocabulary: "an abundance of caution", "keeping vigilant is the key to success", "the quiet war is not over", and "elimination".

The first day of "freedom" (another phrase offering a respite of sorts) reflects our progress so far, but comes with a warning: while the coronavirus lockdown has been eased, "recovering from the damage it has wrought will take far longer". [60] As April draws to an end, new cases remain in single figures. [61] The message, though, remains the same. The Director-General of Health makes it quite clear: "We haven't eliminated it and we haven't eradicated it. Elimination, as I say, is not a point in time. It's not we've got to the end of alert level four – we've eliminated it. Our elimination goal continues into level three." [62]

March and April 2020 have, undoubtably, been tough months, with 33 days in lockdown having taken their toll on emotions. The 'quiet war' continues, the need is to be vigilant, there is still work to do; our emotions and well-being will continue to be tested. Even with the freedoms a new word slips into our vocabulary — "clusters" — and how they can spread the virus. Social distancing is still in our armoury, reminding us that we must stay vigilant. Once again, setting our emotions on edge.

MAY–JUNE 2020: A RESPITE OF SORTS IN SIGHT

The currency of progress is still the daily case number, but there is a subtle shift in focus as attention is directed to those days where no new cases are reported. This leads to somewhat obsessive behaviours, as each day we wait with bated breath for the 1pm conference to begin. The focus is soon refined with the phrase "no new cases today" is coupled with "Are they happening in sequence?". What is the significance of this? The sequence of no cases gives us hope that a respite may be in sight. It is also an acknowledgement of the success of the government's policies. By early May our first "no new cases today" since lockdown began is recorded. While seeing this as "encouraging", Dr Bloomfield adds: "But the key test would come later this week. That is when cases that have emerged since the move to level three are likely to become symptomatic". [63]

The welcome news of "no new cases today" continues as May progresses, and with it our hopes rise that a sequence is forming. But, alas, our hopes are dashed as new cases emerge, and it is not until 12 May that we again hear the phrase "no new cases are reported" and then the news stays the same for three days in a row for no cases — the sequence we were waiting for.

In anticipation of this, on Monday, 11 May, Prime minister Ardern announced, following the Cabinet meeting, the move to risk level 2 and what it would entail. The level 2 roll-out will be in three stages, starting on Thursday, 14 May, with the opening up of much of the economy, and limited social interaction and travel around the country. The following Monday, 18 May, will see schools and early childhood centres open, and finally bars will be allowed to reopen on Thursday, 21 May. [64] Ardern concluded the announcement by thanking "the team of 5 million" for the sacrifice they had made during the lockdown, and asking everyone to "play it safe" in level 2. It is a step-by-step, watch-and-see approach, with "no guarantee" [65] as to when New Zealand will drop to level 1. The phrase "the team of 5 million" will become perhaps the most powerful phrase of the pandemic, as it reflects that collaboration is the most powerful tool we have to win this quiet war.

As the month heads towards June the encouraging signs continue. The number of cases continue to fall and stay in single figures, and the number of days with no cases increases, and the sequences begin to lengthen.

But May is not finished yet. The Budget is delivered on 14 May, with commentators describing Minister of Finance Grant Robertson's Budget as ""acting decisively to cushion the Covid-19 crash when the country was locked down in late March". [66] The wage subsidy is extended, and hospitals and district health boards are described as "winners", and a $50 billion Covid-19 recovery fund is announced to be spent over four years. [67]

There are other developments, too, designed to mitigate the risks that opening up our daily lives and freedoms in level 2 may have on contagion. The most significant of these comes into effect on 19 May, when the "Covid Tracker app" becomes operable. Introducing it, the PM describes the app as "a digital diary", which provides "national consistency to help New Zealanders record where they've been and when". [68] Yet another term to add to our pandemic vocabulary.

A week later, a Vaccination Task Force is established "to develop a Covid-19 vaccine strategy with the aim to secure a vaccine — safe, effective and in sufficient quantities — at the earliest possible time". [69] The Government is putting $37 million into this Covid-19 vaccine strategy, as well as "lobby[ing] internationally to ensure New Zealand and the Pacific Islands get a fair share when it is developed". [70] "A global effort is well underway to develop and test various vaccine candidates," Health Minister David Clark said. [71]

May proves to be a crucial month for the country's pandemic strategy and planning. May provides us with three more phrases that reflect the changing nature of the virus and the tools we have to fight it. They are the "Covid Tracker app", "national consistency" and "pandemic strategy and planning".

As May draws to an end, a glimmer of hope emerges as the sequence of no cases reported grows, culminating in 12 days by 3 June. We dare to wonder whether elimination has been achieved, and even whether there is going to be a risk level change. Our emotions are palpable, driven by our expectations of what might happen.

We don't have to wait long, and it comes with a sigh of relief. On 8 June Prime Minister Ardern announces Cabinet's decision that New Zealand will move to level 1 at midnight. "Today we are ready," she says, before going on to describe level 1 as being "where life feels as normal as it can in the time of a global pandemic". However, vigilance is still the key; "as long as the threat of Covid-19 remains in the world ... it remains here". [72] Reflecting on the move to level 1, Ardern points to "the rapid transmission of the virus and the way it can move very, very quickly. Days can make a big difference ... involving a continuous flow of decisions in quick succession ... and balancing science against political calls. [73] While May has been driven by expectations of some sort of respite, like other months the unpredictability of the twists and turns of the pandemic's journey means these are somewhat dampened, summed up by the pandemic mantra that "vigilance is still the key". And note the phrase that illustrates the government's planning and intentions as it manages the pandemic: "balancing science against political calls".

After 24 consecutive days without a new case of Covid-19 in New Zealand, on 16 June two new cases related to the border are announced. Our "confidence is shaken" the headline rings out. [74] These two cases identify gaps in the border controls, prompting the government to set up a review and to oversee border management. [75] Two days later, another border-related case is reported. As June draws towards its end, the increase of flights into New Zealand, is mirrored with an increase in Covid cases entering the country. "All are recent arrivals into the country and all remain in isolation." By the end of June the number of active cases is 22, all are in isolation; [76] another phrase — "cases in isolation" — to add to our ever-extending pandemic vocabulary.

JULY–OCTOBER 2020: A SECOND WAVE

July begins with the announcement that an All Government Response Group has been established. This Business Unit "will continue to provide assurance of national level oversight and coordination of government agencies' responses to COVID-19". [77] After 102 days without community transmission, on 11 August the prime minister brings us unwelcome news: "new positive cases of COVID-19 in the community ... have been identified in Auckland. On

Wednesday the 12th the Auckland region (Auckland Council area) will move to Alert Level 3 for three days until midnight on Friday 14th of August. The rest of New Zealand will move to Alert Level 2." [78] Within two days, active cases reach 36. The following day 13 new cases of Covid-19 are reported, and the prime minister announces that Auckland will remain at alert level 3, while the rest of the country will remain at level 2 for 12 more days, until 26 August. [79] And with this surge comes another phrase which quickly assumes familiarity and enters into our pandemic vocabulary: the number of new cases and their timing are now being described as occurring in "waves".

Amid all this uncertainty, on 17 August, the prime minister announces a four-week delay in the 2020 general election in response to the COVID-19 pandemic. This is only the fourth time in the country's history that an election has been postponed. [80] On 24 August the pandemic brings us more unwelcome news: Auckland will continue at alert level 3 until 30 August, and the rest of the country will remain at Alert level 2 for a further 12 days. [81] August has been a tense and exhausting month, particularly for Auckland. Emotions are high and nerves on edge and are being juggled across a range of activities and responsibilities as the lockdown continues to stretch out.

More is yet to come, and Aucklanders brace themselves. On 4 September, the prime minister confirms their fears: Auckland will remain at new alert level 2.5, a new level to match the prevailing conditions, until at least 16 September. [82] (This alert level saw changes to the number of people allowed to attend social gatherings, funerals and tangihanga, as well as mandatory mask wearing on public transport). Sadly, on the same day two deaths are reported, bringing the total number of deaths to 24. On 21 September the government announces that, apart from Auckland, the country is moving to level 1; for now Auckland will remain at level 2.5 for a further two days, before moving to alert level 2 with no extra restrictions. [83] On 8 October Auckland finally joins the rest of the country at alert level 1. [84] Sighs of relief all round. It has been an exhausting emotional journey since July. This ever-changing scenario and need to respond accordingly sees the government in September likening it's Covid-19 response to a "rolling maul of initiatives". [85]

More initiatives are to follow. On 12 October it is revealed that the government has signed an agreement to purchase 1.5 million COVID-19 Pfizer and BIONTECH vaccines. [86] Five days later the election is finally held, and the headlines carry the enormity of the result: "Crushed it: Jacinda Ardern claimed historic mandate in Labour landslide as Judith Collins and National suffer devastating loss". [87] In the first time under MMP, a party has won an outright majority of the vote. Prime Minister Ardern "claims a mandate to accelerate ... and a party that governs for every New Zealander". [88]

Any euphoria in the governing labour Party is short-lived, though: after 22 successive days of no community cases, a case emerges on 18 October. Yet, although it is described as a community case, it is believed that the virus was contracted at the border rather than via community transmission — the case and family are in isolation. And while other cases follow, they are all related to the border. Reflecting these complexities of the origins of cases, the definition of new reported cases continues to be refined, with those cases in "managed isolation" being described as such, and being distinguished from cases at the border and from community transmission cases.

TOWARDS SUMMER AND THE END OF THE YEAR

With relief the country heads towards summer, and thoughts turn to what summer will offer. The quiet war is not yet over. On 2 November Prime Minister Ardern announces the appointment of Chris Hipkins to a newly established role, that of the COVID-19 Response Minister, with "responsibilities for all aspects of our ongoing response". [89] She makes the significance of this role clear by adding: "It's critical we have our most experienced Ministers leading the ongoing Covid response to keep New Zealanders safe from the virus." [90]

On 5 November another tool is introduced to help detect the virus, when a Covid-19 wastewater testing pilot scheme is rolled out around the country. [91] On 16 November, following a 10-day delay due to pandemic disruptions, 140,000 students at last begin their NCEA and Scholarship exams. [92] On the same day it is mandated that face masks are to be worn on Auckland public transport and all domestic flights. [93] In the five days from 21 to 26 November, 12 cases are reported, all of which have known origins.

As summer beckons, we are introduced to two phrases that in the coming year will become a feature of the pandemic: "wearing masks" and — reflecting the mantra of following the science — "wastewater testing".

In the last month of what has been a turbulent year through the twists and turns of the virus's journey, it is time to take stock. "Looking back," PM Ardern concludes, "I'm incredibly proud of what our team of five million has achieved, but I also want to acknowledge the huge sacrifices and hardships many have had to face to get us where we are." [94] It is also a time to look forward, and on 15 December Ardern announces a Covid-19 resurgence plan for summer [95] – i.e. how people must prepare and react in case of a summer outbreak . By 19 December, New Zealand has agreements in place that secure enough Covid vaccines to vaccinate everyone in the country, as well as our neighbours in the Pacific "if the governments of those [countries] accept the offer". [96] After an exhausting and tumultuous year — in which a cupboard full of pandemic phrases simply reminds us not just about the twists and turns of the pandemic's journey but how completely they have ruled our emotions — our lives and our resilience have been well and truly tested. So, now feels the right time to enjoy summer — in a Covid way, of course.

CHAPTER 2:

New Zealand and the Pandemic 2021–2024

ANOTHER PANDEMIC YEAR

2021. Another year, and another torrid period on our pandemic journey. Times of turbulence by now seem to be the trademark of the pandemic's path. It is all about cases in managed isolation, issues in MIQ (Managed Isolation and Quarantine), new variants, protests, misinformation and conspiracies, the development of a vaccination programme, mandates, rapid antigen tests (RATs), lockdowns, community transmission, and the ins-and-outs of alert-level changes. While it may seem a familiar path, there is a palpable sense of change in the language of the pandemic, reflecting the evolving mutations of the virus and the journey we are all on. It is the same for our emotions and our resilience, as a sense of fatigue accompanies the feelings we experience as we are no longer impartial followers in the pandemic's journey.

These changes may also be driven by the dramatic context that is beginning to surround the path of the pandemic; "the other pandemic … the first digital pandemic [of misinformation and conspiracies] … the unintended consequences of the things we have collectively invented." [1] As Harari succinctly expresses it: "Humans were always far better at inventing tools than using them wisely." [2] Now we are having to manage and cope with two pandemics adding to our worries, uncertainties and anxieties. But the pandemic's journey isn't over — far from it, it is just getting more complex. By 24 January the first community case since November is reported. [3] This requires us to calibrate our carefree summer attitude somewhat to once more focus our attention on the here and now, and what is immediately ahead of us, remembering the rules we are intimately familiar with: being vigilant, maintaining social distancing, hand washing, keeping to the coughing and sneezing protocols.

This year will be dominated with the planning and management of the vaccination programme. It is a critical step in the fighting of this quiet war, and offers significant possibilities of ongoing health and freedom gains, all of which helps explain the tensions that surround it. A significant first step comes when the government confirms on 25 January that they have "granted the suppliers Pfizer and BioNTech indemnity from any claims that may arise from the use of the vaccine". [4]

February continues this emphasis and is another busy month, particularly in the planning of the vaccine rollout. On 3 February it is revealed that the Pfizer/BioNTech vaccine has been granted provisional consent for use in New Zealand, [5] and a week later the government gives formal "approval for the Pfizer/BioNTech vaccine as 'suitable for use' to those 16 years and older". [6] The government isn't getting ahead of itself, though; it is well aware that it will be a long time before the country can enjoy the degree of reassurance engendered by community-safe vaccination levels. Although an end goal is in sight, this is no time to take the eye off the ball, when Covid-19 is still very much here. So in between these vaccine announcements, on 8 February, the government announces that employers can "receive a $350 payment if their employees cannot work from home while awaiting a Covid-19 test result". [7] While public health remains a priority, the individual economic impacts are not being forgotten.

This need to remain focused on the Covid-19 response becomes apparent a week later when three community transmission case are reported, seeing Auckland move to alert level 3 on 14 February, and the rest of New Zealand going to level 2 until midnight on Wednesday, 17 February. When making the announcement the PM explains that "the alert level change came out of an abundance of caution and would be reviewed every 24 hours". [8] However, there are clearly a number of factors in play to be balanced, and on 17 February, although three new community cases are reported, [9] the prime minister puts Auckland down to alert level 2, and the rest of New Zealand to level 1, from midnight. She adds: "As ever, if you are sick, please stay at home

... This continues to be one of our most important restrictions." [10]

The vaccine rollout is about to kick off, but with the limited supply of vaccines available, a schedule of vaccinations has been drawn up, initially focusing on vulnerability due to occupational exposure and then to health status. Just three days later, on 20 February frontline staff are preparing to get their first dose of the Covid-19 Pfizer vaccine. [11] "Plans are coming together for thousands of border workers [also nurses, cleaners and security workers at quarantine hotels] to be immunised for Covid-19 by mid-March ..." [12] Two days later Auckland joins the rest of New Zealand at alert level 1. [13] The next day a single new community case is announced, [14] and on 24 February the "first South Island border workers get vaccinated as [the] second batch of Pfizer/BioNTech arrives ... as the immunisation programme starts rolling out in the South Island." [15] The next day only one new community case is reported. [16]

But just when things seem to be moving in the right direction, the very next day the prime minister announces that from six o'clock the next morning Auckland will move to alert level 3 and the rest of the country to alert level 2, for a period of seven days. "The main thing we are asking people to do is to stay home if you can, to avoid any risk of spread." [17] The importance of this lockdown reflects the nature of the current cases and the possibility that contacts may take a while to show up.

March unfolds in much the same manner as the preceding two months: cases in managed isolation, concerns about people not following the rules, vaccinations, lockdowns and testing. Thousands of people in Auckland have been tested. And there is more see-sawing in alert levels in response to changing levels and modes of transmission. On the first day of March the prime minister is urging people to follow the rules associated with their alert level. [18] On 5 March there is good news, with Ardern announcing that "in the absence of widespread community cases", at 6am on Sunday, 7 March, Auckland will be moving alert level 2 , and the rest of the country to alert level 1. [19]

On the day following the switch to the new alert levels there is more good news, with the government revealing that it "has purchased enough Pfizer/BioNTech Covid-19 vaccines for the whole country ... guaranteeing that every New Zealander will have access to the vaccine, after securing an additional 8.5 million doses". [20] This is timely, as the very next day the first large-scale

Covid-19 vaccination clinic is due to open in Auckland. [21] On the same day the government announces the establishment of "an independent group to oversee continual improvement in [the] Covid-19 response ... chaired by Sir Brian Roche." [22] On 10 March the plan for the rollout of the Covid-19 vaccines is revealed, "ensuring Free, Fair and equitable access to everyone in New Zealand". [23] In the same period of all these new initiatives — 8–11 March — another 16 new cases are confirmed. The good news is that all of these new cases are emerging in managed isolation, and are not the result of community spread. This allows the PM to announce that at midday on 12 March Auckland will be moving to alert level 1, adding: "I know everyone in Auckland will be looking forward to a weekend with fewer restrictions, but we are asking that everyone keeps up the good habits that help[ed] us deal with cases [as] they emerged." [24] Even with the loosening of community restrictions, this encouraging transmission trend continues: until the end of March all of the new reported cases are from within managed isolation. It is another month where preparation, planning and learning are key to the government's management of the pandemic. For the "team of 5 million" it is another turbulent time where anxieties, worries and concerns follow from the twists and turns of the virus.

APRIL–JUNE 2021: PREPARATION, PLANNING AND REVIEW

The trend continues into April, with all of the new cases being reported are in managed isolation. In the first seven days of April there are 34 such cases; by 18 April there are another 13 cases reported; by 29 April another 21 cases are reported. Parallel to this, the vaccination programme is gathering pace. By 8 April nearly 2000 people have completed their training to become Covid vaccinators, the government "hoping to draw on thousands more as it prepares to roll out the largest vaccination campaign in our country's history". [25] That same day the government announces it has established a new scientific advisory group, chaired by respected epidemiologist Sir David Skegg, "to advise it on crucial Covid-19 decisions, including any changes at the border and the ongoing vaccine roll out". The Covid Response Minister explains that "having such a group was "to ensure future decisions were informed by the best available scientific evidence and strategic public health advice". [26]

On 13 April, another tool is added to the armoury with the passing of the Covid-19 Public Health Response (Required Testing) Amendment Order 2021, which makes saliva testing mandatory for border workers. [27] Two days later it is announced that the Director-General of Health Dr Ashley Bloomfield will lead a background briefing for media organizations to update and provide more detail on the Covid-19 vaccine rollout plan. [28]

On 23 April measures are announced, with a view to making the borders stronger by establishing a new "high-risk country" designation. [29] Allied to making the border stronger, a week later it becomes mandatory for all workers in managed isolation and quarantine (MIQ) and government agencies at the border to be vaccinated. [30] April is another good illustration of a month that follows the mantra of preparation, planning, learning and review.

While initially May brings disappointments for those hoping for Pacific travel, 18 May excitement is building as "the Cook Islands travel bubble begins". [31] The next day the government reveals it has "invested $1.4 billion in New Zealand's Covid-19 vaccination programme to ensure every New Zealander can receive a free vaccination". [32] At the risk sounding repetitive, May is another month where the focus is primary on preparation, planning and learning.

June begins with the unsettling news on 5 June that about "3800 border workers haven't been vaccinated yet, nor have about half of the 50,000 household contacts of border workers who are meant to be at the top of the priority queue". [33] In response, the Ministry of Health explains that the slower-than-anticipated reported rate is "the product of timing and delayed updating of the testing register". [34] There is more comforting news on 8 June: "Pfizer has scheduled delivery of an estimated 1 million doses of vaccine to New Zealand during July. These consignments will double the total number of Pfizer we have received this year to more than 1,900,000 — enough to fully vaccinate almost 1 million kiwis." [35] Nine days later PM Jacinda Ardern details the plan for vaccine rollout for the general population. It is structured in age groups, following the approach commonly used overseas. "From the end of July, we will enter a new phase of our vaccination programme when we start receiving the bulk of our vaccines and are able to broaden the rollout considerably to the wider population." [36] With Medsafe, the government medical regulatory body, giving the Pfizer vaccine provisional approval for use in 12–15-year-olds on 21 June, the government a\says it "is likely to give the final sign-off later this month". [37]

Two days later Wellington's alert level is raised to 2 after an Australian tourist tests positive after visiting the city over the weekend. [38] The same day the national museum Te Papa announces it will be closing after becoming a location of interest for Covid-19. [39] On 25 June, New Zealand receives the news it has been dreading, when NSW officials confirm that the traveller has the "Delta variant of Covid-19" [40] —a new Covid-19 variant which is far more highly transmissible than its predecessors. Travelling woes continue when, due to the city's new Covid scare, a group of passengers is removed from a Wellington flight bound for Rarotonga. Nevertheless, the Cook Islands government decides to keep the broader quarantine travel bubble open. [41]

At midnight on 29 June Wellington region returns to level 1 alert status. [42] On the last day in June, modelling begins to establish when New Zealand will achieve herd immunity against Covid-19: "The modelling shows 83% of all New Zealanders need to be vaccinated against Covid-19 before we can safely remove public health restrictions. Although the report added the proviso is based on data from earlier variants so the percentage may need to be higher now with faster-spreading variants." [43]

As with earlier months, the new cases are generally emerging from those newly arrived back in the country and staying in Managed Isolation. However, the Wellington scare highlights the reality that any part of the country is now vulnerable to Covid-19 infection and the new variants as border entry is eased; not just Auckland, which hitherto has been the only point of entry for incomers from overseas. Overall, though, June has been another disruptive, trying and frustrating month for all, as the virus and its variants twist and turn, needing close monitoring and quick interventions. However, the themes of preparation, planning and review are ever-present, despite the twists and turns of the virus or perhaps because of it.

JULY–OCTOBER 2021: LOCKDOWNS AND THE VACCINATION ROLLOUT

In its 2 July edition of *The Economist* ranks New Zealand second, behind Hong Kong, on its "normalcy index" in terms of "how much they've returned to normal during the pandemic". [44] Other good news follows when on 7 July

Covid-19 Response Minister Hon Chris Hipkins announces that 500,000 New Zealanders are now fully vaccinated (i.e. have received the two shots required to establish immunity), adding: "It was a significant milestone in the rollout of the vaccination. I am confident, the Government is confident, and New Zealanders can be confident that our vaccine rollout is ramping up and gaining pace." [45]

The vaccine rollout pace does not flag. On 19 July "the largest shipment of Pfizer vaccine [370,000 doses] to date has arrived in New Zealand two days ahead of schedule, and doses are already being delivered to vaccination centres around the country". [46] On 28 July, people aged over 60 years are invited by the prime minister to book an invitation to be vaccinated. Covid minister Chris Hipkins also announces that the weekend of 30 July and 1 August will see the country's first mass vaccination being held, in South Auckland. "More than 15,000 people are set to be vaccinated over those three days. Another mass vaccination event will be held six weeks later for second doses.". [47]

The number of new cases reported in July followed the continuing trend, where the greater number were emerging in managed isolation, among them were a number of border incidents involving mariners being put in isolation as a precautionary measure.

The following month sees another development with PM Ardern on 12 August setting out a plan to start reopening New Zealand's borders, "starting with a trial this year of home isolation or shorter MIQ stays for selected travellers", to be "followed by the phased resumption of quarantine-free travel in the future". [48] However, the optimistic mood abruptly changes when, on 17 August, it is revealed that a positive case of Covid-19 has been identified in the community in Auckland, "and at this stage there is no known link to the border". [49] The last community case was in June in Wellington. That there is now a community case, and one whose origins are uncertain, along with the arrival of highly-transmissible variants from overseas, calls for a rapid and ruthless response. The PM places all of New Zealand on alert level 4 from 11.59 that night. Auckland and the Coromandel — areas where the new case lives or has recently visited — will be at level 4 for seven days, whereas the alert level for the rest of the country will be reviewed after three days. [50] By 19 August there are 11 new community cases, bringing the total to 21, of which 12 are confirmed as part of the new outbreak; by 23 August there are 35 new cases, making a total of 107. [51] Given this growth in community cases, on 23 August the PM decides that "Alert level 4 will remain in place to keep New Zealanders safe"; it will be reviewed for the whole of New Zealand on 27 August, and for Auckland on 31 August. [52] By the end of August, the total number of cases has reached 612. The country is grappling with the fast-moving Delta variant and the focus is on containing the outbreak.

But the one thing the pandemic teaches you is that you have to keep your eye on a range of fast-moving targets. So, in the shadow of the lockdown preparation, planning and reviewing still needs to be maintained. That this is happening becomes apparent as August ends, with a pair of announcements: on 19 August we learn that "following Medsafe's approval of the Pfizer/ BioNTech Covid-19 vaccine the vaccination programme is extended to 12–15-year-olds", [53] and on 22 August that record keeping is to "become mandatory for most events and businesses … to ensure the government can contact-trace quickly" and "to ensure people keep a record when they visit". [54] In an effort to restrict the community spread of the virus, contact-tracing is a proactive tool whereby the infected person provides information on the persons and places of contacts they had over the period in which they could be infectious and asymptomatic. Their individual contacts and people who may have been at the identified places can then be alerted, asked to take a Covid test, and to isolate for a period of time to ensure they do not have Covid and are not infectious.

The last of August saw "all of New Zealand south of Auckland" moving to alert level 3, with Auckland and Northland remaining at alert level 4. [55]

September began with the unfinished business from August. The case numbers on 1 September set the context for the month, and reflect those months that preceded it: 75 new community are reported, with the total cases reaching 687. [56] In response to where the infections transmissions are clustered, the next day sees Northland move to alert level 3 at midnight, [57] while Auckland remains at alert level 4. At the same time the rest of New Zealand will move to alert level 2. The PM called the move to "level 2 Delta" – another tweak to the alert level, and named after the fast-moving Covid strain. This move sees restrictions in level 2 areas eased on household bubbles, and "businesses can open, people can return to work and children can go off to school". [58]

Ten days later there is some positive news when it is announced that the government has "secured an extra half a million doses of the Pfizer vaccines from Denmark that will arriving in New Zealand within days ... these dose along with the 275,000 doses purchased from Spain last week provide an additional 775,000 to New Zealand's vaccine supplies." [59]

But, as we have seen, vaccination was only one weapon being wielded in this unremitting quiet war. On 17 September "experts called on the Ministry of Health to improve its mask wearing guidelines to ensure New Zealanders are protected in the wake of highly transmissible variants of Covid-19". [60] Three days later, "a virtual lobby release of MIQ vouchers" was unveiled. [61] Although an effort to try to formalise and make fairer access to MIQ for the many people overseas wishing to return to New Zealand and its limited MIQ facilities, the system will prove to be problematic and attract much criticism.

On 21 September Auckland moves to alert level 3 with the next Cabinet review of alert levels promised for 4 October. [62] The next day, after "assiduously avoiding any talk of targets" up until now, the Covid-19 Response Minister and the Director-General of Health give a target for vaccination, "saying they want 90% of the New Zealand's eligible population vaccinated". [63] By the next day the total cases for the current outbreak total 1123. [64]

Another alert level change is announced on 25 September, with "Upper Hauraki moving to Alert level 2." [65] Three days later, "changes in the rules governing people being able to leave Auckland" are announced. [66] By the end of the month the total of cases reaches 1249. [67]

September is another busy month, featuring the havoc unleashed by the Delta variant, coupled with numerous changes in alert levels, the easing of travel rules, and changes in how to book space in MIQ. All of this gives Aucklanders some longed-for breathing space and light relief, allowing them to move towards a "new normal" type of living under Covid-19. But the "quiet war" is not yet over.

For the first week of October the rolling daily average was 29 new reported cases. On 2 October came one of the first overt expressions of the unease that some parts of the community were feeling as they chafed against the seemingly never-ending and -changing pandemic requirements. It appears some of the "team of 5 million" are tiring of the demands of personal sacrifice for the greater good, especially in Auckland where the lockdowns have invariably been longer and harsher. So they "took to the streets to rally against an almost two-month lockdown". [68] Fed-up they may be, but the very next day sees proof that Covid is not done with us yet. On 3 October the spread of the virus means that parts of the Waikato are to move to alert level 3 for the next five days. While the promised 4 October Cabinet review of lockdown settings will proceed unaffected, it will exclude the Waikato. [69] On 5 October, the PM announces the outcome of the Cabinet review, setting out "a roadmap of a number of steps for Auckland to carefully move out of Covid19 restriction. Auckland moves to step 1 Alert level 3 but several key changes will occur." [70]

Community cases continue to march on. In an effort to stem the contagion, on 6 October the Ministry of Health introduces a "shorter gap" of "three weeks between the first and second doses of the Pfizer vaccine". [71] The following day, the continued spread of the virus in the Waikato sees the government extend the Waikato alert level 3 boundary. [72] In a ghastly game of "Tag", as the virus spreads, other alert level changes follow, Northland going to alert level 3 on 8 October. [73] And, remember, this frantic game of catch-up all takes place in the first week of the month, as the quickly spreading and mutating virus leads us on a macabre dance.

By 11 October, the number of cases in the outbreak totals 1622. [74]

In spite of these daunting statistics, there is an undiminished resolve to conquer Covid by whatever means. On 12 October the next defensive salvo is shot, with "the launch of New Zealand's first-ever 'Vaxathon' that will take place on 'Super Saturday' the 16th of October. It is designed around the fact that vaccination is ...by far the biggest and most powerful weapon we have in our fight against Covid-19'." [75] The success of the Vaxathon is measured in numbers, "with 129,995 doses administered — 39,024 first doses and 90,971 second doses by 10pm on Saturday night". [76] On the same weekend "there were an estimated 2000-plus people tightly congregated on an Auckland Domain field — many without masks". A counterpoint is captured by the reporter at the scene: "while speakers are pushing the case for freedom from alert level restrictions ... above Auckland Domain was a light aircraft with a banner to counter the freedom protest reading 'Love NZ — Get Your Jab Bro'." [77] This latter example of freedom to express oneself is community-focused, not individually-focused, and is done at a distance that does not risk endangering anyone to exposure to Covid.

Preceding the Vaxathon, on 13 October the Ministry of Health launches what it describes as "new possibilities on horizon — My Covid Record website was launched ... the first step in our work towards providing vaccination certificates". [78] This builds on an announcement made two days earlier, on 11 October, whereby "vaccinations are mandated for the two workforces — education and health and disability sectors". [79]

On top of these signs of protest and planning, there are more alert level changes: on 19 October Northland moves to alert level 2, while Auckland remains at alert level 3 (step1) and Waikato at alert level 3. [80] As the month ends, a further flurry of announcements is announced: in parts of the Waikato restrictions will be slightly eased and will move to level 3 (step 1); [81] and on 28 October MIQ stays are shortened for vaccinated travellers from 14 to seven days followed by isolation at home for three days. [82]

Also on 28 October, the Pfizer vaccine is granted provisional approval for two more years. [83] On the same day, another government-approved trial launches, with 300,000 rapid antigen tests (RATs) arriving in New Zealand and being distributed to some of the country's largest businesses, expanding the tools available to find and stamp out Covid-19. [84] On 30 October, for the third time in six weeks, there is a rally in Auckland Domain of a large number of anti-lockdown protesters, "expressing their dislike of Covid-19 restrictions and the vaccine rollout". [85] The following day, 143 new community cases are reported. [86]

NOVEMBER–DECEMBER 2021: LOCKDOWNS, ALERT LEVEL CHANGES, VACCINATION MANDATES, AND PLANNING AND REVIEWING

On 2 November the northern parts of Northland move to alert level 3 "following two unlinked community cases reported in the Far North". [87] The previous day alert level changes have been announced in the two most recent hot-spots, the Waikato and Auckland by PM Jacinda Ardern, with Covid restrictions being eased slightly in Waikato from 2 November, and Auckland going to alert level 3 (step 2) the following week. [88] On 15 November the PM announces that Cabinet has agreed that the next day "a move to Alert level 2 can safely take place" for Waikato. [89] A few days earlier, on 11 November, Upper Northland has been moved to Alert level 2. [90]

As these alert level changes have been taking place, vaccination mandates are also being announced, and cover a range of sectors in the workforce. First cab off the rank: by 6 November "workers in the corrections sector are required to have their first dose and second dose by 8th of December." The vaccination mandate "will be extended to Police and Defence force with the first dose 17 January 2022 and the second by the 1st of March 2022."[91] When the legality of these vaccination mandates is challenged, a decision in the High Court indicates that the legislation surrounding vaccinations mandates "is compliant with the New Zealand Bill of Rights Act".[92]

Sadly, on 10 November a death is reported.[93] By this time, 89% of eligible New Zealanders aged 12 years and over have had their first dose, and 79% are fully vaccinated.[94]

On 17 November the government launches the vaccine pass: "My Vaccine Pass is an official record of a person's Covid-19 vaccination status and will provide access within New Zealand that requires proof of vaccination ... 'The Minister of Covid Response urged fully vaccinated New Zealanders to "request their pass ... to get ready for summer ....'"[95] On the same day Jacinda Ardern announces that Auckland's boundary settings will change from 15 December, "ensuring travel out for all vaccinated people or those with a negative test result", adding that the "country [is] better prepared — 82% New Zealanders fully vaccinated, compared to 23% three months ago".[96] On 23 November it is announced that workers covered by the My Vaccine Pass mandate need to have their first dose by 3 December and be fully vaccinated by 17 January 2022 [97]

On 25 November the government announces an "investment of $1.5 million into testing and home isolation; information about management of Covid-19 and of cases isolating at home".[98] This investment "will boost end-to-end support for people who get Covid-19 in the community".[99]

November has been another month in the shadow of the Delta outbreak. Throughout the month new cases have consistently clocked in at over 100 a day. But a subtle change has appeared in the "pandemic vocabulary", suggesting that a new theme is emerging, expressed in the idea of self-management. This theme is about offering us the tools to self-manage Covid-19. It stems from the belief that Covid-19 will be with us for some time and so, much like the flu, we will need to take responsibility and manage Covid-19 ourselves. Strategies and tools are being developed and will be available to all New Zealanders. A mantra of best practice for self-management suggests: mask up, get vaccinated, get tested, stay at home and isolate for seven days when you test positive, and register.

December comes, again with dreams of summer, but with no abatement in the daily community cases being reported. The rolling average of daily cases reported for the first week is 121. The Traffic Lights levels system of the Covid-19 Protection Framework, announced by the prime minister on 29 November, is being implemented on Friday, 2 December. Introducing the new system, PM Ardern explained: "... the traffic lights are turned on for all of New Zealand, as we move forward safely into the next phase of our world-leading COVID-19 response ... We are now in the strongest position to move forward into the next phase ... Our next phase is focused on minimising the impact of COVID-19 and protecting people. Northland, Auckland through Taupō, Rotorua and districts, across the Bay of Plenty into the east coast and further down the North Island to Rangitikei, Whanganui and Ruapehu districts will move to Red. The rest of the North Island and the whole of the South Island will move to Orange." [100]

"At this time [29th November], vaccination rates of eligible New Zealanders are 85% fully vaccinated." [101] On 3 December, as part of the traffic light system, it becomes a legal requirement to "provide the My Vaccine Pass to enter places that have vaccination requirements in place under the traffic light system". [102] This requirement covers events, and businesses, including hospitality; they may legally choose to implement a vaccination entry requirement for customers, coupled with strict social rules. Universities begin announcing mandates., with students and visitors requiring vaccine passes to come onto the campus from 4 January 2022. [103]

On 13 December, Prime Minister Ardern announces changes to traffic light system, saying "Auckland and all other red regions, excluding Northland, will move to Covid-19 framework setting orange at 11.59pm on Thursday, 30 December". [104] On 16 December, there comes mixed news. New Zealand's first case of the even more infectious new Covid variant, Omicron, has been detected in a recent international arrival through whole genome sequencing. [105] But the good news is that New Zealand has hit the 90% fully vaccinated milestone. Covid Response Minister Chris Hipkins announces this milestone with a "Give yourselves a pat on the back, New Zealand." [106]

On 21 December the planned response to the Omicron variant is announced, with the Cabinet agreeing "a suite of precautionary measures to keep Omicron out of the community for as long as possible". The suite is made up of four measures:

1. reducing the interval between the second vaccine dose and the booster shot from six months to four months;

2. temporarily increasing the length of stay in MIQ to 10 days for all travellers, with no self-isolation component;

3. pushing out the phased border re-opening to the end of the February 2022 ; and

4. using the traffic light system to manage the outbreak.

The plan recognises the need for a swift and comprehensive response, given Omicron's "bewildering speed" of transmission, even if "questions linger about its [potentially lower] severity". While adopting a cautious, tough stance, the government tries to placate fears, pointing to "a number of advantages on our side. We have over 90% and rising of the population fully vaccinated, we still have our border protections and MIQ in place, school has finished for the year[,] and we are heading into summer when we are outdoors more." [107] [108] On the same day the government confirms that Covid-19 vaccinations to protect tamariki are to begin on 17 January. [109]

Eight days later the Ministry of Health confirms that a border-related case with the Omicron variant has briefly been active in the community in the Auckland CBD earlier in the week. [110] As December ends, the shadow of the Omicron variant colours what may lie ahead. There is a palpable sense of foreboding as the new year beckons, reinforced by concern over the presumed turmoil that will likely accompany this next phase.

JANUARY–MARCH 2022: OMICRON, PROTESTS, PLANNING AND PREPARATIONS

By early January 2022, border cases reflect an "unprecedented" number of Omicron cases coming into New Zealand. [111] On 17 January the programme to vaccinate and protect children aged 5 to 11 against Covid-19 duly begins. There are 476,000 children in this age group eligible to get their first dose from this date, and a second dose at least eight weeks later. [112] On the same day, anyone 18 years and older who has received two doses of Covid-19 vaccine is now eligible to book a free booster (six months after their second shot) [113] The following day the government postpones the next MIQ lottery draw due to the spike of Omicron cases at the border. It is reported that there has been "a 10-fold increase in positive Covid-19 cases at the border compared to last month". [114] That day there are 14 new community cases with 30 at the border. [115] The first community transmission of the Omicron variant in New Zealand has also been reported. "To date, there have been 440 Omicron Covid-19 cases detected at the border since December 1, compared with 32 cases of the Delta variant." [116]

On 21 January the government extends the isolation time for all Covid-19 cases from 10 days to 14 days, in response to Omicron. [117] It is becoming clear that expert advice is to throw everything at the outbreak. Two days later the PM announces that the whole of New Zealand will move into the Red setting" of the traffic light system, explaining "our strategy is to slow the spread of Omicron down". [118] Two days after that there is a further ratcheting up of the response: the laboratory processing capacity of PCR Covid-tests is increasing to 58,000 tests processed per day, backed up by accessibility to self-testing RAT tests being improved. [119] The next day, 26 January, the Government announces a three-phase Omicron plan that "aims to slow down and limit the spread of the outbreak". [120] Three days later, Prime Minister Ardern enters self-isolation after being deemed a close contact of an infected person. [121] On 31 January, the Omicron variant of Covid-19 is declared to now be the dominant variant in New Zealand. [122]

By this time in the pandemic's journey, the vocabulary is beginning to subtilty change away from its customary focus on regulations, mandates and a fleet of other protocols, which have been the customary instruments to govern our behaviours. Now, the language focuses on all of us being invited to take a much greater degree of personal responsibility on our own: if you test positive, you would know to wear masks, isolate from others (i.e. at home), and get vaccinated. It's a mantra that calls us to act responsibly and, where we simply initiate behaviours that are self-directed.

A GOVERNMENT LOOKING AHEAD: FEBRUARY 2022

February kicks off with some good news, the OECD reporting: "New Zealand's coronavirus elimination strategy has paid off so far. Strict confinement measures were implemented quickly helping to limit the Covid-19 health toll. This strategy, together with measures to protect jobs and incomes and highly expansionary macroeconomics policies, laid the foundations for a rapid [economic] recovery." [123]

On 2 February a $1.5 million government boost to the Prepare Pacific Community Vaccination Fund is announced." [124] The same day also sees an announcement that the booster interval will reduce to three months - "from four months – the shorter interval only applies to the Pfizer vaccine." [125] A slew of announcements follows, with an announcement the next day that, as part of the government's "reconnecting plan", the border will be reopening in stages from 27 February: "On the 27th the border will reopen to vaccinated New Zealanders from Australia at 11:59pm. It reopens to New Zealanders in the rest of the world on 13th of March." [126] Another announcement that day decrees that all workers are "legally mandated to be vaccinated and ... must wear a medical-grade mask while working in public-facing roles". [127] All this in the shadow of Omicron, where the rolling average for the first seven days of February is 170, with case numbers increasing rapidly as many school communities across New Zealand face "the entry" of the Omicron variant. [128]

But for many months now there has been another battle brewing on our shores, on the Tuesday evening of 8 February it erupts as dramatic scenes start to unfold, as *The Dominion Post* describes: "Wellington rang with the sound of car horns and rage as a convoy descended on Parliament grounds and clogged the streets ... in what could become a days-long-anti-Covid-19 vaccine mandate protest. Some among the thousands who arrived in Wellington pitched tents on Parliament's lawn [in] the evening, or turned the surrounding streets into makeshift campsites. The convoy involved people who came from all corners of New Zealand to let Parliament know that they don't like Covid-19 Government mandates. As has become a theme with anti-vaccine mandate protests, other causes were on display: opposition to the three waters reforms; Prime Minister Jacinda Ardern or the 'lying' mainstream media; and support for Donald Trump and the United States. ... As the evening wore on, a protester reiterated they wouldn't be leaving until politicians ditched the mandates." [129] The protest is to last for 23 days.

As the protest heads towards its third week wet weather does "little to slow [the] protest at Parliament". [130] *The Dominion Post* again describes the scene. "There were at least 1000 people on the lawn in the shadow of the Beehive ... with around 750 tents erected in the area ... Police ... said they had 'serious concerns around the health and safety' of people at the concert.

A Change.org petition calling for those outside Parliament to leave was approaching 50,000 signatures ... One of a number of groups at the protest issued a press release calling for an end to the mandates on March 1, and urgent negotiations with the Government ... [There are] mounting calls from the city and iwi leaders for an end to the occupation and anti-mandate protest clogging the central city." [131]

Meanwhile the virus is not slowing down. Numbers continue to increase, with the seven-day rolling average ending on 14 February standing at 468. [132] Within two days, new daily cases in the community reach 1160, with new daily cases the next day reaching 1573. [133]

Planning and management of the virus continue, notwithstanding the protest and its demands. On 14 February the PM announced that New Zealand will move to Phase Two of the Omicron response at 11:59pm the following evening, at which point the period of home isolation will reduce. Prime Minister Ardern explains that "the increase in Covid cases is not unexpected and the country will stay in Phase Two as long as daily cases remain between 1000 and 5000 cases". She adds: "the way to handle this period will be the same as previous times [although self-isolation for positive cases reduces from 14 days to 10 days, and for contacts from 10 days to seven days] — test, vaccinate and isolate if sick". [134] RATs are available to facilitate this phase. She then advises "the protesters via Morning Report to go home and take their children with them". [135] Far from protesters heeding her advice, the very same day the anti-mandate protest in Christchurch's Cranmer Square Christchurch begins.

On 20 February new daily cases in the community reach 2522. [136] This is almost a year to the day from the start of the vaccination rollout, New Zealand also "reaches 95 percent of the eligible population vaccinated – first dose and 93% second dose ". [137]

As February turns into its last week, planning continues apace with an announcement on 21 February of a new financial support for businesses affected by Omicron, with a new targeted Covid Support Payment becoming available for businesses struggling with revenue during the Omicron outbreak. [138] On 24 February new community cases reach 6137, with the seven-day average of community cases hitting 2911. [139] This triggers the decision that New Zealand will move to Phase 3 of the Omicron response. The Minister for Covid-19 Response says: "Most have been gearing up for this and it will not come as a surprise. However, the move to phase three will not mean a 'sudden lurch' in terms of additional restrictions or movements, because the traffic light system has been designed to smooth things out already." In Phase 3, the minister explains: "... the priority now shifts to isolating those with Covid-19 and their household contacts. Rapid antigen tests (RATs) will be the primary means of testing for Covid-19 and will be available from thousands of sites. Millions more are expected to arrive over the coming days ... We are asking New Zealanders to accept a much greater degree of personal responsibility." [140] The following day the Ministry of Health offers resources on how to take a RAT and how to report the RAT result. [141] On 28 February the government "removes the self-isolation requirements for vaccinated travellers to New Zealand and enable[s] Kiwis to come here from the rest of the world sooner". [142] As February comes to a close, the protests continue.

MARCH 2022: PROTEST ENDED, OMICRON, AND REGULATIONS AND MANDATES

March begins dramatically. New community cases stand at 19,566 and the seven-day rolling average of community cases is 10,689. [143] On 2 March the police clear the anti-Covid mandate protesters from Parliament grounds in Wellington. Under the heading "What you need to know", *The Dominion Post* reports: "Police took back control of Parliament on Wednesday afternoon, 87 people were arrested as a result of the police operation and seven police officers required hospital treatment. Protesters were seen throwing pavement bricks, chairs, small explosive devices and other detritus at police, who pushed back with riot shields, water cannons and pepper spray. Some protesters have been in possession of various weapons. Multiple fires were lit, including tents and the Parliament playground. Protesters were fuelling the fires by throwing rubbish, tents, and LPG bottles on them." The next day it is clear the dispersal is not complete: "Anti-mandate protesters remain scattered in different groups around the Wellington area, as the clean-up of Parliament grounds continue[d]." [144]

Radio New Zealand (RNZ) describes the previous day's events thus: "There were chaotic scenes yesterday as Police moved in to break up the long-running protest outside Parliament ... The [Wellington] council says it will give the area a 'deep clean' given there have been people at the occupation with Covid-19 … The area is currently a police work site, but will be handed back to the council once the operation to clear it is complete." [145] *The NZ Herald* reports: "In a press conference on Thursday the PM said the damage to Parliament is something she never expected to see, and was akin to a 'rubbish dump'. [146] "The damage is indeed extensive, and it is not until 24 June that "Parliament Grounds officially reopen after [the] protest." [147]

As the protest in Wellington comes to an end some Wellington protesters "head to Cranmer Square, Christchurch to join the anti-mandate occupation there." [148] Residents living nearby say "the ongoing disruption and noise is callous and selfish, and has driven some to tears and out of their homes". [149] On 10 March the three-week protest ends with protesters "peacefully leaving the central city park". [150] "All that remained in the square were two full rubbish skips provided by the council for the protesters", [151] although the council is planning to re-sow the lawn.

But protests continuing or ending are not diverting the virus's path, and by 8 March new community cases reach their peak of 23,894 with the seven-day rolling average at 18,669. [152] Two days later the Novavax COVID-19 vaccine becomes available "for adults aged 18 and above who wish to have a different Covid-19 vaccine option". [153] The previous day the Minister for Covid-19 Response has announced that from Friday, 11 March, the isolation period for Covid-19 cases and their household contacts will reduce from 10 days to seven days from Friday. He goes on to say "there needs to be a balance between effectively controlling the outbreak and the flow-on effect for business and essential goods and services such as transport and food supply". This reduction follows the science, which has found that in most cases transmission occurs within seven days. [154] On 16 March, Chris Hipkins, in his role as education minister, announced that "nearly a million more rapid antigen tests (RATs) are being made available and easier to access in schools and early learning centres". [155]

An order is issued on 20 March excusing "critical workers delivering a critical health service" from the isolation regulations. [156] Five days later changes are made to the Red Traffic Light settings across the whole of New Zealand in a further effort to balance limiting the spread of the virus against the economic and social toll of isolation and limited social contact. The main changes focus on capacity limits: "Indoor venues that require Covid Vaccination Certificates (CVCs) will have their capacity limits increased to 200. Venues that don't require CVCs — their capacity remain the same until 4th of April. Outdoor capacity limits will be completely removed. No requirement to wear mask outside but face marks are still required on public transport." [157]

On 31 March the Minister of Health announces that more Covid medicines are available for the most at-risk New Zealanders, "boosting its comprehensive suite of medicines to treat Covid-19". [158] This last day of the month ends with another strong message encapsulating the month's slow shift toward a more balanced approach between caution and freedom, between regulation and self-responsibility. All of the measure that have been put in place — including the new self-management protocols — will undoubtedly save lives. On a day when new community cases are 15,250 and the seven-day rolling average of cases is 14,515, [159] now is the time for all of us to continue to play our part.

APRIL–JULY: OMICRON, MANDATES REDUCE, TRAFFIC LIGHT SETTINGS CHANGE, AND MORE SOMBRE NEWS

In April, as in previous months, efforts are dominated by the Omicron variant. The seven-week rolling average is 14,171. [160] Over the next seven days there is sad news, with 17 deaths being reported. The rolling average of community cases is now 11,791. [161] To counter the virus's twist and turns and its rapid transmission, refinements and new initiatives in managing this journey need to be swift and often. Vaccine mandates narrow on 4 April to "only health and disability, aged care, prison and border workforces", in accordance with "guidance … centred on public health advice". [162] Three days later, the Minister for Covid-19 Response announces "around 36,000 rangatahi aged 16 and 17 years will be eligible to receive a booster dose". [163]

Over the next four days new community cases fall below 10,000, encouraging the government to announce on 13 April, with an "abundance of caution", that all of New Zealand will move to the Orange setting. It came with the advice that "those who have not got [their] booster are urged to do so", and the Minister for Covid-19 Response cautioning that "the traffic light system may be used in response to a combination of Covid-19 and influenza". [164] The government was clearly having an eye to the approach of the winter months, when respiratory illness is more common, and when people are confined together indoors more in the cooler, wetter weather. Perhaps this is why on the same day the Ministry of Health asks the suppliers of RATs to prioritise its orders over those of private businesses. [165] There is a marshalling of resources for any potential consequences of greater freedoms and colder weather. On 14 April, Medsafe approves a third drug "for the treatment of mild to moderate coronavirus disease 2019 (COVID-19)". [166] The stats for 30 April show that over the month the seven-day rolling average of community cases has almost halved, standing at 7415, and while the seven-day average of deaths reported has fallen, too, there are sadly still 11 deaths. [167]

MAY: MANAGING OMICRON AND INFLUENZA

May begins in a way that reminds us that we are still in a pandemic with the fast-moving Omicron variant, with the grim statistics remaining stubbornly high. On 1 May new community cases are 5656, and the seven-day rolling average of deaths remains at 11. On the same day "a person with the BA.4 variant of Omicron" is detected at the border. [168] The Ministry of Health reports: "[T]he arrival of the sub-variant in New Zealand is not unexpected. At this stage, the public settings already in place to manage other Omicron variants are assessed to be appropriate for managing BA.4 and no changes are required." The Ministry further reassures the public: "there is currently no evidence it's more transmissible … [although] it takes a little time … to assess whether it is more infectious or dangerous". [169]

On 2 May New Zealand reopens its border to visa-waiver countries. New Zealand declares itself "'back on the map' for international tourists". [170] New Zealand clocks up 1 million confirmed cases of Covid-19 on 11 May. [171] Even so, with modelling suggesting that the true number of infections could anywhere between two and four times higher, [172] Dr Ashley Bloomfield admits: "It's likely only half of New Zealand's Covid-19 infections are being reported." [173]

As we head towards winter, concerns surrounding dealing with both influenza and Covid-19 emerge. "As Covid continue[s] to evolve, and the creeping concern of its long tail of chronic illness, … at this point in time the virus remains a much bigger public health risk." [174] However, the government warns that "thousands of people could be hospitalised with respiratory illness daily over winter, including more than 1000 with Covid-19 alone at what could be a 'quite high' peak". The Director-General of Heath outlines the modelling that underpins the planning for winter: the winter months may see a resurgence of Covid-19, alongside influenza and respiratory syncytial virus (RSV) outbreaks. [175] as the government's former scientific adviser Sir Peter Gluckman reminds us that Covid-19 "is unprecedented and unfinished". [176] *The Dominion Post* headline of 13 May captures the mood: "It's not over: Vigilance urged." [177] Four days later experts predict that Covid-19's second peak is "expected to hit as early as June". [178]

By 19 May another headline from *The Dominion Post* relays sobering news: "What you need to know as New Zealand death toll hits 1000 Covid-19 deaths." [179] Up until now, those planning to enter New Zealand have had to produce evidence of a negative Covid test taken within 48 hours of embarking. On 19 May, the Covid Response Minister indicates that it is likely this requirement for pre-departure testing will end soon, reflecting the government's change of focus as Covid-19 becomes "part of the 'new normal'". [180] "Against a shaky global economic backdrop", the finance minister Grant Robertson announces the 2022 budget that "has tried to balance the immediate political and pay packet pressures created by rising prices, while also providing significant amounts of money for longer term Labour reforms: health in particular". [181]

On 24 May, the updated My Vaccine Pass becomes available for downloading — "another step in the 'new normal' theme". [182] The next day the predicted fresh wave of Omicron infections stops New Zealand from "moving into the most relaxed pandemic setting for at least another month"; Covid-19 Response Minister Chris Hipkins explains that this is "as the hospitalisation rate from the virus increases". [183] As another month of twists and turns ends, the news remains sombre: there are 8346 new community cases reported and the death toll has reached 1172. [184]

JUNE: MORE TWISTS AND TURNS OF OMICRON, 'IT'S NOT OVER — VIGILANCE URGED'

The situation as June begins is neatly expressed by the opening paragraphs in a piece in *The Dominion Post*: "Winter is upon us and so are the season's ills, as a number of Covid-19 subvariants circulate. A number of Omicron subvariants are in the community in Aotearoa: BA.1, BA.2, BA.4, BA.5 and BA.2.12.1. On [3 June] the first case BA.4 and BA.5 (four cases) were reported in the community ... The Ministry of Health ... [says that] this 'is not evidence of a second wave of Omicron'." [185] Variants and subvariants are to dominate the month with the government later in the month, on 22 June, outlining "its plans for future Covid-19 variants". The Covid-19 Response Minister Dr Ayesha Verrall reveals that the government has undertaken "preparatory work to combat new and more dangerous variants of Covid-19". [186] Earlier, on 8 June, it is announced: "Major health reforms to become law." [187] The aims of these reforms are to give New Zealanders access to dependable quality care when they require it and places an emphasis on the idea of the 'healthspan' – i.e. to help people live longer in good health.

Everyone is encouraged to get their flu shots and Covid-19 boosters, and to ensure all other vaccinations are up to date this winter, as a way towards mitigating the inevitable pressures on the health system. For its part, the government was facing renewed calls to ease the building pressure in the health system by "address[ing] a 'bottleneck' that may be preventing overseas trained doctors from finding work in Aotearoa'. [188] Health authorities are "also concerned about a drop in childhood immunisation rates ... for a more contagious disease: measles ... Our best defence is immunisation" [189] On 16 June the new Covid-19 Response Minister Hon Dr Ayesha Verrall confirms 19 May's prediction by announcing that the pre-departure tests requirement for travel to New Zealand is to be removed from June 20. She explains: "we've taken a careful and staged approach to reopening our borders to ensure we aren't overwhelmed with an influx of Covid-19 cases". [190]

As the middle of the month arrives new community cases amount to 6133 and deaths reach 1348. The seven-day rolling average of community cases is 5983, a drop from at the previous week's 6202. [191] The predicted winter storm starts hitting the health system, and by 22 June "flu [and- staff illness] cause new hospital pressures ... leaving the health system under immense pressure", [192] eliciting a "dire warning from health front line". [193] A welcome piece of news comes on 28 June: a second booster (fourth dose) is now available, although health officials are "pessimistic on uptake of second booster", citing "Covid-19 weariness" [194]

On the last day of the month the Ministry of Health updates its advice for people who have already had Covid-19 and are displaying new symptoms. [195]

On the same day the Covid-19 Response Minister reveals that consideration is being given to changing the current Orange traffic light setting and that an announcement will be made shortly. [196]

June has proved to be another turbulent month, where tensions are palpable with surfacing concerns and worries about a potential second wave, and the need to tackle increasing Covid-19 weariness. It seems an increasingly tall order to ask us to stay alert, be vigilant, and follow the rules, even when we could acknowledge that it is these rules that save lives.

JULY: WINTER WOES, CONTINUING TURBULENCE AND MANAGEMENT EFFORTS, AND DECIDING WHEN IS A WAVE A SECOND WAVE

The number of cases as July begins suggests it will be another turbulent month. The heading "Covid cases jump" sets the mood, with new community cases at 6984 and reported Covid deaths reaching 1529. The seven-day rolling average of new cases is up to 6422 against 4737 a week ago, while that for reported deaths is 12. [197] In the face of these statistics, the Covid-19 Response Minister concludes that "the country will stay at the orange traffic light setting", adding: "We can continue to manage the virus at orange, but are putting in place a range of additional measures to help manage a recent rise in cases." [198] Changes to the health system coming into force on 1 July see the 22 district health boards replaced by a single entity, "Health New Zealand". [199] On just the second day of July, it was reported that "Schools [are] in 'survival mode'." [200]

As if Covid with its flotilla of variants, flu and RSV are not enough, a week later the Ministry of Health reports New Zealand's first case of Mpox (formerly, Monkeypox). Hitherto largely confined to Africa, the first widespread community transmission outside of Africa sees the WHO this month classifying it as a "public health emergency of international concern" (which it will revert in May 2023 as the outbreak is brought under control). But the last thing we and the health system need now is another virus joining the party! The ministry tries to quell concerns, making it clear that it has "taken steps to prepare for the arrival of Mpox", and reassures "there is no evidence of community transmission here". [201]

With an eye kept on Mpox, the main focus remains on the virus that *is* doing the community rounds. On 14 July the government outlines a plan to provide free masks and Covid-19 RAT tests. [202] Another piece of potential good news comes off the back of the new "one-off simplified residency pathway", which "has seen nearly 6000 health workers, about 14,000 construction workers and 761 teachers" apply for a fast-tracked resident visa. [203]

This potential boost to the workforce, and in particular to the health system, proves timely, as we are facing a second Covid wave as cases of the subvariant BA.5 spread around the country. [204] On 5 July, the Omicron subvariant BA.2.75 is detected in New Zealand for the first time. [205]

That "the second Omicron wave has hit" is reported on 13 July, along with the expectation that hospitalisations are expected to rise. The highest daily number of cases since April is recorded: 11,548, and hospitalisations reach a height not seen since 4 April. [206] The Covid-19 Response Minister warns: "We are in for a tough few weeks ahead. Cases will continue to rise. There will be a lot of pressure on the health system ... as [the] new wave rises." [207] This is alongside "cases of influenza remain[ing] high as Aotearoa faces one of the 'most challenging' seasons it has seen in years". People are again encouraged to get a flu vaccination. [208]

Medical professionals voice their concerns. "Doctors across all aspects of patient care say the health workforce is at risk of a 'catastrophic collapse'." [209] Low staffing levels put patients' lives at risk, as medical staff having to ration the care they can give "means neglecting our patients". [210] At the same time, calls to the 24/7 over-the-phone health service Healthline rise by 40%. [211]

The government reinforces the message that face masks and RATs are freely available to anyone who wants them, even as the Covid-19 Response Minister acknowledges that "the next challenge is getting people to use them". [212] The Director-General of Health reinforces the message that we all need to "do your bit for this next period of time, for a couple of months just to help us get through winter", as modelling of the BA.5 outbreak has shown cases peaking towards the end of the month. Both Bloomfield and Verrall urge us all to wear masks "as often as possible". [213]

On 20 July changes are made to the way Covid deaths are to be reported. "Instead of reporting all people who died within 28 days of a Covid-19 infection, those who died because of the virus, or for whom Covid-19 was a contributing factor in their death, will be reported formally." This change to classifying the cause of death at the actual time of death — not up to 28 days later — means deaths can now be categorised in a "very timely" way, making the data more relevant to the current status of events. [214]

On 22 July there is a change in the mask rules for schools: schools are to "enforce a mask-wearing policy" for all students in Year 4 and above. [215] At this time the question of whether the latest wave has peaked is still being debated. Experts tell us that if the previous week's drop in the seven-day rolling average continues for six days in a row, this will be "a good sign." Perhaps understandably this ray of hope is served with cautionary provisos and the fact of it still being in winter, meaning "It's hard to be sure." [216] On 29 July the ministry reports 7605 new community cases and 1479 deaths. The seven-day rolling average of community cases comes in at 7618, but there are 799 people currently in hospital, including 25 in intensive care. [217]

Two days earlier Dr Ashley Bloomfield has held his last scheduled news conference as the Director-General of Health. He reports that, Covid-19 case rates are trending downwards across all of New Zealand and "the 'worst-case scenario' previously modelled [is] now unlikely". His colleagues describe his contribution as a "Herculean effort", and point out that this last news conference is his 307th since the pandemic began., His briefing have been marked by "his presence, wisdom and reassurance" and, as noted by another colleague, "would be missed", [218] including by all New Zealanders. The other news at this briefing is that, from 31 July, the border will reopen for all students and visitor visa categories, including the maritime border. [219]

July ends with a widespread feeling that "everyone around me has caught covid", which is unsurprising when statistical modeller Professor Michael Plank says "the best estimate [is] that more than 50% of the population had caught Covid-19". [220]

These first two chapters will be familiar to you, since their content is still likely to be etched in your recent memory. But because dates are a rather blunt instrument except for historians, they don't give that sense of the diversity of thought during this time or the meaning and rhythms of the pandemic, which are better reflected in the subtleties of the changing language during the pandemic. This is why in the following reflections I have attempted to explore the context that surrounds the dates and give you my ideas of where the meaning lies. You, in turn, can build your own reflections and capture what it all means to you.

SOME REFLECTIONS

The gap between acknowledging regulations and then complying with them

Embedded in this Covid-19 timeline is what has been described as Covid-19 weariness or pandemic complacency. So to try to understand these feelings we need first to frame them in terms of the gap between acknowledging what's required and then accepting it — compliance. Why is it that we can acknowledge what it is that we must do — especially when in most cases it means helping to save lives, including our own — but simply don't do it. Rather than just getting on and doing it, we don't. What is stopping us? The key may lie in what intervenes between the acknowledgement of the rules and complying with them. Emeritus Professor Cory Keyes, in his seminal 2002 paper, introduces us to the concept of "languishing", which he describes as "emptiness and stagnation, constituting a life of quiet despair ... individuals who describe themselves and life as hollow, empty, a shell, and a void". [221] Author Adam Grant describes languishing in terms of what the feeling is *not*: "burnout — we still have energy. It wasn't depression — we [don't] feel hopeless. We just felt somewhat joyless and aimless." [222]

The feeling of languishing

We can, perhaps, sense it when we hear it creeping into our everyday language in the rather loosely used phrase "I'm over it". Perhaps it represents a coping mechanism to simply express a feeling that we can't explain because we don't understand why we feel the way we do. Perhaps used as a coping strategy it is meant to give us a sense of control, but even then, as Jane Bowron suggests in her piece on *Stuff*, the idea of control is doubtful, as using the phrase leads you to think you "can ignore the virus ... and it will go away ... you wish" But what you are experiencing may be the feeling of languishing, and this can't be dismissed simply by uttering a phrase like "I'm over it"". Even so, we may think that using the phrase "I'm over it", as Bowron suggests, "Give[s] us licence to stop keeping up with, and being informed about, the latest developments in the battle against Covid, and to stop wearing masks." [223] And in doing so, while it may not quell the feelings you're experiencing, it does change how you appraise events.

The feelings of languishing are often expressed in ways that simply attempt to capture its essence, such as feeling "blah", [224] "like running beyond empty". [225] It has also been described in terms of "feeling restless, apathetic or empty" [226] or "the mental rut you're going through". [227] "Languishing" was proclaimed "the mood of 2021". [228] Adam Grant describes it thus: "You might not notice the dulling of delight or the dwindling of drive. You don't catch yourself slipping into solitude; you're indifferent to your indifference." [229] The relevance of the feeling is also captured when it is described as "the pandemic-fuelled feeling known as Languishing. Showing up for life, but living without purpose and aim." [230]

When interviewed about his new book *Languishing: How to feel alive again in a world that wears us down*, Emeritus Professor Cory Keyes describes languishing in this way: "Do you feel aimless and numb inside ... People who are languishing almost feel nothing. They describe it as being numb or dead inside. I call languishing the neglected middle child of mental health, since it falls between mental illness and mental well-being ..." When the interviewer suggests that it's "a normal part of life to sometimes feel this way", he agrees, adding: "So are sadness and fear. But normal doesn't mean you must stay there and wallow in it ... People who languish feel stagnant too. They are not growing, and humans are meant to grow" And when he is asked "What can people do to help themselves flourish?", he responds: "There are five activities that research shows help people feel more joy, gratitude, hope and other emotions. I call them the five vitamins. These are: *learn*: Creating stories of Self-Growth, *connect*: Building warm and trusting relationships, *transcend*: Accepting the inevitable plot twists of life, *help*: Find your purpose, *play*: Stepping out of time; These everyday experiences of fun don't require equipment, stadiums or fields, boundaries or rule books; they require nothing but imagination. The only 'rule' is that you derive joy from a moment that might have otherwise passed you by, ... play takes you out of time, even if only for a few minutes ...The only way to stay flourishing is to remain committed to these habits." [231]

Languishing is one way to understand the disconnect between acknowledging regulations and then not complying with them, and it may well be the significant key. But there are other factors in play, too, that illustrate the complexity of what it is we are trying to understand. When we think of the pandemic and the government's battle with it, at the same time there is another battle going on: the government's battle with false news and misinformation. It is clear that "when scientific findings threaten people's sense of control over their lives, conspiracy theories are never far behind ... mak[ing] it harder for Scientists to seek the truth". [232] This is another facet in the puzzle of why compliance doesn't necessarily follow acknowledgement. At the beginning of the pandemic "[t]he underlying science was evolving daily, so there was no expert consensus or body of established research to draw on. And there were plenty of people willing to exploit this information vacuum, creating a secondary epidemic of misinformation ... It didn't take long for bad actors to weaponize this confusion to spread misinformation." [233]

Loneliness

Other factors are also in play, complicating the relationship between acknowledging regulations and complying with them. One of these may be loneliness. "The covid-19 global pandemic and subsequent public health social measures have challenged our social and economic life, with increasing concerns around potentially rising levels of social isolation and loneliness." [234] Others describe it as the "Loneliness Pandemic" — "the psychology and social costs of isolation in everyday life". [235] "Loneliness transcends borders and is becoming a global public health concern affecting every facet of health, wellbeing and development ... social isolation knows no age or boundaries ... [Loneliness] is an underappreciated public health threat." [236] "The COVID-19 pandemic seems to have brought our frenzied speed of modern society to a grinding halt and has literally crushed the wings of unlimited social interaction." [237] "We should expect major impacts on individual and community wellbeing;" [238] including behaviours that lead to questioning compliance.

Covid fatigue

Another factor that shouldn't be overlooked is the idea that it is most associated with 'Covid fatigue' where people are simply driven to be complacent. Being complacent is another mechanism to understand the gap between acknowledgement and acceptance — compliance. Hence the calls from Dr Ashley Bloomfield "to do your bit for this next period of time, for a couple of months just to help us get through winter", and to "again — recommit. We are not through this yet." [239]

Tracy Watkins argues in her *Stuff* article: "Our day of reckoning with Covid is here, and ... the Government has largely done all it can, through measures like vaccination. It really is up to us to do the rest." [240] It proves easier said than done. The presence of languishing, misinformation, loneliness and complacency makes it harder to achieve compliance, but it perhaps also makes it easier to understand why this is so. But the harsh reality is, even if we are 'over it'. We can't give up because "the pandemic hasn't ended." [241]

Some final reflections

When reflecting on the pandemic over each year it seems that a number of themes express our experience and how the pandemic has been managed. Looking back to 2020 the themes that emerged would be:

- "Going hard and going early" with elimination in mind.
- Decision-making focused around "an abundance of caution".
- The communication plan and the power of the phrase "the team of 5 million".
- Focusing on the science and research and not on the politics and misinformation.

When commentating on the government's strategies and management, writers express their views in different ways. For example, "Although new variants have been challenging these successes, the government remains deeply committed to care." [242] The power of the expression "the team of 5 million" resonates with the research on collective coping and communal coping and the power of the community. As Robin Nelson writes, our interdependence with others is a powerful key, simply expressed as: "Our fates are bound together. Taking care of others is taking care of ourselves." [243] A sentiment that Dr Bloomfield would endorse, as he says at his last media conference: "The one big lesson I take away is we tend to underestimate the capability and capacity and resourcefulness of our communities, and in fact providing them with the resources and the information to get on and do the right thing can lead to success." [244] An editorial in *The Listener* at the time of the first lockdown expresses the same sentiments: "for now all New Zealanders should ... not look for scapegoats ... but should put their energy and patience into being part of the solution by looking after themselves and looking out for their neighbours". [245]

In 2021 the themes reflected the twists and turns of the virus and its variants, where there is tangible sense that the preparation and planning strategies are maturing from the experience gained thus far in managing the pandemic.

- The introduction of alert levels – the shift in policy from containment to mitigation.
- The preparation and planning of a vaccination rollout.
- The introduction of, and transition to, the traffic light system from the former lockdown alert levels.
- An emerging theme that edges us towards the idea of individual responsibility through offering the tools to self-manage the virus.

This shift is not towards "more directives" or "policing rules", except when they may provide boundaries for behaviours, but towards offering solutions and guidelines where we are "given the tools" to police ourselves and engage in self-management. In essence it is just getting us mentally ready to accept Covid-19 "is here to stay — [and hence] how do we live with it?"

When you think in this way you understand the reason to shift to the traffic light system and the dispensing with other regulations: the exception being wearing masks. "In the future, routine testing might become part of everyday life. People with imperceptible symptoms who test positive would know to wear masks, isolate from others [at home and get vaccinated]." [246] A mantra that calls us to action and, which is already firmly fixed in our minds. As Tracy Watkins says in her thoughtful piece: "It is really up to us to do the rest … [and] in return the government would use the time well to prepare us for the inevitable wave once it hits our shore …" It is, as Watkins heads her piece, "Our day of reckoning with Covid is here, and what have we done?" [247] This represents "what the 'new normal' [may be like, and making it] a cliché that needs to be retired … but perhaps not yet, because we are entering a new phase of adaptation" [248]

2022 is defined through two words: "planning" and "preparation". The theme of self-management is the governing force as the Omicron variant arrives.

- Omicron and variants arrive.
- Protests emerge against government-imposed restrictions.
- Winter sees the usual seasonal emergence of influenza and RSVs,

along with the indoor conditions that promote the transition of these respiratory viruses along with Covid.

• Self-management and RATs tests are introduced.

In 2022 we have moved to phase 3 of the Omicron response. Planning during the pandemic has a maturing feel to it. Using its growing experience in managing the pandemic the government has taken the time to direct its attention to test what strategies we are comfortable with and prepared for. In essence, the line between mandates and self-management is being established, and 2022 is an example of this maturing process. The Covid Response Minister explains: "Most have been gearing up for this and it will not come as a surprise. However, the move to phase three will not mean a 'sudden lurch' in terms of additional restrictions or movements, because the traffic light system has been designed to smooth things out already." In essence, phase 3 is about self-management and acknowledges what our individual responsibilities are. In phase 3, the minister adds: "... the primary priority now shifts to isolating those with Covid-19 and their household contacts. Rapid Antigen Tests (RATs) will be the primary means for Covid-19 [identification] and will be available from thousands of sites. We are asking New Zealanders to accept a greater degree of personal responsibility." [249]

2022 has been a tumultuous time with the government battling Omicron, influenza, winter woes, and protests. Protests have focused a spotlight on the delicate balance between "doing our bit" and the government imposing regulations — and, in particular, mandates. In the end, the government has opted for tilting the balance in favour of "doing our bit", through encouraging individuals to take on personal responsibilities through self-management. This decision follows the government having probed what we are comfortable with and what we are prepared for. In preparing us to make this transition, the government likens the Covid-19 virus to the influenza virus, which will be always with us. Having established the context, the government importantly gives us the tools to exercise these personal responsibilities. Interestingly, Karin Reed and Joseph Allen in their book *Suddenly Hybrid* note: "[O]ne thing that is universal though is how the pandemic transformed our orientation towards our health and well-being. We wash our hands more. We use hand sanitizer. And it is understood that we should not go to [work] when we are sick." [250] So in 2022 the groundwork has been laid by the government and now it is up to us.

A POSTSCRIPT

This chapter ends with a postscript. The pandemic has certainly been a journey dominated by twists and turns of the Covid-19 virus, its variants and sadly deaths, not to forget the emotional toll. However, international voices have reflected positively on the way the pandemic in New Zealand has been managed. For example, even now when thinking back — although the memories may still be raw, or perhaps sometimes even difficult to remember — we did have at times during the pandemic glimpses of what the "new normal" might look like. And, difficult as it may have been, our efforts are acknowledged in our country's ranking on the *Economist normalcy index:* "New Zealand was ranked second on a list of countries ordered by how much they've returned to normal during the pandemic." [251] The "The Covid-19 pandemic measures saved 2750 lives, caused life expectancy to rise... the researchers looked at excess deaths, a measure defined as the difference between how many people died during the pandemic, from any cause, and how many deaths would have been expected had there been no pandemic. By being quite strategic, New Zealand has produced the lowest mortality in the OECD." [252] Finally, at the World Health Assembly in 2023 a participant says: "We in the WHO think of New Zealand's response as one of the best in the world and really setting an example for other countries." [253]

AN ADDENDUM TO THE POSTSCRIPT AND NEW DIRECTIONS AS WE HEAD TO 2023 AND 2024

On 13 September 2022, most of the Covid-19 rules, in the form of the traffic lights Protection Framework, are removed, in acknowledgement that "overall COVID-19 case numbers and hospitalisations [are] trending downwards, along with a highly vaccinated population and increased access to antiviral medicines". [254] Nearly a year later, on 14 August 2023, the government announces that the last masking mandate and isolation requirements will be lifted, adding that nevertheless "while not mandated, the Ministry of Health guidance is to stay at home for five days if you're unwell or have tested positive". [255] Reflecting on the pandemic, the newly-minted Sir Ashley Bloomfield says: "It's clear we're past the worst of the pandemic. It feels like we're out the other side, and that is the sense I have both in Aotearoa/New Zealand but also internationally." [256]

But even though the regulations have been lifted the virus is still evolving, and certainly hasn't gone away. In April 2023 epidemiologist Professor Michael Baker makes a call "for Covid-19 to be top of mind as we enter a fourth wave of cases". At this time New Zealand is seeing a sharp rise in Covid-19 infections and, although the majority are likely to be reinfections, Covid is still damaging our health. Baker argues for Covid-19 to be "an ongoing issue that must be prioritised", especially with the 2023 general election approaching. Even if we are feeling "Covid fatigue", Baker reminds us that reducing case numbers depends on everyone acting responsibly". [257] Even though the World Health Organization has downgraded Covid-19's official status from pandemic to "global health emergency", the reality is that it is still very much a pandemic, and is, as Professor Baker points out in May 2023, "still New Zealand's number one killer when it comes to infectious disease", meaning "people should make sure they were vaccinated and take sensible precautions". [258]

As 2023 moves closer to Christmas the headlines point to an "Enormous amount of Covid around", with the current wave being larger than the fourth wave experienced earlier in the year. Professor Baker says that this suggests that "the pandemic threat is continuing to evolve in unpredictable ways ...The factors driving these pandemic waves are likely to include a mix of waning immunity, continuing Covid-19 evolution, and changing human behaviour, including relaxation of protective measures and some degree of response fatigue and complacency." [259]

By 21 December 2023 the headlines continue to reflect a situation where "Covid could yet ruin Christmas, New Year", with infection levels back to the highs of January meaning "Covid could yet wreck thousands of Kiwis' Christmas or New Year". Predictions are that between now and the end of the year 12,000 people will become infected with Covid-19, with 720 people ending up hospital and 50 dying. Professor Michael Baker says, "Covid-19 was not behaving like an endemic at the moment. This virus can still surprise us." University of Canterbury Covid-19 mathematical modeller Professor Michael Plank points to the new JN.1 variant as the likely culprit fuelling the year-end surge, being "probably the fastest-growing variant seen this year". He suggests the reason for this is that "JN.1 has picked up mutations which allow it to spread rapidly in a wider part of the population than BA.2.86 could." Professor Baker concurs that JN.1 is the rogue element, making it "not possible to predict when the current wave would reach its peak, as it could be quite prolonged if the JN.1 variant became more dominant". [260]

As the fourth anniversary of Covid-19's arrival in New Zealand approaches, "one thing is clear — the virus isn't going anywhere". If anything, Professor Baker says, "the pandemic has become more intense in the last few months, with this latest wave larger than the previous one". He further predicts that this could be a sign of things to come, that oft talked-about "new normal". "In the future we could experience two major waves of COVID-19 each year, and we need to beef up our strategy to deal with them ...It's getting ahead of our immune system and we need a different way of working ... We need to get on top of this ongoing pandemic. It's not going away, if anything it's getting worse." [261]

The new year sees measure targeted at responding to the reality of the lingering and evolving presence of Covid in our lives. In February 2024 it is announced that RATs will remain freely available until the end of June. [262] Under the headline "Covid Booster supported" the message is clear: "Public health experts are urging people to get boosted against Covid-19 as they head back to work, as the country still grapples with a fifth wave of infections." [263]

The fifth Covid-19 wave which appears to be driving this latest spike in infections offers, Professor Baker says, "a glimpse of our long-term future with the coronavirus". While there is regional variation, with the wave perhaps peaking in some parts of New Zealand, but rising in others, longer term, Professor Baker says, "a 'national approach' was needed to manage these peak periods". He has "singled out several priority areas he felt required addressing, including promoting boosters; supporting to help people self-isolate, and consistent policy for ventilation standards and mask used in healthcare settings". The week before, Professor Baker and colleagues have called on the government to "set up a dedicated centre for disease control — like that in the US, and now being established in Australia — to better prepare for future pandemics". [264]

Looking to the future raises numerous questions, such as "What's going on with Covid-19?" and "Is this just how it's going to be forever?'" Public health experts and epidemiologists turn to known science and to modelling in an effort to provide answers to an anxious public. Their answers are, perhaps predictably, "yes and no". While Covid-19 clearly isn't going anywhere, immunologist Professor James Ussher, from the University of

Otago says: "But how it will behave and change in the months and years to come remains the million-dollar question, as we're seeing the virus move from the pandemic phase, transitioning into an endemic virus … What the pattern will look like isn't clear." In the meantime, as Professor Plank concurs, "it is here to stay" and unlikely to be eradicated in the near future, explaining: "Certainly not with the tools we currently have available … it's impossible to get rid of Covid." [265] In another interview Professor Plank reveals "Covid-19 has not yet become seasonal in the way influenza is, but it is settling into a more regular cycle of peaks and troughs." [266] Covid-19 looks likely to join the two main respiratory viruses circulating before the pandemic: respiratory syncytial virus (RSV) and flu. This has serious long-term implications: "hospitalisations will continue to be higher than they once were, straining healthcare systems". And yet Plank admits that even after four years, there is much yet to be learnt about the virus, "particularly when it comes to long covid and the risk of repeat infections". This calls for vigilance and means that "We still have to maintain our work to deal with covid, but deal with it in the context of everything else," writes Grace Wade. [267] A Royal Commission into the COVID-19 response has been set up, and will report after gathering feedback on any additional topics that it may need to look at. Public consultation is now open, and feedback can be given until 24 March 2024. [268] The Inquiry's focus is on what have we learned from the pandemic, and our response seems to be the correct one.

As the last days of May 2024 draw closer, they bring the news that "New Zealand is at its highest peak for the virus in 18 months", with seven deaths alongside the 6636 weekly total of new cases. Professor Michael Baker offers a context for these disheartening statistics: the biology hasn't changed, but there is more pressure for people to go back to work and school. He feels the Budget due this week offer an opportunity to break this pattern by allocating more money towards the Covid-19 response: "It was important for health and productivity that the government continued to fund booster shots, RAT tests and the anti-viral medication."

Reading such statistics leaves us ruminating on "the million-dollar questions" that now haunt our thoughts: Is this just a shadow of the reality of our future — is this how it's simply always going to be from now on? The nuanced answers of the experts suggest that while crystal-ball gazing may be a fool's game, one message — one we are very familiar with — comes through loud and clear: Covid is still here and disrupting lives — so be vigilant and mask up. [269]

COVID: THE RESHAPING OF SOCIETY AND ITS FUTURE

There is no doubt that the pandemic has reshaped society and its future. It has touched every corner of society. Nowhere has this reshaping been more obvious than for those who have had to reimagine their working lives. It is abundantly clear that "the workplace of today, has totally different expectations than it did pre-pandemic". [270] As Professor Julia Hobsbawm says: "[T]his moment is therefore both exciting and uncomfortable ... Wherever we end up working life has been due for a shake-up for a long time." [271] "The pandemic altered the paradigm for the world of work, forcing a grand experiment [for some] workers across the globe." [272] This experiment is still a work in progress, and its progress will be tracked across the chapters that follow. It is clear why the pandemic has become the vehicle of change and transition for work, and also how it has triggered "philosophical questions about work [which] were not asked before Covid-19 ... People are now asking searching questions about the nature of work, and its meaning to them." [273] With this paradigm shift, "It comes as no surprise that stress and mental health issues (often work related) can be viewed as a modern pandemic." [274]

But this change in the nature of work also sent a tidal wave of change and transition that quickly rippled out to all corners of society. Lockdowns and continued sporadic isolations — as well as initiating a need to accommodate work and economic realities within these confines — provided much-needed time to reflect not just on the relevance of the status quo but more significantly on the patterns of change emerging that may need confronting. The examples are many, all hastened by the pandemic and the accompanying changing nature of working lives, with the design of the city centres crying out for change to respond to the changing patterns of retail shopping, transport systems, the ideas that surround 'the 15-minute city', alongside the need for more sustainable cities — to mention just a few.

And it doesn't stop there. There is the need to reflect on how we express economic growth and the nature of that growth itself, the need to reflect on whether traditional measures of gross national product (GNP) actually reflect what is really valued and how it accounts for our well-being. Then there is a need to reflect on the subtle changes to work, the changing nature of careers – they become less ladder-like, work–life balance becomes more nuanced, and is described more in terms of work–life integration, or work–life navigation expressing a journey that responds to life transitions, leadership that reflects empathy, trust and social connection, and the need to acknowledge the difference between what you want to do and who you want to be. These issues will be discussed in the chapters that follow.

Finally, the pandemic as a vehicle for reimagining working life gets its energy from a theme that early on in the pandemic became a talking point for researchers, commentators, practitioners and managers, coalescing around addressing some of the following questions. "What lens are we choosing as we look ahead? Are we viewing the future as an extension of a predictable past, or are we viewing the future as a broad set of new opportunities that will reflect whatever we think is possible? In other words, are we viewing the future through a fixed or growth mindset … are we creating and innovating? … The intersection of the future of work and what we're now experiencing as the Covid-19 era represents a fault line [a vehicle] in our lives, a uniquely instructional moment. We're invited to reimagine how we work, … and how we build our careers, our companies, and our communities." [275] It is, as Jeff Schwartz writes, "the need to shift to new ways of working, new frames, new expectations, and new possibilities … accelerated by the pandemic". [276]

When we reflect on the pandemic, we are naturally, immediately drawn to think of it in terms of illness, lockdowns, regulations, mandates, alert levels, trauma, anxieties, worries, uncertainties, protests, disruptions and restrictions, and of course grief and death. But the pandemic has proven to have many faces, and reflecting on it as a "uniquely instructional moment" gives us the chance to explore the opportunities ahead of us and the future person we want to be. This gives us a sense of hope, the key element in building resilience. This sets the context for the chapters that follow, and the debates and discussions that flow from thinking in terms of the pandemic as a vehicle of change and transition, and the hope that stems from thinking about it as a "uniquely instructional moment" that should be grabbed and pursued.

CHAPTER 3

Reimagining our Working Lives

INTRODUCTION

As the pandemic has continued to weave its path, we have watched, witnessed, experienced it and learnt about the twists and turns and convulsions of the virus and its variants. It has touched every corner of our lives. There have been no boundaries that it is unwillingly to cross, all seemingly with the intention of sweeping in a future that, while not entirely unexpected, was not actually expected to arrive as rapidly as it has. The pandemic's presence was soon to be felt in many fields like scientific medical discovery, economics, politics, the designing of inner cities, reimagining retail shopping, heightening the different expectations between generations, the importance of lifelong learning, the ideas of what constituted good and essential work, and, of course, the remodelling of work and the reimagining of working lives. All of the intrusions and implications were accompanied with animated conversations, discussion, debate and collaboration.

This chapter is designed to capture the debate and discussion that has accompanied the remodelling of work and the reimagining of our working lives. I have structured the debate by keeping in mind the driving force: *why do we work in the way that we do?* I have cited a collective of international and domestic voices: authors, researchers, academics, practitioners, commentators, all of whom have been involved in the debate, conversations and discussions that have led to what is believed to be the new vision of work for some. This vision is presented as a product of international collaboration and discussion and debate. I hope you will think about the vision and the debate that surrounds it, and reflect on whether it fits your experience, and your hopes, aspirations and well-being.

BEFORE THE PANDEMIC — "CHANGE WAS CLEARLY AFOOT"

Nine years before the term "pandemic" was confirmed with regards to the emergence of Covid-19, creeping into the writing of researchers was a sense, that in terms of paid work "change was clearly afoot", and that organisations and work were in a state of "perpetual motion". [1] "The last decade of the twentieth century brought a rapid growth in the flexibility of employment contracts. Part-time work, staggered hours, condensed working weeks and 'flexi-time' spread. Remote and home-based working increased with the introduction of mobile-technologies" [2] Over the next decade terms like "alternative work" and "nonstandard work" were filtering into our language, describing the restructuring of the nature of work, with the conclusion that "this sort of work 'appears' to be here to stay ... [and is] firmly rooted in the new world of work". [3] Other descriptors were to quickly follow, capturing the "extraordinary growth" of what was called, "boundaryless and contingent employment arrangements", [4] possibly foreshadowing the arrival of the "Gig Economy". [5]

A NEW AGE

"We have entered a widely heralded 'new age' where work organizations are undergoing profound changes ... the very nature of the 'business model,' which dominates organizational thinking is changing." [6] It appears, as other researchers add, "that the time is ripe" [7] for developing new theory and for contemporary theories to be refined. These changes to the structure of work are already questioning what it means to be employed, and require us to now give attention to refining traditional ideas of what employment means. There is a growing sense that these changes are also sharpening the distinction between jobs and work. As the decades progress "work will become more of a tradable commodity rather than a job", [8] and "organizing work into packages called jobs is failing to meet the demands of swiftly changing businesses". [9] "Working lives will be made up of a variety of diverse work and work experiences." [10] All of this raises questions "about the nature of work and our relationship with it ... and what does this tell us about the way we work". [11] So what are the forces that are driving these changes where the future shape of work is being reimagined?

Some of these forces are ones we are already well acquainted with, and include globalisation and advances in technology, and form a broader business context of change that is well accepted. Other forces are more subtle and are specifically directing the changes in work. These include the new generations of Millennials, and Generation Z, whose numbers are ever-expanding in the workforce, and they are becoming agents for change and for new ways of working and new routines. "They are young, globally connected and digital, and they're standing up to call out the errors of our past." [12] "Generation Z workers will be the biggest change agents ... and their dominance and connectivity to each other will become a groundswell that busts through our ageing and irrelevant practices." [13] Generation Zers "are made for this urgent moment ... and they are only getting started". [14] Generation Zers are often described as "digital natives" [15] or the "internet generation" [16], and they have now prompted "new behaviours [that have been] shaped by new technologies ... like social media and the web" [17] and how they share data.

"A new generational workplace means new employee behaviours, approaches, attitudes, and expectations about work and the workplace." [18] Their "impact will overshadow the influence of past generations", [19] and their influence will continue to be felt for some time, as later they will be joined by the Alpha Generation. Other "demographic and social trends, particularly the changing role of women, all point to the need for a fresh approach to work. [That is why] we are poised for a revolution in working practices." [20] It is not all about new generations, although their influence is readily apparent: "the future employee isn't just a younger employee it's an employee with new attitudes about work and new styles of working" [21] regardless of age. So "the transition to new ways of working, leading, and building organizations has already started." [22] But who would have thought that a pandemic would wrench these changes from the shadows of academic journals and books, so that suddenly there they are, right in front of us, as we witness, not without trepidation, how quickly they are accelerated from theory to reality.

THE PANDEMIC AND REIMAGINING WORKING LIVES

Even without Covid-19 and the pandemic "no debate topic elicits a more emotional response than the future of work". [23] Let me assure you that I am not trying to predict the future of work, but we are exploring the research and contemporary practice to try to understand why we continue to work in the way that we do. What follows is a framework built around the research that offers new directions as to why our working lives are changing. Remembering that "your future is what you shape it to be". [24] While immersed in lockdowns, protests, the rules and regulations, and the twists and turns of a devastating virus, who would have guessed that "Covid-19 will ultimately make things better by speeding up changes [to work] that were already under way". "Thanks to the rise of remote work, more people will have more flexibility over when, where and how they earn their living ... This is forcing managers to become better communicators, improving employees' job satisfaction. It is also stimulating helpful ... changes in employment law ... reduc[ing] inequality, and coming up with better-designed systems of employees' rights" [25] and protections.

The pandemic is in every sense where "occasionally, the world engineers a moment in time that's so big we're compelled to stay relevant. For all of us, 2020 and the events within it was that moment." [26] "To say COVID has been a struggle for many of us is a huge understatement. But it has also helped us realise what's important to us and what truly matters." [27] Surprisingly, the pandemic has also given us time to reflect and explore what is significant to us and what are the things that give us a sense of well-being. The new age "requires reflexivity — the capacity to both reflect on and to make decisions about what it is we want to become". [28] The power that lies within the pandemic is that it offers a "uniquely instructive moment" where "We're invited to reimagine how we work ... [it] is actually about the opportunities, the resilience, and growth that we can leverage to do things differently, to establish new priorities and new patterns, and to create a new order in our lives ..." [29] It is, in this way, "a second renaissance", whereby "we have an opportunity to redesign our world ... and underpinning it will be the idea of bringing humanity back to the workplace". [30] Others call it "the Great Pause, [we are] being handed opportunities to re-examine the boundaries that surround the things that really matter... The question is, what are you going to do with your chance?" The Great Pause is "an opportunity to go in a new direction. To rethink your career and your contribution." [31] Others see it as "we are on the cusp of a new Reformation, but this is a reformation of the workplace from the ground upwards." [32] Arundhati Roy describes it as "a portal [of opportunity] ... a gateway between one world and the next ... ready to imagine another world. And ready to fight for it." [33]

WORKING FROM HOME

The immediate impact of the pandemic on work was the need to work from home. The day before our first experience of a lockdown. The prime minister requested that "all businesses which can have staff work from home, do so. ... [W]ith the public service having ... put all the necessary arrangements in place to ensure staff could work from home during a pandemic ... other organizations put ... strong systems in place to effectively work from wherever we are, we have implemented our full working from home policy ...". [34] Who would have imagined that it would have been "a global pandemic that would require the wholesale migration of nearly entire companies to remote work in a matter of weeks". [35] This moment is being described as "a brave new world beyond the industrial-age belief in the Office ... the time is right for remote work". [36] Other authors describe this moment thus: "the good news is that we can change ..., but only if we commit ourselves to refiguring the place of work in our lives. Right now, our priorities are backward. Instead of changing our *lives* to make ourselves better workers, we have to change our *work* to make our lives better." [37] "Our world is changing at an extraordinary pace, and what will go are many of the beliefs about what work is and how it is performed." [38]

The word "remote", as in "remote working", "connotes distance, barriers, separation", [39] and doesn't really capture what is at the heart of this new working style where the emphasis is on "a fundamental shift to a new, different relationship between employees and employers. There is no going back." [40] It is a significant and dramatic upheaval and transformation to the way we work. This helps to explain why researchers and commentators have worked through a range of descriptors to give a sense of what is going on. These descriptors include: "flexible working arrangements", "working from home" (or "WFH"), "the digital-nomad workforce", "working from anywhere" and "hybrid working" (splitting time between working from home and in the formal work space). *Keep in mind that not all workers will have access to hybrid arrangements.*

The sense is overwhelmingly that, however these working arrangements are described, they reflect the future of work. This sense is reinforced by a headline in *The Dominion Post*: "Our year in the future of work". [41] "Leaders who think that what has happened across the last year has been a blip, and that we will 'return to normal', are wrong." [42] Mike Burrell, the executive director of the Sustainable Business Council, said that the work arrangements forced on us by our alert levels 3 and 4 lockdowns simply "gave hints about the future of work". [43] "[It] isn't just the future – it's the *present*. Now is your chance to catch up." [44] "It is now inconceivable to argue that remote or flexible work is impossible when people have been doing it, against all odds, for months." [45] Over time — and accompanied with endless conversations, discussion and articles — a consensus seemed to be building around designing hybrid working for some.

Professor Jarrod Haar at AUT puts it this way in an article in *The Dominion Post* by Brianna Mcilraith: "the future of work was hybrid". He adds: "We are still obsessed with the 9am to 5pm which frankly, makes little sense … Workplaces needed to tailor work more around getting tasks done and productivity, rather than being present in the office … This would give people the opportunity to work less and enjoy life more." [46] The subheading of the article gives Professor Haar's comments a context: "The pandemic has caused some soul-searching in the workforce, and the result is a hybrid approach to employment." [47] Other New Zealand voices echo Professor Haar's views. The Sustainable Business Council's Mike Burrell says: "Flexible working, and working from home at least some of the time, is here to stay." He adds: "It was [also] important to take a deeper look at flexibility in sectors where that was harder to achieve, and that was where technology stepped in — for example remote manufacturing." [48]

Felicity Caird of the Institute of Directors is reported as saying that the stress surrounding the pandemic, "job security and the changing nature of jobs … [means] work has changed significantly and it won't go back …

But to make the most of the disruption, workers have to be supported and upskilled." She adds that "the focus on mental health and wellbeing will grow". [49] Her comments resonate with those of Council of Trade Unions economist Bill Rosenberg, who tackles the same theme when he says: "It also requires employers to stand up and take an active role in helping prospective and actual employees get trained and up their skills, facing up to reality, if you like." [50] Their comments are set in the context of *The Dominion Post* article headed "Our year in the future of work".

"The pandemic has revealed that, for [some] employees, we can break the relationship between work and place." [51] Other voices have joined the conversations about hybrid working. When in March 2022 the government changed the scope of the traffic light system's Red setting, "public sector agencies [were] in no rush to bring back workers back into the office", saying that "staff will be able to use flexible working arrangements such as working from home, adding that they "had always encouraged flexible working environments, and while the pandemic had necessitated more people working from home, this policy would not change". [52] In her piece in *The Dominion Post*, Janine Starks asks "whether 'working from home' [has] a future". Her answer is affirmative: "what does appear to have legs in the wider employment market is the hybrid model. It's an extension of flexitime and the most likely candidate for an increase in productivity, while balancing the other needs of training, career progression and employees maintaining their social mojo." [53]

Professor Cary Cooper "believes the best solution is hybrid working — a mixture of in-office days and working from home", adding that "research has shown that giving an employee some autonomy — knowing that their manager trusts them — leads to less sickness absence and more overall productivity — there is no doubt that this hybrid working is the way forward". [54] So all eyes are on hybrid working, "The transition to hybrid work and a focus on the *what* instead of the *where* present a true chance for a revolution around inclusion not only at work but *through* work." [55] More supportive evidence, if you need it, comes from workers themselves: "Working from home (WFH) is now the most searched-for-term on *Seek* ...". [56] Couple that with "researchers [finding] flexible working can reduce the risk of heart attack ... Having a better work–life balance is so beneficial to health that some employees who work flexibly end up with heart health equivalent to what they had 10 years earlier. The findings are likely to add to the debate about whether working from home more often, as more people have been doing since Covid, improves their health. They [the researchers] also suggest that working in a stressful environment raises the risk of a heart attack or stroke ..." [57] "You can't have the sort of culture that we've created — the 24-7, always-on, technology-based culture — without a rethink. The victims of that new world are the people who are now signalling there has to be a rethink." [58]

Research and practice are certainly coalescing around the hybrid model and supporting it when we reimagine our working lives. Accelerated by a pandemic which in every sense "was [a] global experience of how quickly change can happen when the purpose is big enough", [59] progressed by technology in its role as a change agent, and generated by the mindsets of Millennial and Generation Z workers. All this reinforces the idea that "the greatest shift required in making the transition ... a success is the shift in our thinking". [60]

We may be able to help you to make that "mind-shift" by answering the following questions you may have around hybrid working. Working from home during a global crisis is not the same as working from home in calmer times, is it? What have we learned about hybrid work so far? What will happen to work–life balance? What will happen to my productivity? Doesn't hybrid working have the greatest impact on knowledge workers and the knowledge economy? Won't it require changes in management styles? Will the office and its format change under hybrid working? Will I need to upskill, and will I need to update the way I think about my career? What type of new technology will I have to get used to? Who will benefit from hybrid working: men or women?

'Working from home during a pandemic is not the same as working from home in calmer times, is it?' "The reality is that given a choice I suspect most of us would want a mix of office time and working remotely." [61] So in "calmer times" you have a choice of locations and can set a routine around your preferences as to where you work. The feelings you have when you are working from home because of a lockdown — where you can't control when the end is in sight and your normal routines are in disarray — will hopefully dissipate. Remember "the future of work won't be as simple as either being constantly present at the office or always working from home.

The options and variations will be endless … We can, and in fact we need to design a working life that fits our preferences …" [62] Writers also tell us "How thinking about 'future you' can build a happier life", and suggest: "We should think about whom we'll be in the future — because doing so has profound consequences for our health, happiness and financial security." [63]

What have we've learned about hybrid work so far? Looking forward "we're not yet in a steady hybrid pattern … neither workers nor businesses have the real-life experience we need yet, [so], the future of the workplace is very much a work-in-progress … it seems the one constant will be change … We're a long way from figuring out 'normal' — but hopefully we will have more answers than questions soon." [64] As we move through the book, chapter by chapter, we will continue to track the progress of the hybrid model and ask whether it has prevailed. The one thing that must be described as a "known" at this point is that "the flexible-work genie is out of the bottle … it didn't take long for huge numbers of workers to figure out how much they liked remote work and all the elements that come with it". [65] The other "known" is that bosses "have called for their employees to start spending at least some time back at their desks … Most companies are trying 3-2 or 2-3 set-ups — but it is not going seamlessly." [66] The challenge, it seems, is getting the combination between working in the office and home working right, and that is complicated by employees' preferences. Formerly research had concluded that "approximately three days is the right in-office number", but continuing research suggests it "may, in fact, be as few as one". Having said this: "Hybrid work uptake is very different within companies … there's really no one-size-fits all across businesses." [67]

"Hybrid work has different emotional impacts." Switching "between two types of schedules, workplaces, and environments [can] be draining", although for others hybrid work "provides a much-needed emotional boost", [68] particularly when they are back physically with colleagues. Any policy needs to "engage the employees in the process, remembering that designing hybrid work arrangements needs to be done "with individual human concerns in mind, not just institutional ones". [69] On the other hand, "companies are figuring out that they need to be flexible and accommodating especially if they want to recruit and retain a diverse workforce". [70]

"For now, however, focus will be on honing the policies and routines that normalise hybrid work, so this stage starts to feel more intentional and less like an experiment." [71] The good thing is that the pandemic has taught us that the best way forward is through the global collaboration of ideas, giving us not just confidence, but also opportunities to share experiences and strategies, "and hopefully mak[e] hybrid work *work*". [72] In the end you will need to look back and "thoughtfully take stock: In the changes you've made, have you created a foundation for the future that everybody in the company will find engaging, fair, inspiring, and meaningful?" [73]

What will happen to my work–life balance? What will happen to my productivity? Looking first to work–life balance, the idea is to get you to think about what does "balance" even mean?' Is it an urban myth and "when does this 'mythical state' occur?", [74] or how when working in the traditional way from "9 to 5" do you reach balance when the equation is not balanced in the first place? It seems the cards are stacked with little flexibility on the work side, making any balance difficult to achieve simply because all the trade-offs were always on the life side. Now that we are thinking in terms of *flexible* ways of working, we will dispense with the idea of balance just for the moment and talk instead in terms of work–life 'integration.' "The question isn't to balance work and life; instead, it's how to better integrate them." [75] It's "not trading off one for the another but finding mutual value among them". It is thinking in terms of the total person, and not the work identity matched against the life identity –– integrated gives you that total person, giving "sustainable change to better not just you but the most important people around you". [76]

Others wonder whether "now that many of us have experienced working from home … if a new concept might emerge … The concept of work–life coherence." [77] If work–life balance sets work against life "the idea of work–life coherence is to unify the two sides … work and life are in a two-way relationship — they are interconnected — so everything works better when they're in flow. When there's some flexibility; in its most literal sense, work–life coherence means we can work in a way that suits [your] life." Both integration and coherence are examples of the long shadow of the pandemic and how it shifts and refines our thinking. We are now being asked to go beyond the idea of balance and express our relationship between work and life in a way that is relevant to twenty-first-century living where we aspire to some form of "harmonious connectedness". [78]

When we come to the issue of productivity the research findings suggest, in general, that our productivity has increased when working from home. The question is why? The answer may lie in what is described as "deep work". [79] Deep work is where "professional activities performed in a state of distraction-free concentration that push your cognitive capabilities to their limit". [80] It is experiencing "the flow", [81] where you are "concentrating, losing yourself in an activity". If we give attention to absorbing things, "we'll experience our working life as more important and positive ... the feeling of going deep is in *itself* very rewarding". [82]

Others follow this reasoning and argue that: "The ability to be alone with your thoughts is, in fact, one of the key advantages of working remotely." Working from home, "you can find a space that fits your work style ... your place, your zone, is yours alone." "If you ask yourself': where do you go when you *really* have to get work done? Your answer won't be 'the office in the afternoon'." [83] That is because offices have become "interruption factories". "Meaningful work, creative work, thoughtful work, important work — this type of effort takes stretches of uninterrupted time to get into the zone. But in the modern office long stretches just can't be found. Instead, it's just one interruption after another... The ability to be alone with your thoughts is, in fact, one of the key advantages of working remotely." [84]

Other authors add their voices to reflect the potency of this debate. Justin Zorn and Leigh Marz describe the world as a "world of noise", where noise is defined "in two words, 'unwanted distraction' ... [that simply is] consuming our attention". [85] We live in an age that is defined by terms like "constant connectivity", "hardwired", an "online world" "and the expectation of being *always* on". [86] So taking time for silence and cultivating it "isn't just getting respite from the distractions of office chatter or tweets. Real sustained silence, the kind that facilitates clear and creative thinking, and quiets inner chatter as well as outer.'" [87] "Silence isn't just the absence of noise. It's a presence." [88] It is important to "weigh the costs ... of the noise we generate", [89] and its potential to create disruptions and distractions, and how this limits our creativity, attention concentration, productivity and our best work, and indeed our lives.

Johann Hari also points to a world that is a "blur" [90] of distractions, and how this blur reduces our ability to focus and concentrate, and how quite simply "we seem to have lost our sense of focus and how we can get it back". [91] How "a life of distractions is, at an individual level, diminish[ing]. When you are unable to pay sustain[ed] attention, you can't achieve the things you want to achieve. ... Through no fault of your own, there never seems to be enough stillness — enough cool, clear space — for you to stop and think." Citing a study from the United States, "that [most office workers] *never* get an hour of uninterrupted work in a typical day", [92] Hari says: "We need to strip out our distractions and to replace them with sources of flow" — that is, deep work [93] — as that is "where you are flowing into the experience itself". [94] He concludes: "Flow expands us"; [95] "It is the deepest form of focus and attention that we know of." [96] So as productivity is maximised by getting in your zone or flow, and as this is often best achieved when you can work from home, it goes a long way to explaining why productivity tends to be improved with remote working.

Does hybrid working have the greatest impact on knowledge workers and the knowledge economy? The "knowledge economy" is a term that has been used widely both in New Zealand and internationally. However, the United Nations notes that "knowledge economy" is not an agreed term: "it must be said that there is no coherent definition, let alone theoretical concept, of this term: it is at best a widely used metaphor, rather than a concept". [97] Nevertheless, the term has certainly filtered into general use, and with its focus on the "production of knowledge and its distribution and use of knowledge and information" [98] its meaning has been extended to describe the economy as "weightless" — a term that some have argued "has stood the test of time". [99] Researchers continue to explore the sectors of the economy that recruit these workers, but there is no doubt their "skills and expertise are becoming increasingly sought after as companies rush to keep pace with change" [100] and because of the value they add to the economy.

It is clear that these workers have embraced boundaryless careers mainly through the roles they play in helping to transition organisations, and the "way that [they] can add value immediately". [101] Jason Walker, the managing director of the New Zealand branch of international recruitment company Hays, cites the important contribution the experience of their work patterns can add to the current discussion of change, because their roles have for some time reflected "in many ways the 'new normal' that is emerging across New Zealand workplaces ... These skilled professionals work alongside permanent employees as needed, creating a blended workforce that can flex in response to project work or the need for unique expertise." [102]

So while it would seem that the "new normal" working arrangements that have turned some jobs on their head are to knowledge workers an accepted routine, with the flexibility they offer simply a way of life plus "the ability to manoeuvre". [103] It could be that these workers — with their employment patterns and the varied experiences they have garnered — have the skills and expertise to work with organisations to assist them through this transition into hybrid working. The impact for them may well come in a different way, because they have the potential to become the change agents because of their familiarity with flexible working, and can advise on the challenges of dealing with personal preferences and the two modes of working.

Won't it require changes in management styles? The simple answer is "yes". However, leadership was on the turn before the pandemic hit, and in many ways was already re-focusing on the issue of managerial control. The loosening of managerial control can be summed up as not ordering workers what to do, but "allow[ing] them to choose to work in ways that best play to their strengths ... Getting hybrid right will be about embracing your people in their entirety." [104] The "defining feature of new work systems is thus ... self-management". [105] Managers need to re-examine their style of managing and question whether it is the best way to motivate employees. If the pandemic has hastened anything it is certainly not any strengthening of traditional views about management control, but beginning to trust people to self-manage and letting them decide how to complete their work. It is this latter style that has a more comfortable fit with twenty-first-century working. If managers are going to make this transition successfully, they need to think in terms of "creating a shared purpose, radical flexibility, and deeper connections". [106] All "with a mindset focused on people and driven by inclusion". [107] It will also require regularly reviewing the changes being made, and asking whether they are "a foundation for the future that everyone in the company will find engaging, fair, inspiring, and meaningful". [108]

It is not just looking at how management styles need to change, but also at the mindsets of those being managed. A new proposal is offering "a new way to approach work, that is centred on four mindsets ... [that] we inhabit and switch between as we go about our work each day[, they] are: learn, clarify, focus and create ... Where we are and how we feel are intrinsically linked — physical spaces that are engaging, fit for purpose and easy to access support us seamlessly transitioning between mindsets." But "above all else, workers want three things — connection, engagement and flexibility". The mindsets we exhibit, and the tools, support and culture we use to enable them "can help make the future of work more productive for everyone". [109]

The best way to describe empathy is as "the essence of human connection"; it is "the human side of leadership". Empathy typifies the twenty-first-century style of leadership, and embraces it, as it lies at the core of the new style of leadership. "It is all about being mindful, fully present, suspending judgement and listening with the intent to learn, absorb and give. Empathy is truly about being there ... It is important to be more purposeful about 'connection' – both at home and work." Empathy is a style of leadership where the belief that "connection truly matters" is at its heart. [110] It offers inclusion through the values of *"belonging* ... A workplace where everyone feels that they belong ... [where] there is every reason for a company to build and to maintain a more positive culture for everyone ... More empathy is needed in the workplace ... The benefits of Belonging are for everyone." [111] Leadership and its fit with the context of the age will go some way to making the possible happen.

Will the office and its format change under hybrid working? The short answer again is "yes". But before the pandemic struck, the call for change and the remodelling of offices had already begun. In this case change can be traced back to the growth of boundaryless working. The pandemic, of course, simply accelerated and gave a sense of urgency for such change. So the "answer is yes, but not in its traditional way". Under the heading "What's the purpose of the office — and do we still need it?" change was occurring. "While the office era isn't over yet, the role the office plays in workers' lives is changing, and it seems natural that the layout of the place should change with it." But a word of caution! "It's still too early to tell just how things will go ... but experts say that being anything less than 'extremely careful'" in rearranging office and work practice would be unwise and pre-emptive, because in the long term it will depend on "how hybrid is structured and rolled out across companies". [112] One overarching vision is that the "office will become a culture space, providing workers with a social anchor, facilitating connections, enabling learning, and fostering unscripted innovative collaboration". [113]

These new features of the office need to be embedded in the organisation's culture, "important aspects of which will include empathy, [connection], cooperation and collaboration". it is worth noting here that the impact of Covid-19 has not only hastened a widespread shift to working from home, it has also meant that workers now have "different expectations of their workplace". [114] "Offices will be designed to offer *'human moments:'* a face-to-face encounter that allows for empathy, emotional connections and nonverbal cues to complement what is actually said." [115]

This new approach "strikes a balance between openness and privacy, incorporating design elements that enable social interactions of many types". [116] What is wanted is "a variety of spaces ... where collaboration can occur in different ways, [with opportunities] to sit down and have a coffee in a booth, lounge spaces to sit and talk and gathering spaces for people to come together in an informal way". [117] Office space should be designed "to create more opportunities for employees to connect", [118] for while "you can't plan for impromptu conversations, you can make then more likely to happen". [119]

Finally, in their book *Where is my office?* Chris Kane and Eugenia Anastassiou write about a "Workplace Renaissance" "Since the turn of the twenty-first century, change has been in the wind ... Then came Covid and this global phenomenon has unleashed challenges we have never encountered before. It has fundamentally changed the nature of demand for offices ... We must accept that the nature of work has changed, this impacts the use of offices and how they are managed ... [The focus now] should be on people and place, not the other way round! ... The workplace should no longer be regarded as a place to contain the people who work there, but as a base from which they are free to explore the new twenty-first century world of possibilities ... The emphasis here is instead of worrying about what the actual space looks like, it is getting the experience right for people which should be the major concern [120] that for some time had been gradually gathering traction in some quarters.

A PAUSE TO REFLECT AND A WORD OF CAUTION

You can begin to see that a number of themes are emerging as we answer the above questions. Once the answers are combined, these themes go some way to begin to tentatively outline what could be described as good management practices. The remodelling of offices sets a new context for leadership with its focus on social interactions, maintaining connections, inclusion, fairness and equity, and the opportunities for informal learning and collaborations. The office may be "less about coming in and doing tasks and more about spending time collaborating and socialising with colleagues", [121] giving you the time to use the office as an informal learning opportunity that refreshes and revives you and allows you to get a better understanding of the ways the organization works. This is all about the transitioning from working from home to office time, understanding individual preferences, and preserving the flexibility that is so important. Each location — home and office — gives you two different contexts that enrich your experience, and allow you to understand the inclusiveness of the work that you do. Perhaps it gives you the coherence that brings work and life together in an integrated way, giving satisfaction and reducing the stress when you are trading one off against the other.

But we shouldn't get ahead of ourselves. The call for caution still prevails. Certainly the pandemic has taught us new ways of working, allowing our expectations to sharpen and focus now on how we *would like* or *want* to work, and it has already given us the flexibility we desire. But the hybrid structural changes are still a work in progress, and are still in a somewhat experimental stage. So while it is possible to sketch tentative outlines of what good management practices would look like, there are still critical questions that need to be asked and answered. So the mantra of being "extremely careful" is still the approach to take.

Will I need to upskill, and will I need to update the way I think about my career? Another "yes". We will be required to become "active learners as part of our commitment to stay informed and relevant". We will need "to focus on when our current skills will be redundant and when we need to build new skills and understanding to support our career progression". [122] Help is on the way as writers emphasise the potential of lifelong learning. Lifelong learning makes us "more resilient to the ups and downs of the modern labour market. Let's recognise that jobs are no longer for life and education is not just for the young." [123] Others express the potential of "renewable learning" that helps you as you transition through work: it is a necessity to employ it "to succeed in today's rapidly evolving world of work". [124] The benefit of lifelong learning is it instils the skill of learning to learn. Lifelong learning offers a regenerative progression where you are "able to understand yourself and be reflexive about the choices you make". It also builds your intellectual capital, as it "is clear that in the future intellectual capital will become increasingly important in the creation of valuable jobs and careers". [125] Others suggest that to make changes and develop your career you need "to expand [your] mental models of development and education beyond the first part of our lives. Lifelong education will require new frameworks, institutions, and financing mechanisms." [126]

You may have noticed that the word "learning" appears across many of the answers to the questions being asked. This is deliberate, as learning represents a "self-directed work-based process, leading to increased adaptive capacity". [127] These opportunities may be through formal learning, such "as *micro-credentials* as they recognise your skills and knowledge in a particular area that employers are looking for. They are aimed at people who want to upskill or learn a specific skill, work with technology that is changing rapidly", [128] and enhance career development. Micro-credentials "will make it easier for people to develop up-to-date skills as they explore multiple careers throughout their lifetimes, as well as allow them to refresh or verify the skills they use in their jobs". [129]

On the other hand, unstructured and informal learning is everywhere. "Workers are demanding 'plug and play' platforms that enable access to smaller bites of just-in-time education throughout their careers ... Renewable learning reflects growing demand for — and familiarity with — new learning modalities, from online talks to curated content, to face-to-face meet-ups to virtual group discussions offered by a constellation of new providers." [130] "Workers also need guidance about various learning pathways." Pressure will build "to self-direct their own learning and decide what knowledge they're missing, where to acquire it, and how to fit learning into daily routines. Not just personalized learning, but personalized career pathing will fast become the new normal." [131]

What are the skills for the twenty-first century? Researchers have identified at least five: *"Flexibility and adaptability skills* — are not only resourceful and adaptable but also able to be flexible. *Initiative and self-direction skills* — to take initiative to learn new ideas, concepts, processes, and applications, which augment their efficiency and effectiveness. Self-directed, not only to cope with change, but to also discover how organizational productivity can be improved. *Becoming self-directed learners* go[es] beyond mastery of skills ... [to] explore and expand one's own learning and opportunities to gain expertise. *Honing social and cross-cultural skills* — to be able to interact effectively with people that they work with or come in contact with. *Productivity and accountability skills* — namely efficiency, effectiveness and high quality … services … producing results. *Leadership and responsibility skills* — a high level of interpersonal skills, an ability to persuade followers, be responsibility for others, facilitate activities and relationships." (132)

Many of these skills fall under the heading of, and are frequently described as, "soft skills". "But this way of describing them 'needs a makeover' … because the description doesn't capture the nature, the significance and role of these skills in the 21st Century. These skills are critical … [their significance] is bound up in how you work and interact with other people … [making them complex,] difficult and critical … they are our biggest strength … [simply because] you can't execute anything without bringing other people along with you." (133) "Focusing on developing … — especially the 'soft skills' — will set [people] up with a great chance of success." The mantra is, "Look around you at what changes are happening in your industry. Learn new skills. Develop wide networks. Be curious — it is what young people will need to do, but [older people] will need to do it too, to make sure [they] stay relevant." (134)

Finally, the shape of careers is predicted to change. "The trend [away] from linear [ladder-shaped] careers ha[s] only been accelerated by Covid-19 …. Nonlinear careers have shaken off their stigma and become the new normal." (135) "Careers will become more fluid and less linear or ladder-shaped. People will have more jobs during their careers and more careers during their working lives." Allied to this change is that "work status will change. From being defined by job, organization and place in the hierarchy, it will increasingly be about a person's skills, reputation and ability to contribute and build networks." These changes have impacts on other aspects of the organisation, "we will need to learn how to separate status from hierarchy". (136) Hierarchical thinking will no longer suit the culture of twenty-first-century organisations. However, it is one thing "to think about what you want to do … but perhaps there is a better question to ask. Maybe it's less about *what* you want to do, and more about *who* you want to be. Who are you and what can that tell you about what you should do next. We shouldn't ignore 'who we are, beyond our identity at work'." (137)

What type of technology will I need to get used to? This is a difficult question to answer because I don't know what you have been using. So here is a rather broad approach that looks at the available technology and its place in working from home. To begin, the writer Sean Peek explores the idea that "technology and inclusion will continue to shape the future of remote work". He begins by making the point that "teleconferencing and telework technology has advanced to the point where some businesses thrive with completely remote teams". He then raises the question of how effective remote working is, before going on to reports survey results that "indicate that remote workers are actually more productive than their office-based counterparts". [138] It is interesting to note from the survey he cites that remote workers were less distracted by their boss than office-based employees. An indirect reference perhaps that supports the idea of deep work and the ability to get into the flow when working from home.

Peek then turns to the issue of how remote work has evolved. He points to how "now, technology affords us the ability to get the same job done, no matter where in the world we are. [It has] enabled us to be in contact with co-workers or clients at any time ... Live video feeds help out-office workers see and speak to another in real time, anywhere with an internet-connection, which is the next best thing to a face-to-face meeting." [139] he then turns "to the current state of remote work", pointing out that "the modern workforce is increasingly mobile, collaborative [and] dynamic, and comprises multi-generations, all with different communication preferences ... all represent unique challenges when it comes to staying connected while on the job".

However, Peek notes: "While the desire and expectations of working remotely increase significantly every year among the workforce, companies are only slowly adopting remote-friendly policies." Companies need to design policies that reflect and embrace the elements of ever-evolving best management practices. Looking into the future, Peek reinforces this view, saying "instead of resisting the change, organizations should improve their remote work policies and capabilities". [140]

The writer Bernard Marr begins by suggesting that the pandemic "will continue to impact our lives in many ways. This means that we will continue to see an accelerated rate of digitization and virtualization of business and society ... As a society, we will undoubtedly continue to harness this newfound openness to flexibility, agility, and innovative thinking, as the focus shifts from merely attempting to survive in a changing world to thriving in it." [141] He first turns to the new reality that artificial intelligence (AI) is everywhere. Pointing to smart phones, he suggests that they are now getting smarter because today smart means that they are "increasingly powered by AI generally, machine learning algorithms — and capable of helping us in increasingly innovative ways … AI has permeated the tools we use to carry out every day work."

Marr points to other technological developments before turning his attention to immersive technologies, arguing that during the pandemic "many of us experienced the virtualization of our offices and workplaces, as remote working arrangements were swiftly put in place. This was a crisis-driven surge of a much longer-term trend." Enter immersive technologies: by 2030, he predicts that "virtual experiences will be available that will be indistinguishable from reality".

In his conclusion Marr explores the issues that surround technology in terms of its "transparency, governance and accountability". Why? Because "for technology to work, we humans need to be able to trust it". He posits that our current unease may be in part because AI "is sometimes portrayed as a black box, meaning we can't see inside it to "understand how it works". However, he argues that this inability to understand AI "may be more to do about its complexity, rather than any malevolent scheme that limits our understanding". While offering a degree of comfort, this of course doesn't lessen our alarm when events occur that concern us about aspects of AI and its potential. Feeling predicated around a perceived lack of control and of unpredictability reactivate feelings of mistrust — "clearly with good reason!" Marr accepts that this needs to be addressed: "Governments too clearly understand that there is a need for a regulatory framework, … and AI solution providers will have to demonstrate [that] their system will not cause physical or psychological harm." These issues mean that all parties have responsibilities to collaborate, communicate and perhaps compromise to reach acceptable solutions that balance any disquiet, leading to Marr to conclude that "this balancing act is likely to become [an] increasingly prominent subject of discussion … as more people become aware of the positive and negative effects on society that AI and other technology trends will have". [142]

Immersive technologies may become part of the package required to work from home. "Immersive technologies create distinct experiences by merging the physical world with a digital or simulated reality. Augmented reality (AR) and virtual reality (VR) are two types of immersive technologies. These technologies share many of the same qualities. However, AR blends computer-generated information onto the user's real environment, while VR uses computer-generated information to provide a full sense of immersion." [143]

Who will benefit from hybrid working: men or women? To begin to answer this question we first explore the issues that surround different types of hybrid working arrangements, and then shift our focus and ask "whether these could have unintended negative consequences for women (or anyone) over time". [144] Remember we have explored many issues of hybrid working while answering all of the questions above, but the last piece of the jigsaw — and perhaps the most complex, but the key to hybrid working — is the need to give some clarity to what arrangements actually constitute hybrid working. At one level "it has to work mutually for employees, employers and organizations alike ... There is not a one-size-fits-all-solution. And that's key." [145] And at another level managers "need to think very carefully ... about the types of working arrangements they'll permit". [146]

To avoid negative consequences, managers "should design and implement policies that can level the playing field ... It is also important and of course, it's always good practice when putting in place such 'far-reaching' working arrangements to schedule formal times to revisit them in the future, thoroughly review how well they're serving all concerned, and modify them as necessary." [147] Others agree with such sentiments, "for hybrid jobs [need] to be carefully designed rather than allowed to develop on their own, because existing inequalities might be reinforced". [148]

"Hybrid working arrangements can be configured in two very different ways: ... 'flexible hybrid' and 'fixed hybrid.' In a flexible hybrid system, the same employee is sometimes co-located and sometimes remote, so their location changes throughout a typical workweek. In a fixed hybrid system, some employees are always co-located while others are aways remote and their locations don't change throughout the week." [149] There is, argues Professor Martine Haas, "some 'cautious optimism' about how women will fare in a flexible hybrid system, however, there are 'compelling reasons to be less optimistic' about how they will fare in a fixed hybrid system, where they work remotely full-time while other colleagues co-locate". [150]

There are at least three elements that disadvantage women in this type of working set-up: "access to mentoring and sponsorship, assumptions that surround commitment and speaking up — and being heard." So Professor Haas explores the need for women to "recognize the risks ... and how they can be minimized" [These include]" *'step forward and take'... for example* asking for resources they need, including mentoring and increasing their efforts to be visible Managers also have a important role [to play in recognising] how the responsibility should be shared and *to create and maintain balance* between remote workers and those in the office [and, as mentioned in the previous paragraph] managers need to review hybrid arrangements thoroughly [to confirm they are] serving all concerned and modify them as necessary". [151]

Others argue that "We're no stranger to [the fact that] hybrid working shapes equitable outcomes ...There's immense benefits to this, but it also carries potential for adverse effects. *Especially for women* is the *'Zoom ceiling'* a new glass ceiling." This brings us to the issue of *proximity* bias: Simply put, "it's the idea that people unintentionally favour employees who are closest to them rather than further away ... [So], what's at stake for women?" Organisations need to "set the tone for a proximity-bias-free workplace" to prevent the careers of those working remotely being jeopardised, and the remote workers "feeling disconnected from the wider team [and managers], and seen as less valuable". [152] Management "needs to [use] its soft skills to maximize their performance and that of their hybrid team ... allow everyone flexible work schedules [so that] the playing field will be hugely levelled ... Managers must be proactive about inviting meeting attendees into the discussion ... cocreate a communication charter ... ensure an organization-wide culture of exceptional communication and actively consider remote employees for opportunities." [153]

There are two points that summarise the crucial issues that reflect "taking away and thinking about" ideas. The first is that there is a clear preference for a flexible model of hybrid working where employees are co-located and sometimes remote, so their location changes throughout a typical week. The second is taking steps to avoid proximity bias, with communication policies or charters needing to be built through a culture that is designed to be collaborative, cooperative, inclusive, supportive and transparent.

SOME REFLECTIONS

Reflecting on the answers to the questions raised, and acknowledging their research base, we need to also take into account a number of adjacent issues or trends. First, the pandemic's acceleration of working from home practice, and of technology that has given us immersive techniques. There is also the generation gap emerging in the workforce, with Millennials and Generation Zers — who think in terms of a digital age rather than an industrial age — looking at the traditional work practices unthinkingly taken over from the previous century, and asking "Why do we work in the way that we do?" Even so, our answers to the questions make it possible to distil from them an opportunity to tentatively talk about frameworks for best management practices; however, as we are dealing with "a work in progress", [154] caution requires that we should stay within the bounds of what we know. And yet attempting to answer the questions has, at the very least, "help[ed] us to understand the decisions you need to make — or remake — to ensure ... hybrid policies are balancing institutional and individual needs". [155]

We need to accept that "we are living in the age of the hybrid work experiment"; "for many, this experiment began months ago, or longer, but we have a long way to go to get it right". [156] So perhaps the last big test lies ahead of us: to clarify what constitutes the hybrid working arrangements we set up, and to ensure that the model embraces flexibility, and "starts with a mindset focused on people and driven by inclusion", [157] feasibility, equity and fairness. This "requires experimentation and rigorous planning", [158] but if we can get it right "we have a real chance to re-define the future of work". The task will be challenging, and it will certainly require "periodically pausing to see what's working and what's not". [159]

Researchers, human resource experts, and practitioners in the field display a rare confidence, arguing that hybrid work is here to stay. Exploring Arundhati Roy's idea "that the pandemic is a portal ... a chance to rethink ... and imagine another world" [160] also gets a strong tick for hybrid working as an opportunity accelerated by the pandemic. "Working from home or working flexibility has been the most obvious example of positive and probably lasting change from the pandemic in New Zealand, thanks to technology. It has the potential to reshape work balance and could have a positive impact on transport and emissions." [161] However, it is important to keep in mind the context that surrounds hybrid working arrangements: whereas those who can access flexible work — typically office workers and those in professional roles —have gained more flexibility since the pandemic, this is not so for those in occupations, such as healthcare, retail, hospitality and manual workers, where flexible work arrangements are harder or impossible to set up. [162] Nevertheless, the Sustainable Business Council's CEP Mike Burrell says, it is "important to take a deeper look at flexibility in sectors where that was harder to achieve, and that is where technology step[s] in, for example remote manufacturing". [163] It should be possible to explore all of the tasks that make up a job to determine how feasible flexibility is.

So while flexible working and home working represent a significant and fundamental structural change to working practice, its application is limited to those workers whose tasks make it feasible. This should be kept in mind when talking about hybrid working, just to keep it in context. The desire for flexibility has been a long time coming, and without doubt this feature gives hybrid working its contemporary value and staying power.

When talking and discussing hybrid working, it would be irresponsible to not mention those other sectors of the workforce that have had a particularly tough time during the pandemic and its fallout. It is important that any discussion of the changing workplace not over-shadow the challenges, disruptions and stress they have had to endure. So to place our conversations about hybrid working in a broader context I have three sectors in mind: small business enterprises, hospitality and tourism. Of course, the boundaries between these three are somewhat porous, and so often when talking about one you are also talking about the other two.

Turning first to small business enterprises, a *Dominion Post* headline captures what they are battling against: "Small businesses face strong headwinds". The strong headwinds to be confronted are "revenues drop, costs increase and labour is tighter than ever before", not forgetting inflation and the rising cost of living. The call for shopping local has never before been as crucial as it is now. On top of those factors there are others: "cash flows, people recovering confidence to go out again [and spend], supply-chain issues, and facing a lack of staff to service a recovery". [164] This last factor is exacerbated by the ongoing uncertainty of when illness might strike staff members and/or their families and contacts, and put any number of employees in isolation at any time.

There is no doubting the stress and anxiety that small business owners have endured and its impact on mental health. While there is a hesitant feeling that perhaps there is light at the end of the tunnel now that the pandemic regulations have gone, doubt and uncertainty lingers, as you can't really predict what's ahead. In October 2022, the government, announcing the extension of its health and wellness support package, acknowledged this, estimating there are about "546,000 small businesses here in New Zealand and up to 1.2 million individuals who are owners or employees. Rolling out the package across the country ... will offer them wellbeing tools to support them as they recover from the pandemic." [165]

The hospitality sector's challenges were felt immediately, just a day before the country went into its first lockdown in March 2020. *The Dominion Post* headlines caught the feeling of the sector: "We're in a pile of pain"; "Nightlife as we know it is heading to a grim new dawn — shatteringly — low patronage, closures, and businesses around the country shedding $10 million a week"; "Entrepreneurs are in 'a fight for [their] lives'". [166] By 2022 the news was no better: "It's a luxury for owners to open that's how bad the labour shortage is." [167] However, all along there has been a feeling of "the utmost respect for the industry's resilience in coming through Covid. They collaborate, they help each other out, they share staff and stock." [168] Public health researchers have also been continuously looking for ways to 'reduce the pain" by providing the hospitality industry with "a 'holistic strategy through developing a people-centred approach" to meet the challenges faced; this included "a flat team structure, an uncertainty-embracing organisational environment, transparent decision-making process and sympathetic behaviours from leaders to facilitate service staff to develop greater coping mechanisms for the unknown future". [169]

However, with the first lockdown it was as if winter had come early, and tourism operators were asking where do we go from here? Uncertainty was everywhere, but international tourists were nowhere. The challenges were dire, frightening and extremely worrying. Looking into the future it was difficult to predict when international visitors numbers would return to at levels where tourism businesses could once more be considered sustainable.

When the first lockdown ended, the tourism industry was encouraged to focus on the domestic market, and the sector showed its resilience as the team of 5 million packed their bags and responded to the call. However, it was not just a lack of international visitors that the industry was dealing with; there was also a shortage of trained staff to cover any upsurge in visitors. Even with a modicum of growth there was still the problem of staff shortages and how the industry could support that growth. A Tourist Industry Aotearoa survey "found that four in 10 of all the people employed in tourism have gone, with a loss of about 90,000 people from the industry". [170] The difficulty was compounded with "Job vacancies attract[ing] little interest." Again, the industry showed its resilience, offering applicants "very competitive packages ... [and] incentive payments ... 47% of businesses were confident of attracting and retaining the workers they need". [171]

August 2022 saw the tourism industry hosting a conference organised around the theme "Navigating the Future". Their, Minister of Tourism Stuart Nash argued that New Zealand needed to attract "'discerning travellers' and not those travelling on a shoestring ... Our marketing spin, it is unashamedly going to be at these high quality tourists." [172] By October 2022 cruise ships began arriving in New Zealand again, and the borders were free of Covid regulations. But challenges remain with issues both old — like the environmental impact of large volumes of tourists — and new — businesses having to consider their financial models and the continuing demand for staff.

But for all of us, we shouldn't forget that the pandemic has given us that "unique instructive moment" [173] to reimagine our working lives and ways of working, even in those sectors that have had it particularly tough. We have a choice. To paraphrase Arundhati Roy: we can move forward "carrying the dead carcasses of our prejudice" and old ways of doing things, or "we can walk through lightly" into the new world "to imagine another world". [174] We *can* change old traditional mindsets and engage in ones that embrace growth and learning across all organisations, and provide working arrangements that allow all workers the opportunities to flourish and build that coherence through all of the different aspects of their lives. If it means that, in amongst the turmoil and challenges, "the transition to hybrid work and [its] focus on the *what* instead of the *where* presents a true chance for a revolution around inclusion not only at work but *through* work", we should take it and make it our unique instructive moment. Doing so "has never been more achievable than it is now. The difference is that now the need for change has never been greater" [175], so, we have a real chance to redefine the future of work.

Chapter 4:

Our Working Lives and the Four-Day Working Week

Even though our pandemic regulations have ended, the pandemic lingers. The virus continues to make its presence felt as new Covid subvariants are identified. The rolling weekly average of daily cases rises, as do reinfections, and the numbers in hospital and deaths. Its presence continues to cut through our working lives, too, and so this chapter turns to another great experiment *the four-day week;* leaving us, once again, to reimagine our working lives, questioning those traditions that have shaped it since the nineteenth century. The uprooting of our working lives also leads to a need to question our understanding of careers and our views on leadership, as they, too, become collateral damage from the virus's journey. The virus has also shone a spotlight on how we assign value to different types of work; how what is considered to be "essential work" in times of crisis often appears to be remunerated in inverse proportions. Finally, the pandemic and its fallout challenge us to refine those characteristics that add value to work.

The virus doesn't care about traditions or the status-quo, and so we have to embark on a journey that requires us to rethink those traditions, even though for many of us they represent a way of life that until now we have just simply taken for granted. Although we have never experienced a pandemic before, one of the lessons that we have had to quickly learn — with its attended emotional cost — is that change is always a pandemic's committed partner. It's not just the change we have had to cope with, but how quickly change happens, particularly in a pandemic, and this adds to the emotional burden we carry.

This chapter, like the previous ones, points to how the virus's path is invariably accompanied by discussions and debates where commentators, researchers and experts, both internationally and domestically, work in collaboration to develop some sense of coherence from these conversations and experiences, establishing what is relevant and what needs changing. I have cited these conversations, discussions and debates with two underlying themes in mind. For those discussions around a four-day week, the driving force remains "Why do we work in the way that we do?" Accompanying this driving force is the question: "Is there nothing we can do better?" [1] Both forces reflect a world in transition, organisations in "perpetual motion" [2] and the challenges of change.

THE ORIGINS OF THE FOUR-DAY WEEK

My interest was aroused when I read a piece in *The Guardian Weekly*, in 2021, that reported "Spain could become one of the first countries in the world to trial the four-day working week." [3] It soon became apparent that this wasn't just an isolated trial but something that has since blossomed into a global movement. Eighteen months later I was reading a piece by Daniel Smith on *Stuff* with the headlines "this is not a crazy idea anymore" and "Are we on the precipice of a four-day working week revolution?" [4] The evidence was mounting, as were the headlines: "'We see huge benefits': firms adopt four-day week in Covid crisis", [5] "The positive benefits of a four-day week: Economics of a four-day working day week: research shows it can save businesses money", [6] and "How do you switch to a four-day week?" [7] So what was it that has catapulted us into a global debate around working hours?

Well, it would be easy to say that it has been the pandemic. However, while the pandemic may well have contributed, it is more about a complexity of other factors that were already on the move to erode the traditional ideas that surround working hours. The concept of work was coming under pressure as researchers were having to make distinctions between standard and non-standard ways of working due to the changing rhythms of working lives prompted by, and aided and abetted by, the digital age, generational issues and globalisation. Adding to the mix were the rising levels of work stress, the growing concerns about health and wellbeing, and general work–life balance.

However, the trigger event that may have thrust the idea of a four-day week onto the table may well have been the questions that are continually being asked about why productivity is still being measured by "the number of hours employees spend at their desk … [particularly] when research showed that productive hours may on average be around 2.5 hours in a standard eight-hour day". [8] The role the pandemic played may have been in the way it exposed the unmet demand for more flexibility in working arrangements, providing fertile ground in which the idea of a four-day week could flourish. However, it is probably more accurate to think of the trigger as an amalgam of all of the factors mentioned above. Quite simply, the four-day week is an idea whose time has come.

But how did the idea of a four-day working week become a global movement? 4 Day Week Global co-founder Andrew Barnes was the driving force — the four-day working strategy has his hallmark stamped all over it. His inspiration to take the idea forward can be expressed through both his philosophy and his leadership ethos: "There is an urgent need to change — in quite an extreme way — how we work, if we are to get the best out of people and commerce, and begin to relieve the strain on ourselves and our planet," he explains; and addressing this led to "a global conversation about the future of work" and then the four-day week concept. [9] The concept of giving staff an extra day off was first trialled by Barnes in 2018 with his Aotearoa company Perpetual Guardian, before being made a permanent set-up when the clear results were "increased productivity and happier employees". [10]

4 Day Week Global co-founder and chief executive Charlotte Lockhart put it this way: "[T]echnology is making more flexibility possible in many workplaces … the reality is we know that the way we're going to work in the future isn't how we've worked in the past.." [11] Companies who have begun to initiate a four-day working week believe that "this is what the future of employment should look like". [12] Organisations around the globe are now piloting the four-day working model in conjunction with 4 Day Week Global, including organisations in Ireland, Iceland, the United States, Canada, Spain, the United Kingdom, Australia and New Zealand. [13] As an example: "[In] what's estimated to be the largest four-day work week ever conducted, 70 companies and over 3,300 employees in the UK are embracing the work–life balance shift, as part of a pilot program to trial four-day work arrangements for the next six months." [14] Looking to the future, the New Zealand Council

of Trade Unions has called for a "mass pilot" of a four-day working week among a clutch of other initiatives. [15]

So what principles drive the four-day working initiative? "The four-day week is *about productivity first,*" writes Barnes, adding, "I cannot be more explicit than that." [16] The next principle emphasises "*the importance of flexibility* ... it is the shove we so desperately need to move the world of work into a twenty-first-century model which meets economic and human needs on an equal basis". [17] Next is "the idea *of mutually beneficial agreements* between employers and employees (providing alternative options as to when, where and how much a person works), [and] have measurable psychological, social and economic impacts". [18] The next principle can be described "as creating a culture, the four-day week is a model of work which can meet the human and economic needs of the modern developed world equally, setting people up to succeed in work and in the rest of their lives.". [19] All of this is captured by "the 100–80–100 rule (100 per cent of the pay, 80 per cent of the time but delivering 100 per cent of agreed productivity)". [20] Finally, the last principle is that it requires "*carefully planned operational changes*" [21] and the need to explore "*a more streamlined schedule in the workplace*". [22]

It has been said that the four-day week is "an employee-led process where the magic bullet is trust". [23] Collectively, the principles outlined above offer transformational change. In his four-day week model, Andrew Barnes has "argued for and demonstrated the value of a productivity-focused, reduced-hour model of work for companies and industries ... No one doubts we are in a new industrial era whose economic ramifications are all but impossible to predict; no one is avowing that human well-being, especially as it pertains to our work lives, is optimal ... no one [is denying] the challenges we face; if we need radical action on climate change, we must be just as radical in changing how we work." [24]

On building a case for a shorter working week, authors Brian Lufkin and Jessica Mudditt focus on "the productivity boost" and "how it boosts health and wellbeing." These two outcomes are now closely associated with the shorter working week, and go a good way to explaining why the model "is gaining traction, particularly in light of recent examples of workforces who have successfully trialled a reduced-hours' week", and also why when we look at the outcomes of those who have already initiated such a scheme we think that "they may be on to something". There are different ways in which you can "remove a portion of your total work time for the week", but the key is that the individual scheme must be feasible to achieving business goals, that the workers themselves select the structure that works for them, and remuneration remains the same. [25]

Researchers continue to explore the "optimal work time" before productivity begins to fall away. But one of the greatest advantages of working fewer hours indicated by the evidence is that people become better workers. One theory is that working fewer hours but having to get through the same amount of work means that workers become more aware of the distractions that can disrupt the normal working day and reduce productivity. So they focus on doing whatever is necessary to achieve the required outcomes, changing "the focus from hours worked to productivity — that is from 'busy work' to the right work". [26]

In their article "The case for a shorter workweek", Brian Lufkin and Jessica Mudditt move the focus beyond just productivity to making workers more satisfied, "happier, healthier, more engaged" [27] These two factors — productivity and worker satisfaction — are, of course, highly correlated, and perhaps is down to workers "feeling more rested" when they are not caught up in the other distractions at work or ... 'personal tasks at work'. This all results in "a health and wellbeing boost", as a greater sense of balance or life cohesion gives them the more energy to do the tasks required in both their work and personal lives. Nevertheless, Lufkin and Mudditt report that experts counsel exercising "caution and thoughtfulness when implementing these models of work", even as they suggest that now could be a good time to give it a go. They cite one of the experts as saying: "We've basically come to an inflection point, as a society that allows us to do this. People's minds are more open ... we're already in upheaval and change." [28] Or perhaps it is fitting to leave the last word to Andrew Barnes: "[Is] there nothing we can do better?" [29]

THE FOUR-DAY WORK WEEK

The heading in *The Dominion Post* "Four-day work week anyone?" captures what was quickly to become a global movement. The column goes on to illustrate just how important this global movement is, quoting workplace expert Gillian Brookes, who expresses its significance in this way: "Businesses will scramble to gain a comparative advantage by adopting the four-day week ahead of their competition. Once that 'tipping point' is reached, it will ultimately become a new default ... as the research showed it created stronger productivity, while providing no immediate extra costs for the business." [30] Another article also illustrates the power of the four-day work week movement, with the arrival of the "long-awaited data from the large-scale UK four-day work week pilot in February — and results were overwhelming positive ... 71% of employees reported feeling reduced levels of burnout; there were also improvements in physical health and well-being ... Employers on the trial also say a truncated work week has boosted productivity and output." Even so, feedback from "a small portion of the trial's participants" indicated that the four-day work week "isn't an automatic solution for all". [31]

There is a very real sense that the four-day work week's time has come, with a commonly-held view being that "if we need radical action on climate change, we must be just as radical in changing how we work". [32] With the technological resources we have available to change the nature of work "a defined work day is long gone, outmoded". [33] Time and again it is being show that where flexible working arrangements are the result of "mutually beneficial agreements between employers and employees (providing alternate options as to when, where and how much a person works)" there are positive "measurable psychological, social and economic impacts." Such arrangements "can meet the human and economic needs of the modern developed world equally, setting people up to succeed in work and in the rest of their lives". [34]

OTHER LONG-TERM CHALLENGES FOR WORK

Although the emphasis has thus far focused on the pandemic as being the vehicle for change in offering new ways of working — particularly hybrid working and the four-day working week — we should not forget that other long-terms challenges face the workforce. Kirk Hope, chief executive of BusinessNZ, says that these include developing "an ... affordable and sustainable long-term model for vocational education — one which delivers a highly skilled, highly productive (and therefore more highly paid) workforce. He also notes: "We're also on the brink of a workforce shortage due to an ageing population, which could see us needing an additional quarter-million workers by 2045 if we don't act on immigration." How we handle these challenges is down to adopting the right mindset, he suggests: "[T]he beauty of adopting [a] forward-looking perspective is that it propels us in the right direction, even as the horizon constantly shifts." [35] We also should not overlook the need to continually create meaningful jobs, as sociologist Professor Paul Spoonley cautiously predicts "that 40% of the jobs in 2023 will not exist in 2033 and 65% of the jobs [future generations] do over their life have not been invented yet". [36]

The other challenge begins with another set of questions "How will Covid-19 shape the longer-term future of the landscape of professional work? And how will the professions respond to the emerging technological challenges? Brevity is no friend to the careful and meticulous evidence-based analysis of Richard Susskind and Daniel Susskind. In their book *The Future of the Professions*, they present their groundbreaking research, which "raises profound questions about the relevance of the professions in an era of ever more powerful technologies". [37] These fundamental, transformational technologies are already becoming imbedded in the future of their working lives, and offer change that challenges the very essence surrounding their professions' future. So while professionals may have won the battle for flexibility, their next battle comes when advances in technology strike at the very heart of what they do, and in this way threaten the future of their profession.

CAREERS AND LEADERSHIP

We now turn to the issues of careers and leadership as we think about reimagining work and working lives. This completes the circle of change around the future of work. These two issues can be described as flowing from the work that you do and where you do it, but even that descriptor is somewhat porous.

As we learned earlier, careers are becoming "more fluid and less linear or ladder-shaped". This means that people are likely to have "more jobs during their careers, and more careers during their working lives", which in turn means they will have to "rely more heavily on marketing their unique skills, reputation and 'personal brand'". Work status will change, too. People will no longer be "defined by job, organization and place in the hierarchy, it will be increasingly be about a person's skills, reputation and ability to contribute and build networks". [38] This brings with it a change in career focus: whereas in the past people acquired specific skills and knowledge and applied them to specific tasks, the name of the new game is resilience and adaptability to navigate an ever-fluid environment. "Resilience involves ongoing reinvention — being able to adapt, reskill and upskill throughout our lifetimes ... We will need to develop and nurture our critical capabilities ... and to be comfortable with technology and data."

This spills over into leadership models and how they operate, with a move away from hierarchies in favour of networks of teams. "Work will increasingly evolve beyond a focus on process to a focus on projects, assignments, and initiatives. Teams and networks will strengthen organizational resilience and become the critical units of organizational performance and professional development." [39]

Writing in *The Guardian Weekly*, Professor André Spicer explores the case that while "career ladders continue to exist, navigating them is much trickier". He then looks at research that has been undertaken into the "range of strategies people can use in negotiating increasingly complex career paths without clear ladders", concluding: "When we think about making our way, we tend to only focus on the obvious career ladder. These are important, but are not the only way to make your way in the world of work. If you look more broadly, there are likely to be other ways forward." [40]

All of this, of course, signals that, lifelong learning will become the tool that allows us to successfully make the transition to the new world of work. Work will become, as Alison Maitland and Peter Thomson suggest, "more of a tradable commodity rather than a job". [41] This means we will "need to become active learners as part of our commitment to stay informed and relevant". [42] This will make lifelong learning much more important, and, by coupling this with micro-credentials (i.e. formal, short, stand-alone courses) changes will need to be made to accommodate this kind of education.

When talking about the changing nature of careers, it is important not to lose sight of those moments that are best described as *serendipitous opportunities*. These are such moments as when, for example, suddenly someone in your network tempts you or draws your attention to a chance to take your career in another direction. Thinking about your career to date, you may already be able to remember those times when a serendipitous moment arrived and has taken you in a direction that you hadn't ever thought about, or perhaps you had thought about it and now the moment arrives to act. Whatever happens, work will likely be a series of transitions, and this is why it will be important to be ready and prepared for when that moment to transition arrives.

The second issue explores the role of empathy not just as a characteristic of leadership, but as a more general behaviour trait that enables you to build social connections that are significant for you. We also capture the importance of empathy in Chapter Six when we look at relationship-focused coping. Empathy is described as "expressing and, being understanding and sympathetic of another person's moods and reflections ... empathetic responding". [43] The word "empathy" has become deeply associated with the pandemic, and gains its power and influence simply because it is a trait that builds the resilience we need to cope with the emotional issues that have flowed during the pandemic. Turning back to empathy as a leadership trait, change leader Dr Harold Hillman describes it in terms of "head, heart and hands." Each reflects that "people like being understood rather than judged — *head* — people like it when they know you have felt what they feel — *heart* — and 'actions really do speak louder than words' — *hand*." Hillman concludes: "for each of us, this powerful trio has made a huge difference in our ability to push through any challenge or to help others to do so. To know and show empathy, practise the rule of three as often as you can." [44] This style of leadership reflects the twenty-first century and its many challenges.

So, the thinking behind flexibility is clear. It sets up satisfied and happy workers. Research also points that workers are more productive and efficient when offered flexible working. However, if flexible arrangements are to be successful. Leadership will need to change, too. Remember that empathy, trust and social connection are now the keys to success, rather than operating traditional top-down management. Julia Hobsbawn identifies the moving of employees away from a rigid nine-to-five, Monday-to-Friday working week towards wanting to "choose how to manage the time [they] spend working in a way that suits [them]". Research results showing clear benefits to both productivity and job satisfaction with working flexibility explain "why discussions around the four-day week have reached an intensity never seen before." These positive outcomes and the changing face of work generally means, Hobsbawm concludes, "there is nothing to lose and everything to gain". [45] In making the transition, remember that it is the three aspects of this new twenty-first-century leadership style — empathy, trust and social connection — that give managers the capacity, and the drive, to manage these new patterns of working.

HOW DO WE MEASURE THE VALUE OF A JOB?

The footprint of Covid-19, almost in its first step, raised questions about, and certainly focused our attention on, how we assign value to different types of work. We very quickly learned what work was deemed as essential to keep society functioning at its most basic level and the population safe and healthy. Put more eloquently, the pandemic caused us to ask "what jobs are truly valuable" and to questioned "why we are content to let our markets reward those in often pointless … roles so much more than those we recognise as essential". [46] With this came the realisation that for some time "we have witnessed the creation of an endless variety of new jobs … It's as if someone were out there making up pointless jobs just for the sake of keeping us all working." [47]

The core of the matter was: how do you develop an absolute measure of the value of a job. When undertaking such a task, economists use the idea of "utility" as a measure of value — "how useful is work in satisfying a want or a need?" [48] But utility comes with its own difficulties, in the sense that economic value may be too narrow in assigning value. Perhaps a better way to think about it is to go back to basics and reconnect with the ideas of "the good work agenda", which considers what attributes make a job good, and returns to valuing work in terms of how it "engages all our skills, talents, capabilities and emotions". [49] Would these latter attributes move us and bring us closer to the *social value* of work?

But thinking aloud about what *should* be the "real value" of a job is made more difficult not only because the boundaries between economic and social value are blurred and at times porous, but also because value has many dimensions, including some that "clearly can't be quantified … like sentimental value", [50] which helps to explain why the "the field of value is always contested territory". [51] This means it is crucial is to continually remind yourself that "the market is at best a poor arbiter of value". [52] There is no doubt that we need to think about what gives work its sense of value and then celebrate its role. Prompted by the pandemic and by the accelerated way in which work is changing, is it now time to refine how we determine value and to think more in terms of how the "good work agenda" defines what makes good work? There is also merit in focusing on "the ways people reflect on the value of their job" [53] and how their job gives (or doesn't give) that sense of making a difference. Finding that out may lead us to better understand work that is sustaining.

We can also think of work in terms of its social sustainability reflecting qualities, such as "a sense of meaningfulness, fulfilment, self-esteem and a life of value" — all of which enhance the quality of working lives. [54] If these attributes make working a richer experience, then they are the ones that we should aspire to. To put it more simply, this is exactly what changes to work practice focusing on flexibility, trust and shorter workweeks are trying to do — make work and jobs more fulfilling and meaningful, and a more valued experience. With the lockdowns and other transmission-elimination strategies turning the spotlight on what work was essential to society's wellbeing, and introducing large-scale remote working, people began to focus on why, up until then, things were still being done as they had always been, and to look at how they *could* be done. A part of this was the realisation that value need not be limited to economic criteria. The pandemic "taught many people that the job does not have to be the way it was", with workers increasingly demanding that it offers a sustainable and rewarding quality of life in return. [55]

This demand reflects the importance of creating meaningful jobs that offer a quality of working life, and a life that is valued. It is important that these qualities are not forgotten, particularly when, as we have seen, sociologist Professor Paul Spoonley is cautiously predicting "that 40% of the jobs in 2023 will not exist in 2033 and 65% of the jobs [future generations] do over their working life have not been invented yet". [56] The hope must be that the creators of these future jobs will have learnt the lessons of the pandemic and design jobs that are far from pointless, and are imbued with qualities of sustainability and meaningfulness, and offer a life that is valued and a working life that makes a difference.

We may have strayed a little from the idea of "pointless and meaningless work", but regained the territory by focusing on the characteristics of good work, and from there what valued work may look like. But it is evident from the recent consideration of our current work status that "we clearly aren't that clever when it comes to creating (or rewarding) jobs people are likely to find meaningful or fulfilling", (57) which makes our return to the work of the "good work agenda" crucial. Meanwhile, employers can also "learn a lot from attending to what helped people be more productive and satisfied" during the pandemic. For example, evidence from the working from home experience reveals that "workers were less distracted by pointless meetings and open office settings and were able to focus on meaningful tasks rather than being burdened by busywork", which raises the question of "how can job environments be places that help people thrive rather than wearing them down." (58) All this simply reflects the pandemic's journey, and because of it there is "hardly anyone [who] has made it through the pandemic with their work life unchanged". (59) Again, this explains why growing numbers of people have been led to ask the question: Why do we work in the way that we do?

REFLECTIONS

This chapter opened with the second big experiment: the four-day week. Talking on RNZ, Charlotte Lockhart, chief executive of the not-for-profit 4 Day Week Global, went straight to the point: "the reality is we know that the way we're going to work in the future isn't how we've worked in the past". She then gave a glimpse of what the alternative might look like: "Flexibility is the key, and a reduced working week doesn't have to be precisely four days, but can adapt to meet business needs ... We are a big advocate of a 32-hour work week. A four-day week is just a catchy title." However, she was quick to point out that "catchy" was not the same as easy — "There is nothing to say it's going to be easy in every industry" — but encouraged people not to be deterred just because they find the idea challenging. She concluded: "There's no reason that the 40-hour work week, which has only become standard in the last 100 years or so, has to remain the same forever ... We've got to look at what is the society we want." (60) As 4 Day Week Global co-founder Andrew Barnes suggests, we shouldn't get seduced by the status quo when the real question that sceptics should be asking is: Is there nothing we can do better? Exploring the options is necessary: "If we need radical action on climate change, we must be just as radical in changing how we work." (61)

As we have seen, the four-day week is an innovation whose time has come. When you examine the outcomes of those organizations who have made the change, the outcomes are always positive, touching both individual well-being and organisational productivity. And don't forget, it is an innovation that captures the demand for flexibility because it gives people time — and there is no escaping that balancing how you use your time is a necessity in twenty-first-century living. Why? Because balance and coherence are continually sought after since they produce the feelings of satisfaction. To support this initiative, it is interesting to read a small column in *The Guardian Weekly* under the heading "100 — the number of UK companies now signed up for a permanent four-day working week for all their employees (a total of 2,600 staff) with no loss of pay". [62] Reflecting on this chapter, it simply illustrates that innovation is no friend of the status quo.

The pandemic has given us a chance to reflect on what we value, and what is important to us and to think about our priorities. Since, for almost all of us, this is the first pandemic we have ever experienced, we are immediately reminded of the moments of excruciating emotional turmoil and disruption and uncertainty. But, as our understanding of the pandemic growths and develops, our experiences give us an opportunity to reflect on the way "the pandemic has created a once-in-a-lifetime opportunity to rethink what the workers among us want from work and our working lives ... We are now faced with some significant choices — do we go back to our old ways of working or do we use this as an opportunity to completely redesign work and make it more purposeful, productive and fulfilling for all?" [63]

Chapter 5:

The Pandemic and Consequences to How We Live

THEY RIPPLING OUT TO TOUCH HOW WE LIVE AND OTHER SOCIAL (ECONOMIC) ISSUES

As the pandemic unfolded, it became abundantly clear that the virus displayed an impatience to show that its goal was that other parts of our society were also fair game to being disrupted. In this chapter I will explore the virus's footprint in its race to ripple out and touch different parts of society. So this chapter turns to how we live, exploring how the virus "may yet have a lasting say on the shape of cities of the future", [1] particularly through ideas of sustainable cities and the 15-minute-city. The virus leaves us a legacy of what is relevant, and what else needs to be refined and rethought, causing us to reassess our preoccupation with economic growth and GDP, and leading us to consider the refining of capitalism. "Occasionally, the world engineers a moment in time that's so big, we're compelled to make change relevant. For all of us, 2020 and the events within it was that moment." [2] The driving force behind the pandemic is the virus Covid-19. So, it is the fallout from the disruption unleashed by the pandemic that has giving us an opportunity to decide what may now be relevant and what needs to be refined.

This chapter, like the previous one, points to how the virus's path is invariably accompanied by discussions and debates where commentators, researchers and experts, both internationally and domestically, have worked in collaboration to develop a coherent sense of what remains relevant and what needs changing. I have cited these conversations, discussions and debates with two underlying themes in mind. The first is captured by slipping into the vernacular and asking whether whatever is under discussion is still "fit for purpose". The second is simply, is whatever is under discussion *relevant* or does it jar against the changing nature of society? Are these things adding value or even capturing what it is we value in twenty-first-century working or living. There is, of course, a porous boundary between the two. Again, the idea is for you to think and reflect on how you appraise them.

REIMAGINING CITIES AND SUSTAINABLE CITIES

You may think that the pandemic has little to do with reimagining cities, but you would be wrong. The pandemic has hurled us with a rather sharp nudge to accelerate the rate of change for cities. "It seems the pandemic, for some, became a moment to reimagine how we see the future of our oldest cities." [3] Why is this? "Because cities can play an outsized role in creating solutions for a more sustainable world", [4] offering us the chance to explore new ways of managing old problems using sustainable solutions. Think of the impact of the pandemic on cities through the work from home requirement and the changing role for the office, the need for space to physically distance, and the impact of these on the future role and configuration of public spaces and how and when people move about in a city. Reimagine the different modes for transport and how they could offer alternative ways of moving around the city. Reimagine retail shopping and the role of online shopping and reimagine if you lived in what were to become more sustainable environments.

The Earth is being put under ever-increasing stress now that over half the world's population live in cities, with whatever is going on in cities is having an impact on the planet as a whole. William McDonough, an architect who has pioneered designs for sustainable development, reinforces the implications of this interconnectedness: "How they reimagine the urban landscape and how they design growth will profoundly influence the future of all life on the planet." He goes on to argue that a way to mitigate this is to design cities that operate in similar way to the natural world. Such design is based on three key principles.

The first principle creates cities that operate in a circular rather than a linear manner: "the linear city is designed around 'take, make, waste,' whereas circular cities are designed to 'take, make, retake, remake, restore'... in this case waste becomes a resource". The second principle describes a positive city, "in that everything is powered by the sun, wind and sometimes by geothermal power". The third key principle is diversity, and refers to how city planners aim for what fits ... carefully to local ecologies ... incorporating natural and cultural history. By doing so, they create possibilities for positive growth that supports life. McDonough contends that if we follow these three urban design principles: "...as we shape the nature of our cities, we will be making places that celebrate both human creativity and a rich, harmonious relationship with the living earth. We will be forging a new geography of hope." [5]

Another perspective is offered by Jonathan Manns in an opinion piece in *The Dominion Post*. "New Zealand is at a turning point," he writes, emphasising "We need to have better conversations about our cities ...The pandemic has thrust health and wellbeing into the spotlight, forcing a reconsideration of how and where we live and work ... Successful and resilient towns and cities are dense, interconnected and human-scale... There are profound technological, demographic and environmental changes afoot." Having identified the need for change, he turns to the work of Professor Carlos Moreno. Manns reveals that, in responding to this need to re-evaluate and reimagine our urban spaces in the light of our new ways of living, Moreno has formulated "15-minute cities", which Manns describes as "a concept in which residents seek to achieve most daily tasks within walking or cycling distance of their home ... It's proven [to be] effective and popular." [6]

Ian Evenden explores the 15-minute city concept — "An idea that's catching on in capitals around the world." Paris has taken it to heart, and there has been interest from Latin America and across Europe. Wellington also entertained the idea of 15-minute city as did Hamilton although their model was built around a 20-minute city. "This changes the city from a dense centre with surrounding suburbs into a series of hubs within which are shopping and entertainment facilities. None of these hubs is more than a 15-minute walk or cycle from where people live, and many people may live close to more than one hub. He sees it as "an intuitive concept and has the capacity to deliver tangible changes in people's lives. For these reasons, it has proven easy to translate into political programmes and policies that transform cities. ... It seems the pandemic, for some became a moment to reimagine how we see the future of our oldest cities." [7]

As the Green Party's transport spokesperson Julie Anne Genter has said, the 15-minute city is "all about sustainable urban development". [8] Ian Evenden describes some of the ways the concept might translate into reality, starting with "reimagining the High Street". This would see city centres turned into "more active areas, dedicated to doing rather than just buying ... That means an increase in cafés, bar restaurants, and cinemas. Post-COVID, open-air markets are increasingly seen as safer places to shop than retailers based indoors." The 15-minute city also buys into the new desire for flexibility in work lives, the blurring of lines between work lives and personal lives, with the focus shifting from fixed hours and locations to productivity, wherever that might take place. Evenden sees that the new design can easily cater for this: "providing [the] public [with] high-speed internet access on shopping streets could encourage shoppers to linger at a café and maybe work there, rather than going home after buying what they need". [9]

Similarly, the Streets for People programme in 2022 was about creating what Transport Minister Michael Wood called a "world that is fit to live for our tamariki", as the government "focused on finding ways to reallocate road space towards active transport options, including walking and cycling". [10] This freeing up of public outdoor spaces from roading was again part of an international trend where the focus was shifting to greater outdoor living. Ian Evenden explains part of what lies behind this is that the Covid-19 pandemic had "left many people appreciating the outdoors more than ever, finding that time spent in nature relaxed them and improved their mental health. With people unable to travel long distances, they sought green spaces closer to home such as gardens and parkland." There are upsides for the planet, too, he points out: "An injection of green into urban spaces can help with carbon absorption, improve air quality and mitigate flooding ... To this end tall buildings [could be] built with vertical gardens on their sides. And for society in general, with a London School of Economics study suggesting "that crime is lower in areas with trees". [11]

With growing urban populations leading to urban sprawl destroying biodiversity, Javier Yanes writes: " ... If there is one type of place where planting trees has a special role and meaning, it is in cities." Governments and councils need to make a concerted effort to make their cities greener: if cities of the future are to flourish then nature must be allowed to flourish. Yanes contends that this would entail city councils having agreements "aiming at having 30–40% of built-up city surface consisting of green spaces." As well as green spaces providing "aesthetic enjoyment, relaxation or recreation ... they meet the United Nations Sustainable Development Goals".

As Yanes points out that "Trees are natural climate control ... [they] not only provide shade, but also cool the air by evapotranspiration; in others words, they allow cities to sweat." This reduces energy consumption with air conditioning systems, citing the World Economic Forum (WEF), which says that "a single tree can cut 3% of a household's energy consumption within five years of planting". Trees can also sequester tonnes of CO2 over their life cycle, as well as reducing air, noise and water pollution. Yanes concludes: [T] hat green cities are able to offer more, [caring socially inclusive communities with a greater quality of life because it offers that community an ability to easily promote wellbeing ...] "Green spaces promote urban biodiversity, which in turn improves the health of trees themselves, and their permeable soils reduce the impact of heavy rains and flooding." (12)

New Zealand has its own cheerleaders for greening our cities. The message in the *Sunday Star-Times* heading is clear: "We need to radically transform our cities for sustainability". In the accompanying article, writing in response to the 2023 flooding in Auckland caused by Cyclone Gabrielle — which "devastated many businesses, destroy[ed] properties, and [left] many workers reticent to return to their jobs" — Associate Professor Boarin and Dr Armoudian of the University of Auckland offer an alternative way of reimaging the structures of cities.. First they outline the unacceptable current situation, where the concrete and metal built environment is inimical to the indigenous flora and fauna that had once flourished where the buildings now stand: "As the planet heats up and the weather grows wilder, those businesses, workers and residents face greater dangers because these types of structures become heat islands that worsen the effects." Then they state "But that future is not predestined", before going on to draw on examples from across the world of how cities are being sustainably transformed to tackle climate change. "Instead of just masses of concrete and metal, indigenous plant-green roofs, vertical gardens, rain gardens and permeable pavements to absorb and manage stormwater run-off, cool hot structures, mitigate the effects of floods, and reduce energy consumption and noise pollution through their natural insulation." As Yanes points out, Armoudian and Boarin highlight the other positive consequences of greening our cities: "[I]ndigenous flora and wetlands, [and] other green spaces will extract pollutants and carbon from air and soil, cool the region, and reward us with vital oxygen, cleaner waterways and enhanced physical and mental health — all while helping mitigate climate change." [13]

OUR PREOCCUPATION WITH ECONOMIC GROWTH AND GDP

Following the virus's tortuous journey "helps illuminate some of the long-standing problems we face, making hidden issues clear. It also provides an opportunity to put them right." [14] This part of the chapter explores how the ramifications of the pandemic have rippled out to touch multiple parts of society, leaving us to ponder what is still relevant, what needs to be refined and rethought, and what changes need to be made. One of these is questioning how we evaluate success as a society. "For over 60 years, economic thinking told us that GDP growth was a good enough proxy for progress." [15] "But in the context of today's social and ecological crisis, how can this single, narrow metric still command such international attention?" [16] Thankfully, the voices of many are "growing a movement in economics to overcome the fixation with this one indicator". [17] If we are looking for courageous changes, the case for tackling our "unsustainable preoccupation with economic growth" [18] is abundantly clear. Perhaps this is fortuitous as, interestingly, "economics advances one crisis at a time ... Sure enough, the recovery from the covid-19 pandemic has given economists another chance to learn ... Discoveries from the recovery" [19]

Economic growth and its consequences are now being challenged, as many are coming to believe that "the preoccupation with growth might lead us to oblivion". [20] The gains are debatable, but the costs are real and mounting, even though they are not always readily apparent: "[T]he environmental costs of this growth — trillions of tons of greenhouse gases in the atmosphere, a poisoned ocean, and the widespread destruction of the earth's natural systems — remain largely invisible". [21] There is growing awareness, though, with the heads of the G20 warning of "the vulnerabilities from unbalanced growth, increased inequality and chronic environmental unsustainability". [22] A headline in *The Observer* captures the growing intergenerational divide concerning this preoccupation with growth: "Are young people poised to put the brakes on endless growth?" Will it turn into another concern that separates different generations? Are Generation Z ready to take the fight forward on the preoccupation of economic growth, in the same way that they have become the driving force in confronting the climate crisis? [23]

Here, we explore the thinking behind this movement. At the core is the idea of "coming into balance", which begins with questioning what the economy is actually for. Those challenging the economic status quo believe that "instead of prioritising metrics like GDP, the aim should be to enlarge people's capabilities — such as to be healthy, empowered and creative — so that they can choose to be and do things in life that they value ... and to do so within the means of our life-giving planet giving them a life of value". [24] Kate Raworth's *Doughnut Economics: Seven Ways to Think Like a 21st-Century Economist*, offers an eloquently expressed deep analysis of the issues, and concludes that thinking in terms of "thriving-in-balance" is fundamental to the twenty-first century. If the goal is to achieve "human prosperity in a flourishing web of life", then we need to view the economy in its entirety. [25]

Justin Zorn and Ben Beachy begin their analysis by questioning "at a time of a massive public health crisis ... why do we measure our economy according to a metric that says so little about our well-being ... [and that bears little] resemblance whatsoever to most people's lived experience?" [26] They argue that measures of success need to encompass a wider remit, including issues like public health, economic equity, climate action: questioning and measuring performance in these area is a practical exercise, "not academic musings", because ... "in government, as in business, we manage what we measure". [27]

The solution, they write, doesn't "abandon the standard GDP measure because it still has its uses"; instead they look to expand it to make it more meaningful. They suggest transforming the measure into a series of four indicators: "G1 being the standard measure, G2 would offer a fuller picture of income, revealing how equitably it is distributed ... G3 look[s] to the future, ensuring that today's output does not hamper tomorrow's by exacerbating environmental challenges or depleting resources. G4 could account for our daily well-being, including, for example, measures of health and social connection" [28] and the quality of our lives and the experiences we value.

They conclude that while metrics "rarely capture the public imagination, this one gets to the heart of a deeply and timely question: How to pursue genuine thriving rather than growth for its own sake. And at a time when people across societies are seeking systemic change, reimagining GDP is one plausible way governments can deliver." [29]

Mark Carney, former governor of the Bank of England, acknowledges that while "continued growth ... is a necessity", it should not be growth for growth's sake — just any growth. "The power of the market needs to be directed to achieving what society wants. That requires measures of income and welfare that reflect our values. Measures that count natural and social capital as well as economic capital. We need a world where we are no longer guided by measures like GDP that were devised a century ago when the earth seemed immortal and when the social norms of the market felt immutable." [30] The growth we need, Carney argues, is "broad-based". [31]

In the United Kingdom, Professor Sir Partha Dasgupta led an independent review on the economics. In his final report, *The Economics of Biodiversity*, he concludes that "in order to judge whether the path of economic development we choose to follow is sustainable, nations need to adopt a system of economic accounts that records an inclusive measure of their wealth. The qualifier 'inclusive' says that wealth includes Nature as an asset. The contemporary practice of using Gross Domestic Product (GDP) to judge economic performance is based on a faulty application of economics ... [as] GDP does not include ... the degradation of the natural environment." In developing the idea of sustainable development, we need to factor in "the demands humanity makes on Nature". [32]

Commenting on Dasgupta's review, Larry Elliott in his piece in *The Guardian Weekly*, echoes the sentiment that natural resources need to be valued more highly than GDP. He argues: "The notion that there is no alternative to the status quo has finally been exploded. That's not to say that the fundamental rethink called for by Dasgupta is going to be easy. But the need for change is glaringly obvious, and the opportunity is there too. That opportunity must not be squandered". [33]

On the behest of French President Nicholas Sarkozy, Joseph Stiglitz, Amartya Sen and Jean-Paul Fitoussi conducted a review on the measurement of economic performance and social progress, exploring the "classical GDP issues". While acknowledging that GDP is "the most widely-used measure of economic activity", they conclude that GDP alone is too narrow a measure and focusing on it alone can be misleading. "GDP mainly measures market production, though it has often been treated as if it were a measure of economic well-being. Conflating the two can lead to misleading indications about how well-off people are and entail the wrong policy decisions." Instead, more prominence should be given to the distribution of income, consumption, wealth and living standards. [34]

Before "tackling the more difficult task of measuring well-being", they recommend looking at the existing measures of economic performance and seeing where they need improving. , "to better reflect ... the structural changes which have characterized the evolution of modern economics". Traditional measures of output and economic performance are inadequate given "the growing share of services and the production of increasingly complex products". They explain what is at stake: "what we measure affects what we do; and if our measurements are flawed, decisions may be distorted ... we often draw inferences about what are good policies by looking at what policies have promoted economic growth; but if our metrics of performance are flawed, so too may be the inferences that we draw." Looking at what can be done within the existing measurement framework is no simple matter. [35]

New Zealand authors have added their voices to this movement. We turn first to the writing and research of Professors Paul Dalziel and Caroline Saunders, who in their book *Wellbeing Economics: Future Directions for New Zealand* point to a rich vein in New Zealand's history of acknowledging the significance of individual wellbeing and catering for it in its world-first pioneering of the welfare state. Now, wellbeing economics offers "a new opportunity for New Zealand to pioneer a further transformation in how a country enhances the wellbeing of its people". [36]

The wellbeing economics framework offers a new direction, they explain: "[I]t is improvements in wellbeing that count, not how the wellbeing is produced; second, it rejects a sharp distinction between economic policy and social policy; thirdly it is sceptical about claims that economic growth will lead to universal improvements in wellbeing, [and] ... finally wellbeing economics argues that policy should be aimed *directly* at expanding the substantive freedom of persons to lead the kinds of lives they value and have reason to value". [37] The focus of wellbeing economics can be summarised with the words "value-added growth". (38) Dalziel and Saunders' detailed work and cogently argued case makes, "an inspiring call for New Zealand's transformation ... to a progressive wellbeing state". (39)

A second New Zealand voice joins the movement. In *Comparonomics: Why life is better than you think, and how to make it even better*, Dr Grant Ryan points us towards "the Speed of Economic Progress (SEP) as an alternative measure of economic growth to GDP". Using "comparonomics", he argues, "seems a lot more useful than traditional economics for long-term time comparisons". (40) Ryan's focus is twofold: (a) what is the SEP measure telling us, and (b) "if things are so much better, why do we feel so bad?"

Turning to (a), Ryan points out that "all [SEP] measures is the relative speed at which things important to us go from impossible to available to everyone". (41) He sees it simply as "a tool that allows you to ask questions so you can prove to yourself that you have a lot to be grateful for". Which brings us to (b), where he suggests that some of our prevailing negativity may be falsely based: "Just because you feel hard done by doesn't mean you are actually hard done by." (42) He explores a number of biases, including those presented in "media — we have evolved to seek bad news, social media, pervasive advertising, negative information bias, and digital screen addiction" and suggests that exposure to these pervasive negative biases goes a long way to making us feel like we do. (43) Moreover, one of the reasons we feel so bad about progress is "that many experts tell us we are not doing well and they are wrong". Using a measurement tool like SEP instead allows "you to work it out yourself", perhaps with more heartening results. (44) Here brevity is no friend to Ryan's detailed analysis or his descriptive writing and the strength of his knowledge.

The final word goes to outgoing Minister of Finance Grant Robertson, who said that when he had taken on the role he was "determined to reshape the fiscal management of the nation to take into account greater well-being and more long-term planning". While this was evidenced in his Budgets, such as the 2019 Wellbeing Budget, he "expressed regret ... that Covid-19 meant that he was not able to fully realise that vision". (45)

REFLECTIONS

Consistent debate about economic growth and its partner GDP transversed the latter part of the twentieth century. However, there is no mistaking that the Covid-19 pandemic has hurled us with unbelievable speed to rapidly refine our understanding about the nature of risk, sustainability, resilience and preparedness. But out of this debate we are presented with alternatives that give us hope: "thriving in balance", "broad-based growth", "inclusive measures of wealth", "genuine thriving rather than growth for its own sake", the "importance of social progression", "value added growth" and "SEP". During a period of radical change when the need is for energising, revising, renewing, we need to adopt creative approaches that fit what the twenty-first century is now about. Picking up on the point made by Justin Zorn and Ben Beachy, if we focus on a measure of "short-term raw output rather than wellbeing, we risk policies that sacrifice what's truly important". [46] Joseph Stiglitz pushes home the point: "striving to grow GDP is not the same as ensuring the well-being of a society". [47]

But wait, change seems to be emerging. In his piece for the *Scientific American* "GDP is the wrong tool for measuring what matters", Stiglitz writes that there is "crystallizing a global movement toward improved measures of social and economic health. The OECD has adopted the approach in its *Better Life Initiative* ... that measures ... the things [that are] care[d] about. The World Bank and the International Monetary Fund (IMF), traditionally strong advocates of GDP thinking, are now also paying attention to environment, inequality and sustainability of the economy." [48] He points out that faced "with the devastating crises that looms — catastrophic climate change and biodiversity collapse" we require, "at the very least, an excellent navigational system". This has been brought into even sharper focus with "the global crisis in human societies that a microscopic virus has precipitated ... Concerns about climate change and rising inequality had already been fuelling a global demand for better measures." He concludes by citing the words of the OECD: "We have been developing the tools to help us drive better: It is time to use them." [49]

One can only agree with Adam Grant, who writes: "I can't think of a more vital time for rethinking ... and lett[ing] go knowledge and opinions that are no longer serving [us] well." [50] It is also important to remember that "occasionally, the world engineers a moment in time that's so big, we're are compelled to make change to stay relevant. For all of us, 2020 and the events within it was that moment." [51]

REFINING CAPITALISM

Flowing on from the 2008 banking crisis, the idea that perhaps a new type of capitalism may be needed slowly began to gain currency. But it was not until 2020's pandemic that the idea of reimagining capitalism seemed to have a resurgence. In these world-shifting circumstances, "it has become easier to suggest that firms have real responsibilities for their people and communities and to talk about the human and emotional dimension of business … and finding that a focus on 'being' is just as important as a focus on 'doing' and [business leaders] are seeking the language of meaning, compassion and empathy as integral part of their lives and their jobs". [52] The aim when reimagining capitalism is "how we can build a profitable, equitable, and sustainable capitalism by changing how we think about the purpose of firms, their role in society, and their relationship to government and the state". [53] The key to reimagining capitalism is that the idea of maximising shareholder returns is yesterday's idea, and firms that "master change" will be those having "a pro-social purpose beyond profit maximization and taking responsibility for the health of the natural and social systems on which we all rely not only makes good business sense but is also morally required … the world is changing". [54]

This sets the context, and drawing from it economists and social scientists have debated on the various new forms capitalism can take. There is *compassionate capitalism,* [55] where the emphasis is on individual flourishing, and *responsible capitalism,* "where the aim is to bring organizations and communities closer together by developing a strong[er] sense of place" and a "more collaborate ethos … [making] commitments and deeper relationships … because businesses can only flourish in the new order by adding a further, broader, vision … in other words a business needs a purpose beyond itself … so that employees can develop a deeper sense of purpose and meaning in their work". [56] Progressive capitalism emphasises social progression, "inequalities and the common good," [57] Finally there is inclusive capitalism, which, with its "structural feature … equality, fairness and a sense of social contract", [58] "presents as an opportunity for business interest and the communities from which they derive their profits to rebuild the social contract between them through a rebalancing of privilege and obligation on more sustainable pathways". [59] A universally accepted definition of inclusive capitalism has not yet emerged, however. [60] With the old order of capitalism being described as "very much under siege" and with "warnings about short-termism ... echoed in many quarters", [61] the challenge for businesses is acknowledging that "the privilege of participation ... carries with it obligation[s] to the broader community". [62]

"The coronavirus exposed and exacerbated the fragility and inequity of the global economic system." [63] The clear message coming from those who are reimagining or suggesting refining capitalism are courageous and urgent: capitalism needs a rebalancing primarily between businesses and the community through a sense of place, trust has to be restored through establishing a sense of purpose beyond itself, and a broader vision is necessary when we reimagine capitalism, and that view is "absolutely necessary... right now". [64] Remember, "moments of existential crisis can turn into opportunities for bold reforms". [65] An emerging theme when thinking about the pandemic's journey, and one to hold close, is: the pandemic is no friend of the status quo.

REFLECTIONS

Summing up: "embracing a pro-social purpose beyond profit maximization and taking the responsibility for the health of the natural and social systems on which we all rely not only makes good business sense but is also a moral require[ment] ... The firms that change with it will reap rich returns – and if we don't reimagine capitalism, we will be significantly poorer." [66] "Business must step up. It is immensely powerful. It has the resources, the skills, and the global reach to make an enormous difference. It also has a strong *economic* case for action. [67] "Is this enough to reimagine capitalism? Of course not! ... But talk is a first step to action, and many firms are acting ... COVID-19 has brought immense suffering. But it has also shown us that business really is as much about 'us and later' as it is about 'me' and now' and that we can move much, much faster than we ever imagined." [68] As Stiglitz and colleagues conclude, their report represents "opening a discussion rather than closing it". [69]

Reminding us of the role of growth and part it plays in economics, Research Professor in Economics Daniel Susskind confirms that we should continue to pursue growth, but adds: " [A]s we do, we must also recognize and confront the tradeoffs involved ... this requires us to consider two moral questions. How much should we care about these other ends? And how much should we care about the future? ... The answer to both must surely be *far more*. The priority we attach to growth means that we care too much about it and too little about everything else; the short-termism that characterizes contemporary life means we put far too much weight on the present and not enough on what lies ahead." [70]

Thinking back across this chapter, the phrases that follow reflect the core of this discussion: the ideas of and the consequences of unbalance growth, the need for broad-based growth, a refined sense of corporate purpose that embraces a broader vision, and a real sense of community not forgetting the wellbeing of society, what we value and what we aspire to.

CHAPTER 6:

Coping with the Pandemic

COPING — ITS DEFINITION AND WHAT THE COPING RESEARCH TELLS US: SETTING A CONTEXT

The concept of coping has not only become central in the field of psychology, it has also worked its way into the vocabulary of society more generally. [1] "The implication [is] that coping is part of the very essence of the human change process. Thus, coping not only is basic for survival, but it also relates to the quality and the ensuing constructive meaning of our own lives." [2] This is why an understanding of coping is important, the more so given that "stress is so much a part of everyday life [and] how people successfully manage stress has [an] immediate personal relevance" for all of us. [3]

What have we learnt from the research about coping? Well, the first thing we have learnt is that coping "is a complex ... process that is sensitive both to the environment, and its demands and resources, and to personality" [4] and of course how much control you have over the situation. The multiple factors at play mean "there is no 'silver bullet' in coping that works for everyone". [5] Therefore it becomes necessary to learn how to "balance the relative use of different strategies", and to realise that "what 'works' in one situation may increase distress in another". [6]

Coping can be defined as "cognitive and behavioural efforts to manage psychological stress". [7] The key to this definition lies with the word "effort", distinguishing coping strategies from other adaptive behaviours that occur in everyday life. "Coping is a subset of adaptational activities that involve efforts ... to manage stressful demands." [8]

But the key to coping is best understood when you think about how the stress process unfolds: first you recognise that the event is making a demand on your resources, and then you assess how confronting the event will be for you. It is this assessment or appraisal that creates the personal meanings you build around the event and its "immediate personal relevance" for you. [9] Its importance lies in the fact that the "stress, coping and emotions" you may experience are simply "dependent on the appraisal you make". [10] The significance of the appraisal process is in identifying your personal context and the role it will play "in direct[ing] the choice of coping strateg[ies]" [11] you make. The message is clear: we must focus as much on how the person thinks about the event, as we do on the nature of the event itself. The power of these personal meanings is simply because how you think influences how you feel. [12] What is "at stake in this encounter ... contributes to the emotion quality and intensity" of the encounter. [13]

To make this clearer, Carolyn Aldwin has established a conceptual framework made up of five types of appraisals or assessments: "harm, threat, loss, challenge, or benign". [14] To this she adds "three additional appraisals sometimes encountered were simply annoyances, others were concerns over other people's problems and the third described where people 'were simply at a loss for what to do next'. [15] This process on how an event is appraised or assessed simply re-enforces how stress is a product of the transaction between "the person and the environment". [16] If you appraise or assess the event in terms of a challenge your coping strategies will be likely different than if you had appraised or assessed it as a threat to your self-esteem or competence. This illustrates why people faced with the same demanding event will cope differently — as each of them has appraised it in a different way, reflecting their personal context. To fail to understand the appraisal process is simply to ignore the most fundamental process that lies at the heart of the stress and coping process.

Having introduced this crucial context of individual appraisal and response, the chapter now moves on to explore possible ways to couple coping with the events of the pandemic. The driving force of this chapter is to get you thinking about how you can build your resources and improve your capacity to cope. It is not designed to evaluate your coping, but to explore techniques and strategies that may give you a sense of fit, and perhaps of immediate relevance to events like the ever-evolving pandemic, and the priorities you may wish to set to help you develop your personal capacity to cope with the hurly-burly of a changing world. But it is important to offer a note of caution: the aligning of the coping strategies is simply designed to give a sense of fit, but you can adjust where you think the different strategies and techniques should sit, so that they better suit your purpose and are more helpful when you think about your coping style.

A SUITE OF RULES

There was, of course, a suite of rules that reminded us that we were in a pandemic, and without doubt these rules were designed to save lives, with their evolution responding to the twists and turns of the virus. More importantly, they offered us a set of behaviours — which became almost second nature — to protect us from the virus. These behaviours included hand washing, social distancing, staying home if unwell, wearing a mask, using the Covid tracker, protocols for sneezing and coughing, and getting vaccinated. It is plausible to think of the suite of rules as a way of giving us a sense that we were acting as a community, as others, we thought, were following the rules as well. With social distancing limiting our behaviour to act otherwise, following the rules was one of the few ways we could express a sense of community. This sense of community may well have flowed from the empowering phrase "the team of 5 million". Or it may simply have been because we are all in it together, caught in the grips of an unpredictable pandemic, and obeying the rules gave us the opportunity to describe our behaviour in a way that reflected communal coping.

MENTAL HEALTH STRATEGIES

Beginning with the advice of classical mental health strategies, we have here collected together a summary of the strong, common-sense advice they generally offer. These strategies are intended to develop your resources and increase your capacity to cope with the pandemic. They include looking after yourself physically — by making sure you eat and sleep well — and just as importantly paying attention to your mental health. The strategies being promoted were designed to develop good habits that would transfer over to a post-pandemic world. The following is a sample: "here are some ways to promote mental wellness: make time for movement — take a walk or join an outdoor exercise ... mental rest — just as you need to get enough sleep, you also need mental rest to recharge your body. Try a new hobby or do something creative to give your mind a break from work and other stressors. Set goals ... set them small and achievable so ... you keep focused and feel accomplished. Seek out a professional ... recognize your anxieties and the time to reach out to those around you and seek help." [17] Others extend the list but capture the same themes: "practice these tips to nurture yourself, improve your mood and help others — be kind, be thankful, deepen your connections, move your body, write down your thoughts, meditate, determine what is really bothering you, play games, dine well, remind yourself that this will pass". [18]

A key message is to remember what we have learned through the pandemic, although specific learnings "will depend a lot on where you live, what your experience has been like, and what you make of it all". The strategies being promoted had a dual focus: helping you cope now, and equipping you for living in a post-pandemic world. They encouraged you to look to a time when the regulations had been lifted, to consider what life would it be like, and what the new normal would be. The message was spread over five themes: firstly, that being with others is the key to happiness, lockdowns notwithstanding. Secondly, reducing stress is good for all. "One silver lining of staying at home is that it's forced many of us to slow down and find new ways to manage stress and anxiety ... and [these] are worth holding onto." Thirdly, that gratitude matters: it's is a powerful emotion that gives us a sense that being kinder can release positive emotions. Fourthly, "We need less stuff than we think ... and [with the presence of a climate crisis beckoning] we can help to build a healthier society if we can consume less and give more." Finally, perhaps what really got us through the pandemic is learning that "We are stronger when we act together." Our mantra was realising that helping others is helping ourselves, and cooperation matters because it's key rests in the power of social connection. [19]

In her article 'Coping with pandemic stress', Melinda Wenner Moyer encourages us "to be flexible, open and honest with ourselves and learn how to take things one day at a time". It is also important to acknowledge any feelings of fear and to not feel bad having them: "It's totally normal that the anxiety is there — it's about managing it ... trying to pinpoint what exactly worries you most at the moment and then identifying aspects of the situation that you can control or make progress on." She also warns us against being too rigid in our thinking, as it makes it much more difficult to adapt to changing environments, whether COVID or another situation. Once again, we hear the words "adaptable" and "flexible": "The idea is to think of problems as obstacles you can overcome (at least partially) rather than as insurmountable hurdles we can do nothing about. There are aspects of this pandemic we cannot control – but by focusing on the things we can tweak as least a bit and by thinking of ourselves as resilient and adaptable, we will do better." She recommends using cognitive-behavioural therapy, which "has consistently been shown to boost mental health", as it "focuses on helping individuals identify, understand and change their thinking and behaviour patterns in these ways".

She also looks at practical ways to cope with living in a pandemic world, including finding new ways to connect. While the limitations of social distancing strain those connections, she advises the reader to take guidance from themselves, paying attention to how one feels: "Trust your instincts and ... be willing to try out new things if the approaches you first choose do not seem to be working ... and keep in mind that the more time we spend in this pandemic, the better we will get at muddling our way through because people adapt surprisingly well to challenging situations." [20]

Trauma and resilience specialists Steven Southwick and Dennis Charney look at evidence-based tactics for building resilience that scientists have identified, including "rethink adversity, forge close friendships and tackle novel challenges". Some of the strategies are geared towards reducing stress, while others help you grow from an experience. "Different avenues for building resilience include learning how to regulate your emotions, adopting a positive but realistic outlook, becoming physically fit, accepting challenges, maintaining a close and supportive social network, and observing and imitating resilient role models." They also focus on a coping strategy called cognitive reappraisal, in which "a person revises his or her interpretation of a difficult experience to make it less negative". There are many advantages to adopting positive framing: "Optimism and positive emotions are strongly associated with good mental and physical health, even longevity... remember, resilience is associated with realistic optimism ... Other resilience-enhancing attitudes and behaviours include perseverance and endurance, toughness tempered by compassion, altruism, dignity in the face of deprivation and potentially growth from suffering." [21]

Dr Steve Taylor also believes that the pandemic provides some positive opportunities, writing: "Surviving an awful experience can lead to some surprisingly positive psychological effects in many people." He believes that one of the after-effect of the Covid-19 pandemic will be post-traumatic growth. "In the midst of the suffering and challenges of our present predicament, we may develop a heightened sense of appreciation, more authentic relationships, and a new sense of resilience and confidence. We may slow down and learn to live in the present rather than filling our lives with incessant activity and constantly rushing into the future." He concludes by pointing to one of the fundamental lessons of the pandemic: "We are all in this together, and we will overcome the crisis only through cooperation. Conflict and competition will only lead to more suffering ... When this is all over, we may find that we are stronger and closer to one another than before." [22]

Remember, another lesson from the pandemic is emerging, and again it is directed at advancing the science. Lydia Denworth expresses it this way: "Fortunately, the unprecedented pandemic is leading to unprecedented science not just in virology but on mental health and resilience. Behavioural scientists are measuring the psychological toll in real time and striving to identify what helps people cope." As a consequence, scientists are predicting: "there will be a whole new science of resilience. We could learn how to help people become more resilient *before* these things happen." [23]

Bringing this section on classical mental health strategies to an end, we simply want to focus on the power of their principal messages to cope in a pandemic. Again, Lydia Denworth provides a useful summary: "[S]uccessfully coping in a crisis means continuing to function and engaging in day-to-day activities. One must solve problems, regulate emotions and manage relationships. These are factors that predict resilience such as optimism, the ability to keep perspective, strong social support and flexible thinking." With most people being able to strengthen their coping skills, it is worth making a conscious effort to do so. Denworth explains some potential avenues to follow: "[P]eople are encouraged to follow classic mental strategies like getting enough sleep, observing a routine, exercising, eating well, and maintaining strong connections. Spending time on projects, even small ones that provoke a sense of purpose helps." She also has a word of warning regarding potentially negative habits, saying "those who consume a great deal of news about a community-wide crisis are more distressed". [24]

COPING THAT FOCUSES MORE GENERALLY ON RELATIONSHIP BUILDING

We now turn to specific coping strategies that have a real sense of fit when weighed against the trials and challenges of the Covid-19 pandemic, and more generally go some way to directing your attention to the importance of relationship maintenance, not just in the pandemic and your "bubble", but beyond the pandemic as well. This involves relationship coping, prosocial coping, perceiving benefit coping, benefit reminding coping, and reappraisal coping.

Tracey Revenson and Anita DeLongis, who have researched relationships in the context of chronic illness, explain the elements involved. "Relationship coping" refers to "efforts to manage and sustain social relationships during stressful episodes ... it involves trying to maintain a balance between self and other[s], with the goal of maintaining the integrity of the relationship above either partner's needs". They then set out the practicalities of what this entails: "Relationship-focused coping modes include working through issues, making concessions, thinking about and examining and reflecting on things and considering the other person's situation, and being empathetic ... Empathetic responding includes attempting to manage or prevent conflict, dealing with the other person's distress ... understanding another person's [position] and efforts, and responding to the other person in a supportive, caring manner as a means to defuse interpersonal stress and maintain the relationship ... It's about active engagement asking how she or he feels and actively involving discussions." [25] Lydia Denworth reveals that an individual's makeup can influence their degree of compliance with pandemic regulations, explaining: "Those high in empathy are more likely to engage in health behaviours such as social distancing ... the positive thing is empathetic responses can be learned and encouraged with proper messaging." [26]

Prosocial coping directs its attention to how your coping affects others, so "a person may delay or not engage in a direct action to solve a problem if that action is perceived as causing distress to another" or they may "use coping strategies intended to buffer or protect another person from stress". [27] Remember that people may experience your coping in a different way than you do: prosocial coping offers a gentler route and awareness as to how others may be affected by the coping you may initiate. Psychologists Susan Folkman and Judith Moskowitz explain that prosocial coping involves "think[ing] carefully about how others feel before deciding what to do", adding that studies have found that "active prosocial coping was associated with better emotional outcomes". Communal coping can also be described as prosocial — "join[ing] together with others to deal with the situation together". [28]

When battling with adversity, perceiving benefit coping describes where some "report that something positive has come from the experience … such as closer relationships with family and friends, reprioritizing of goals, and greater appreciation of life", or finding that everyone is safe or has tested negative to the virus. Folkman and Moskowitz explain that the way this may work is by capturing that moment of feeling that "something positive has come from the experience", which then "provides respite from distress and helps to replenish resources and sustains further coping". These potential positive outcomes are motivating researchers to increase their efforts "to study the process by which persons experiencing stress arrive at the conclusion that they have experienced benefits from the stress". [29]

Benefit reminding coping examines "where the individual reminds himself or herself of the possible benefits stemming from the stressful experience". Folkman and Moskowitz say we now need to understand more clearly "the interplay between positive and negative emotions during both acute and chronic stress". [30]

Much in the same vein, reappraisal coping can be summed up as: "Is there a less destructive way to look at this situation? Or am I catastrophising or exaggerating its potential negative impact? Or is there something that I can learn from the experience, or is it possible to grow stronger as a result?" Southwick and Charney explain it as being where "a person revises his or her interpretation of a difficult experience to make it less negative". [31] Remember that appraising the stress changes during the coping process.

This means that a fundamental step in the coping process is evaluating how you are appraising events, as those appraisals are a straight line to your emotions, and will influence your choice of coping strategies and the context that you build around the event itself.

OTHER COPING STRATEGIES

Exercise — the healing power of walking

One of the outdoors activities that was allowed during the pandemic was exercise, and generally involved staying close to home and walking around your local neighbourhood. We follow the science, which has for some time explored how much walking you should do each day — focusing on the daily number of steps taken —and so is our initial focus. Then we explore the health benefits from walking, and the role of exercise as a strategy to offer those who do it the enjoyment of the solitude it provides. When thinking about the story of exercise we need to begin by looking at how in our everyday life those once-routine movements we did have almost disappeared, explaining why our contemporary lifestyles are regularly and simply described as sedentary. In his book *The Miracle Pill*, Paul Walker argues that "there is hope ... even in an environment designed against human-powered motion, [that] change can be easier than you think". There is no need to go rushing off to the gym: "it is still possible to experience movement and exertion as a regular part of your life. When you make something routine, normal, even forgettable, you no longer need to carve time out of your day to do it, or feel guilty when you don't. Instead, it embeds, becomes permanent. When this happens, it feels almost as if you have been let in on a secret ... The consequences that follow for your wellbeing can be astounding ... It is just being active ... What is the best activity to do? ... [T]he one that you'll do and keep doing." [32] Psychologist Professor Marc Wilson says: "It is no surprise that physical wellbeing is associated with psychological wellbeing ... At a basic level, we're more able to engage in physical activity when we feel psychological wellbeing. It refills our emotion coping reservoir, it is a reciprocal relationship." [33] Ageing expert Dr Norman Lazarus confirms that "our lifestyles determine the state of our bodies". [34]

Physical exercise like walking, simply because it was allowed during the pandemic, turned into an important coping strategy. Resilience experts

Southwick and Charney explain the way it is beneficial: "It can enhance resilience by protecting ... people against the negative effects of stress ... it can strengthen attention, decision making and memory, empowering people to better shoulder stress." In many respects, they say, exercise has assumed the mantle of a "stress inoculation". [35] We were not only encouraged to take exercise, but also to think of it as a practice that could be continued beyond the pandemic. To turn it into a habit and think of it in this way: "There are 1,440 minutes in a day. Perhaps you can find 30 of those to exercise, set yourself challenging but realistic goals, exercising is better than doing nothing, if you aren't exercising at all, start by taking the stairs instead the lift, or call a friend to schedule a walk once or twice a week, and identify what motivates you." [36]

While "the best activity is ... the one that you'll do and keep doing", the focus has certainly turned to "the healing power of walking ... Don't balk at a walk," writes Jono Lineen. "There is a reason people have been doing it for millions of years — it's exceptionally good for us ... walking is one of the most effective ways to improve our state of mind ... [not forgetting] how it promotes our sense of empathy ... and when we walk our bodies remember that is what we are meant to do." [37]

After establishing that walking was beneficial, the research quickly turned to how many steps you should do. But it is all too easy to become fixated on the pedometer screen and lose sight of the overriding message, which is to go out and just do the exercise. Olivia Shivas, writing a piece in *The Dominion Post* under the heading "No need to walk 10,000 steps a day', supports the idea that getting out and exercising is the message that people need to hear, adding, "realistically, an adult's ability to reach a target for a daily step count depends on their health ... Rather than counting how many steps you take a day, we should be participating in 30 minutes of moderate-intensity exercise for at least five days [a week]." This message is reinforced by a cardiologist cited in Shivas's article, who advises "the number of steps you take a day doesn't really matter, but instead people should adjust the time they are sedentary or inactive, during the day and be physically active instead". [38]

But researchers have persisted in determining the ideal number of steps to be trotted out each day, and the consensus that has now emerged is 7500 steps. [39] As one of the researchers involved says, "for some people the idea of 10,000 steps might be out of reach and if they think actually if I get off the couch and do something, it's still benefitting me. Ten thousand shouldn't be the obstacle that holds you back." [40] Other researchers chip in with the same message: "So, if you don't move much, or are unfit, you can be sure to get a massive benefit from doing just a bit more than you currently do", adding: "When we walk 7,500 steps — which takes about an hour or less and corresponds to about 5–6 kilometres — our chance of dying from any cause in the next two years is about 40 percent less ... We should be mindful that the researchers looked only at mortality, yet our health and our capacity to live a happy, independent, and active life until mortality is really important to us." [41] Lazarus encourages us to think about the difference "between healthspan and lifespan — how long we live and the state of our health during those later years". [42] "We reap the benefits regardless of whether the steps are accumulated throughout the day — working in the garden, walking to and from the bus stop, taking the stairs at work — or in one session, where separate research suggests there are more health advantages when we push our pace a little ... walking is just one of a 'physical activity diet' that includes slow and relaxing exercises, those that get our heart rate pumping, and those we enjoy doing just for fun." [43]

Just when we thought the number of steps was settled, though, recent research has suggested that "walking at least 3967 steps a day started to reduce the risk of dying from any cause, while 2337 steps a day reduced the risk of dying from cardiovascular disease. Above these cutoffs, each increase of 1000 steps a day was associated with a 15% reduction in the risk of dying from any cause, while an increase of 500 steps a day was associated with a 7% reduction in dying from cardiovascular disease." The lead researcher Professor Maciej Banach says, "Our study confirms that the more you walk, the better. We found that this applied to both men and women ... In addition, our analysis indicates that as little as 4000 steps a day are needed to significantly reduce deaths from any cause, and even fewer to reduce from cardiovascular disease." He concludes: "[I]n a world where we have more and more advanced drugs to target specific conditions such as cardiovascular disease, I believe we should always emphasise that lifestyle changes, including diet and exercise, might be at least as — or even more — effective in reducing cardiovascular risk and prolonging lives." [44]

And, as luck would have it, just after I had written the section on the number of steps, I came across a research paper cited in the *New Scientist* that legitimises the idea of walking 10,000 steps a day! "Taking between 9000 and 10,000 steps a day really can make us healthier … [It] seems to reduce the risk of an early death or heart-related event, adding legitimacy to an idea that has been criticised as unscientific. The origin of the belief that people should aim for 10,000 steps a day is unclear, but it has been linked to a marketing campaign promoting pedometers in Japan." The article goes on to cite a study by Dr Matthew Ahmadi at the University of Sydney, Australia, and his colleagues, which has recently been published in the *British Journal of Sports Medicine*. Dr Ahmadi's study "suggests the figure could hold merit … The researchers calculated that the optimal number of steps a day is between 9000 and 10,000, with the benefits then starting to tail off." The *New Scientist* article then goes on to cite the opinion of Dr Dale Esliger at Loughborough University on the Ahmadi study: "This paper helps the field take a great stride forward. It does appear to support the notion that the originally non-evidence-based 10,000 steps target may indeed be about right." [45] So, now you have a range of research-based step goals, and you can choose from the different targets which one you wish to achieve — depending on you being comfortable with it, and indeed your body being comfortable with the target you set.

It seems other medical doctors would concur, too: "It's the best medicine we can recommend. Just going out for a walk." Another says "I think you really can get mental health and physical benefits from just short, brief movement breaks", [46] while another describes it this way: "This research shows us how good walking is for our health. If you packaged the benefits as a pill, we would be hailing it as a wonder drug." [47] Professor Grant Schofield at AUT says: "It's worth saying that New Zealand has an inactivity, low fitness problem and it's changed quite a bit. Twenty years ago, we were one of the fittest countries in the world, now [we're] in the bottom third of the OECD." [48]

"But what makes walking so special?" asks Alistair Hall. "For starters it's the most accessible — it can be done anywhere by anyone. All that's needed is shoes and walking attire. There's also a huge body of research that points to numerous health benefits. Besides the obvious fitness gains, regular walking has been shown to reduce the risk of cardiovascular and metabolic disease. It improves the health and strength of bones and muscles. Long term, the risk of cancer, particularly of the breast and bowel, can be reduced. Walking, especially in nature, releases endorphins into the brain which reduce stress and muscle tension. It lowers the heart rate and blood pressure. And it's tiring, so we sleep better." [49]

The evidence keeps mounting, as do the headlines". Under "Prescribed time in nature linked to improvements in anxiety, depression and blood pressure", Donna Lu writes in *The Guardian:* "Researchers say there are interlinked benefits across mental and physical health from prescribed time in green spaces or near bodies of water ... Doctors sometimes use nature-based social prescriptions programs — sometimes described as 'green prescriptions' or 'blue prescriptions' — to advise patients to spend time in green spaces or near bodies of water." [50] In "Prescribing nature: the restorative power of a simple dose of outdoors", Lu writes: "Access to green space has also linked to a reduced risk of loneliness and some have even suggested that interacting with microbes in the environment may be beneficial for our immune systems ... Experts suggest that spending time in nature may not have the same barrier to uptake as exercise." [51]

Just to reinforce this message of time spent in nature, Lydia Denworth begins her article "Greenery improves body and mind" by recounting how during the worst of the Covid pandemic she went on socially distanced walks, taking refuge in the outdoors. She writes "I think everybody got that nature seemed to be the solution for a lot of the stress issues that people were dealing with", before going on to recount the now familiar health benefits for blood pressure, immune systems, cardiovascular disease and improved sleep. She then turns her attention to the "convincing evidence that time in nature reduces depressive symptoms, alleviates stress and improves cognitive function." She concludes by saying that although many of these studies are aimed at policymakers rather than individuals, "they remind us all of the importance of seeking out greenery wherever we live". [52]

Just, as I thought I was heading in the right direction, to get people moving, here is an interesting twist. Under the heading "A better pill to swallow — could fitness tablets really work?", David Cox writes in *The Guardian:* "Exercise-mimetic drugs have long been a goal of science. As a new trial begins, it is hoped they could aid not just the sedentary, but elderly people and those with disease or disability." It appears that even the researchers sensed a certain irony in their work: "Giving a drug that promotes the benefits of exercise they say, well, what are we treating? Why don't they just exercise?... [but] in the end, they comment, 'if we were actually able to do this, I think these would be really terrific medicines'." [53]

However, the "The message is still clear. *Just go out and move.*" "The more we study physical activity," writes Professor Daniel Lieberman, "the more we realize that it doesn't really matter what you do. You don't have to do incredible strength training ... to get some benefits of physical activity. There are all different kinds of physical activity, and it's all good in different ways ... If 10,000 steps feels out of reach, it's OK to shoot for less — just so long as you're focused on movement." [54] Dr Norman Lazarus concurs: "We have known about the benefits of physical activity for some time," he says. "Move and your heart responds, and then every other system responds to that movement." [55] So, why not take it up and get out and try it? As Karen Nimmo writes, "what is good for the body is good for the mind", before issuing the challenge "are you match fit?!" [56] Sir Ashley Bloomfield, after participating in 2024's Southern Cross Round the Bays in Wellington 2024, said: "People are a lot more aware now of the benefits of physical activity for physical health, but also ... the direct benefits on mental well-being ... That's especially important when we see the increase in mental health issues for people — not just young people but right across the age spectrum." [57] But as Kirsten Rose, a physiotherapist at the Auckland Physiotherapy and Health Collective, reminds us: "exercise is only fully of benefit if recovery comes with it". [58]

As we age, we need to reflect on what Greg Macpherson suggests in his book *Age Less: The new science of slower and healthier ageing*: that we adopt a "longevity mindset". Here, as with Dr Lazarus's work, the focus is on "healthspan — the portion of a person's life that is lived in good health, free from chronic diseases or disabilities". He goes on to make it clear that if you were to ask any researcher working in the field of ageing "for their key recommendation for increasing healthspan and longevity, without fail they will answer exercise". He adds: "Nothing else compares to exercise — no drug, supplement or diet even comes close. If you are serious about increasing your healthspan and living in the best health possible for as long as possible, then you must make regular physical activity part of your lifestyle. The good news is that it doesn't take as much as you imagine. A 30-minute walk every day is ideal, be it outdoors or even doing your shopping. What is the best exercise? It's the activity that you like and will continue to do." [59]

Other experts agree. In *New Scientist* Michael Marshall writes: "for moderate-intensity exercise more is still better: your risk of dying early, say from a heart attack, will keep decreasing the more that you do. There's no such thing as too much exercise if it's moderate-intensity aerobic exercise." [60] Other writers also endorse Greg Macpherson's view, such as Grace Wade, again writing in New Scientist: "the best exercise is ultimately the one you will be able to stick with ... but I think for most people, we just need to get out there and get moving". [61] Returning to Greg Macpherson's longevity mind set, he recommends "the importance of establishing regular exercise habits "that can be maintained through what he calls the "longevity work week". He suggests that workplaces offer "structured daily 60- to 90-minute programmes that focus on improving health and increasing lifespan, within the work day, instead of the four-day work week that is currently gaining traction." In doing so: "The time given back to employees would be slightly less but ultimately both employees and businesses would achieve significant benefits." Finally, just to set these ideas in a context: "the foundations for longevity, revolves around exercise, diet, good sleep, stress management, and forming deep bonds with the people in your life". [62]

Now let's explore a benefit of exercise that few of us would have ever dreamed of when it comes to walking: solitude. It is Professor Cal Newport who draws this benefit of walking to our attention in his book *Digital Minimalism*. He describes solitude — which he defines as "freedom from input from other minds" — as "a key property of walking". With walking being "a fantastic source of solitude" and encourages us to "spend more time alone on your feet". The resulting experience of solitude "allows you to think through problems that are worrying you and gives you time for self-reflection on some particular aspect of your life that needs more attention ... [Doing so] simply makes you happier, more productive, more creative, more new ideas; an understanding of the self, and closeness to others." Living "in a world that has fast become 'solitude deprived'" means that walking gives you these benefits, because it offers a significant opportunity to simply put "solitude into an otherwise hectic life". He explains that the new challenge is how to find enough solitude "in the hyper-connected twenty-first century". The answer, he says, "spending more time alone on your feet". [63]

Newport offers another "excellent mechanism for generating" solitude in your life: writing a letter to yourself. He explains that "it not only frees you from outside's inputs, but also provides a conceptual scaffolding on which to sort and organize your thinking ... the key is the act of writing itself. This behaviour necessarily shifts you into a state of productive solitude — wrenching you away from the appealing digital baubles and addictive content waiting to distract you, and providing you with a structured way to make sense of whatever important things are happening in your life." As Newport points out, writing is "a simple practice that's easy to deploy, but it is also incredibly effective". [64]

This practice would certainly resonate with those using writing as a therapy. Other researchers would agree, having found that writing down thoughts and then shredding them relieves anger. Their research showed that "writing down your reaction to a negative incident on a piece of paper and then shredding it or scrunching it into a ball and throwing into a bin, gets rid of anger." One of the researchers said, "[W]e expected our method would suppress anger to some extent ... We were amazed that anger was eliminated almost entirely." This research "builds on research on the association between the written word and anger reduction as well as studies showing how interactions with physical objects can control a person's mood." The researchers concluded that, "the meaning (interpretation) of disposal plays a critical role in reducing anger". [65] This would indicate that writing down any negative thoughts could be an effective coping strategy during the pandemic. It is certainly one that can be done anywhere, and it appears to have a liberating effect.

One of the lessons we have learned from the pandemic is "We are all in this together ... When this is over, we may find we are stronger and closer to one another than before." [66] It takes nothing more than a quick read of this chapter to get a sense of the significance of social connections in our battle with the pandemic, and is an immediate reminder of how they have been strained by the pandemic, simply reinforcing their importance. It also raises the question of how important the physical element of social interactions may or may not be. "Should social media closely mimic face-to-face, or can less intense forms of communication leave people feeling connected? We do not know yet, but it is likely those studies will now get funded when previously they weren't." [67] When casting your eye over this chapter, you could count the number of times developing strong relationships are mentioned among the coping strategies and the building blocks of resilience. So to emphasise the importance of social connection, we explore its role in the way it offers wellbeing and satisfaction. Remember: "Our fates are bound together. Taking care of others is taking care of ourselves." [68]

Social connections

In his piece 'Better connected' in the *New Scientist*, David Robson begins by asking: "If you were to take one step to improve your health, what would it be: change what you eat, be more active or invest more times in your friendships? Most people know that diet and exercise have huge impacts on well-being. Fewer realise that social connection is just as important." Robson then describes how numerous studies have shown that people can be protected from some common medical condition when they feel "supported and loved", with an active social life reducing the risk of premature death by as much as 30%. Similar benefits are experienced in the workplace, where "good relationships are linked with greater creativity and job satisfaction — and a lower risk of burnout". Robson concludes "The obvious upshot is that we should put more effort into building strong and meaningful relationships" and that not having strong relationships is "as bad for your health as being overweight, physically inactive or drinking too much alcohol". Robson explains that such social support "helps soothe life's stresses via emotional and practical means." He concludes: "Given all this," [Robson emphasises] that it is no wonder medical authorities are now paying serious attention to the importance of relationships. I am convinced that we all have the potential to find greater connection, along with all the benefits for our health, happiness and creativity that it brings. The social life you crave is closer than you think." [69]

The surprising power of habits and routines

The ideas around habits and routines have been in my mind especially since a proportion of all we have been discussing so far could be classified as falling under the heading of "habits and routines". So we begin this last section on autogenic (self-generated) techniques talking about habits and routines and the surprising source of power and potential they have. In his book *Atomic Habits: Tiny changes, remarkable results*, James Clear suggests that the most effective way to change habits and keep them going is "to focus not on what you want to achieve, but on who you wish to become", saying that "the most practical way to change who you are is to change what you do … does this behaviour help me become the type of person I wish to be?" Clear outlines 'a set of rules to follow when trying to establish a new habit: "make it obvious (cue), make it attractive (craving), make it easy (response) and make it satisfying (reward)". These cues quickly become normalised and invisible. Context — that is, time and location — is one of the most common cues. It is important that the opportunity is attractive, too, as this acts as a motivational force, helping to establish the habit: "make it easy to do it right, and then comes the reward — we are more likely to repeat a behaviour if we make it satisfying". [70] He explains: "This is one reason meaningful change does not require radical change. Small habits can make a meaningful difference … And if a change is meaningful, it is actually big. That's the paradox of making small improvements." [71] Applying the set of four rules — cue, craving, response and reward —offers "a new way to think about your habits" and establish them. [72]

There are two other strategies, like the strategies mentioned above, to build your resources and improve your capacity to cope with the pandemic and its fallout. Following the classical mental health strategies, one is making sure you get enough rest, as rest "is essential to help our overstressed bodies and minds repair themselves". [73] The other strategy is ensuring you have some downtime or time-out, as this gives you the break that calms the mind, frees the mind and takes you away from troubling events, and simply refreshes you.

The necessity of rest

In her book *The Art of Rest*, Professor Claudia Hammond indicates that a problem of modern life is that we tend to have "a rest deficit": "We always feel we must be doing something … being busy." Hammond roots this concept of "busyness" in the context of modern life. "Modern work practices, modern lifestyles and modern technology have combined and conspired to make life in the early twenty-first century ceaselessly demanding." The consequent rest deficit, "both perceived and real, is damaging in many ways", particularly with regard to work-related stress. *The Art of Rest* is "a call for rest". We need to reframe rest as an essential, not a luxury. "We need to start valuing it, validating it, vaunting it." [74] In order to do this we need to have a clear understanding of what "rest" means, because "people intuitively understand the word, but struggle to pin it down precisely". Hammond characterises rest as "an activity that is restorative, intentional, relaxing", noting that significantly "to fully relax, people must give themselves permission to rest". [75] Allocating time for meaningful rest — and then making sure to take it — is another coping method that helps when battling the pandemic.

Professor Hammond's book draws on her research on "the rest test", where she is the lead investigator. The book is full of people's favourite restful activities: "spending time in nature, being alone, listening to music, reading, doing nothing in particular, a good walk, a nice hot bath, daydreaming, watching TV and practising mindfulness". [76] Utilising such waking rest activities "in the right doses ... can be a vital process for the optimal functioning of our bodies and minds. [They offer] our capacity to recover." Incorporating rest into a good work–life balance also helps protect against stress-related illnesses. [77] Dr. Liam Drew's article 'Relax to the max' also shows how "the ideal microbreaks [downtime] at work ... can increase vigour, reduce fatigue and improve well-being." [78] Professor Hammond also endorses the value of the microbreak: "There's research showing that we tend to postpone breaks as a reward when we finish what we've got to do ... whereas microbreak studies [downtime] indicate that it is more beneficial to build regular downtime into a busy schedule." [79] Taking a break and engaging in downtime is a coping strategy that will help you not to overthink the new Covid world, as it leaves you a moment to ease your mind, replenish and refresh yourself, and allows your mind to rest.

In taking a break, many choose walking, although it "might seem like the antithesis of rest". [80] However, Professor Hammond tells us that some people "feel they can only rest their mind when they exert their body." [81] This is not as contradictory as it may initially appear, as "walking frees us not just to think, but to think deeply. Is that restful? Well, sometimes it is in thinking about the most profound questions that we find the deepest peace." [82] What's more, numerous people say that doing nothing makes them restless. [83] In the end, how you choose to rest "will be down to your preferences and choices". [84] As with many of the other techniques we have covered in this chapter, they need to become an important part of your lifestyle, which will be easier to establish as a habit and benefit from if it is something that gives you pleasure, rather than being another chore to tick off.

The cult of busyness and downtime

While the idea that we have to be busy all the time certainly seems to have wormed its way into twenty-first-century living, it doesn't have to be like that. Perhaps "busyness" has become a means of coping with the pandemic and its long tail, as it takes you mind away from the ebbs and flows of the pandemic. Probably, and perhaps more likely, busyness has become a ritual that has been embedded in your working life, and then simply slipped from one domain to another as we sought out ways to cope with the pandemic. And the fact that busyness is so ubiquitous is that it has become a status symbol. But, as psychologist Adam Waytz points out: "[W]hen it comes to corporate life, busyness is not a virtue, and it is long past time that organizations were lionizing it … The idea of long hours and 'always on' [remains, however, and] even as the long-term damage of this becomes clear, individuals continue to mindlessly overwork … Even an epoch-changing pandemic could not shake this aversion to idleness.." [85] Yet Zhanna Lyubykh and Duygu Gulseren say that "counter to the popular narrative of working long work hours … research suggests that taking breaks within work hours not only does it not detract from performance, but can help boost it". [86] So it makes sense, advise Tony Schwartz and Catherine McCarthy, to focus on "manag[ing] your energy, not your time… To recharge themselves, individuals need to recognize the costs of energy-depleting behaviours [like working long hours] and then take responsibility for changing them, regardless of the circumstances they're facing." [87]

Living under the tyranny of busyness is exhausting and touches all aspects of your life. But Schwartz and McCarthy say "the good news is that taking breaks can help employees to recharge and short-circuit the negative spiral of exhaustion and decreasing productivity." [88] Dr Liam Drew tells us: "Microbreak studies indicate that it is more beneficial to build regular downtime into a busy schedule … as brief as 10 minutes long from demanding activities, with studies showing that short periods of rest that are completely detached from your job can increase vigour, reduce fatigue and improve overall well-being." [89] Wellbeing support service providers Love Living advise: "Think of microbreaks as tiny investments in your wellbeing. They can be simple as stretching your arms and legs, taking a few deep breaths to centre yourself, looking way from your computer screen to rest your eyes, walking around your workplace to improve circulation, engaging in a brief, light-hearted conversation with a colleague ... They're not about escaping work, but rather enhancing the quality of work by ensuring that employees remain refreshed and alert throughout the day.." [90]

Richard Watson, in his book *Digital Versus Human*, writes: "Looking out of the window and thinking is generally seen as monumentally unproductive, which is monumental nonsense. First, we need a break. We can't permanently exist in a state of flight or fight ... Second, wasted time is not time wasted ... [S]pending a few hours walking alone, marinating your mind in magazines, or chatting to mates could well be the most productive thing you do all day, because it can lead to new insights and ideas ... [F]or its only when our minds are unoccupied and empty that a real self-awareness occurs ... that we are more receptive to new ideas when our minds are allowed to wander ... Indeed, the real value of work is not what we produce for others, but what work produces in ourselves." [91]

Professor Cal Newport would certainly endorse these sentiments, as he has written that "the relentless overload that's wearing us down is generated by a belief that 'good' work requires increasingly busyness — faster responses to email and chats, more meetings, more tasks, more hours", and invites us to consider instead "how we might transform [and reimagine] our modern understanding of professional accomplishment" [92] Reflecting on "these tumultuous years" of the Covid-19 pandemic, Newport says "what started with the Great Resignation has become the Great Exhaustion". [93] In a piece for *Time* magazine, Emily Ballesteros points out that the frenetic pace of work means that "most people aren't surprised to hear about 'the great exhaustion.' We know that we are tired, and we see it in the choices we make every day" [94] where work intrudes and seemingly effortlessly takes over our lifestyles. Even so, Amy Arthur wonders: "are [we] ignoring the signs that our bodies are running on empty? ... [Where] current advice to keep fatigue at bay is almost always to 'do more.' The idea seems to be that one can push through exhaustion by sheer will without repercussion ... But fatigue itself can perpetuate the conditions in which it thrives." She thinks we should look for another solution to the exhaustion epidemic: "Instead, we need to 'do different' or 'do smart' ... as when work takes over your free time, research has shown that it leads to reduced vigour and lower overall well-being." [95]

Ballesteros points out: "The good news is that there are things within our control that can improve our quality of life and make you feel energized ...

[A]t the end of the day, how we feel is determined by small decisions we make. How much sleep we get, prioritizing a morning walk with a friend, consuming media thoughtfully, refusing to discuss work and work stress when we off the clock — these small things make a big difference, but we must do them consistently and relentlessly. We can't wait for changes to come from the top down; we must address the factors of exhaustion within our control to ensure we live healthy, peaceful, and satisfying lives." [96]

Closing in on the cult of busyness, Dr Dougal Sutherland, a clinical psychologist at Wellington-based Umbrella Wellbeing, would seemingly also agree. "We're under constant pressure to busy ourselves, some of it self-generated … and you can't really do anything enjoyable until all the work's done. And when's the work done? Well, the works never finished. There's always more work to do." He suggests a shift of focus to sleep and non-sleep rest. "Both help us recharge and recover on a physiological and mental basis, and without that we simply don't function as well as we could." [97] When reading Dr Sutherland's piece, I am reminded of the words of eminent economist John Maynard Keynes: "For we have been trained too long to strive and not to enjoy." [98]

SOME REFLECTIONS

Five themes have accompanied this chapter so far. The first theme is *doing something is better that doing nothing, particularly if it gives you confidence, a sense of achievement and hope*. The second theme leads us to a question and an answer: *What is the best activity? It is the one that you will do, and keep doing*. This leads us to the third theme: *it must be embedded in your lifestyle*. The fourth theme, which in many ways embraces the other themes, is all about *who you wish to become* — managing your "future you". The last theme you may not have noticed, or may not have picked up on it yet: *hope*. As psychologist David Feldman says: "Hope is a way of thinking that pushes us to take action." You persist because you have "an abiding belief in yourself and your capabilities. It's tempting to lose hope today, but that would be surrendering a vital power." [99] This helps to explain why hope is such an important ingredient in building resilience.

REFLECTING ON THE FUTURE YOU

Earlier in this chapter we wrote about the pandemic giving us a "unique instructive moment". Tony Schwartz argues that we should, "view the future as a broad set of new opportunities that will reflect whatever we think is possible". [100] This theme has permeated the pandemic's journey, with writers sharing their views on capturing this moment in different ways. Lisa Leong and Monique Ross have suggested that "our current state of upheaval could rise to the second Renaissance ... We have an opportunity to redesign our world through a second Renaissance ... that will unravel some of our assumptions about how we work ... that have long been crying out for a new approach." [101] Karen Mangia has described it as a Great Pause, saying: "You and I are being handed opportunities to re-examine the boundaries that surround the things that really matter ... But even in the midst of a global upheaval, there's still a chance to move forward ... are you ready to change with it?' [102] Professor Lynda Gratton adds: "it also requires each one of us to take a more thoughtful, determined and energetic approach to exercising the choices that are available to us. It requires reflexivity — the capacity to both reflect on and to make decisions about what it is we want to become." [103]

Professor Rick Snyder's focus is on coping: "Life is filled with experiences that push our repertoire of thinking, feeling, and behaving. We are expected to learn and grow from the events that initiate our coping responses, with the implication that coping is part of the very essence of the human change process. Thus, coping not only is basic for survival, but it also relates to the quality and the ensuing constructive meaning of our own lives." [104] Coping with stress is "an intrinsic part of the fabric of action and experience" With colleague Kim Pulvers, Snyder explains the function and mechanism of coping: "Coping thoughts, feelings and actions ... occur in response to 'big' events, that is, events that shake the customary senses of stability or threaten to undermine the usual activities of people. Additionally, coping is typically not a single response, but a series of responses, initiated and repeated as necessary to handle the remaining, continued, or transformed nature of the stressor." [105]

Lydia Denworth explicitly ties stress and coping into the Covid-19 experience. "This is the first time in living history we've had a global lockdown that's gone on for such a long time ... This is different from other forms of stress because it's not just one domain of your life ... People are dealing with relationship or family challenges, with financial and work challenges, and health." [106] In this context, Andrea Gawrylewski makes the link to resilience: "It takes perseverance and determination, to be sure, but an array of tools can help us build our resilience: friendship, goal setting and a positive mindset." [107]

We can view the pandemic as an opportunity to revisit our priorities and values, to look at our lifestyles and perhaps make changes. In doing so, we can pair Tony Schwartz's mantra to reflect on "whatever we think is possible", [108] with David Feldman's advice of "not losing hope as that ... would be surrendering a vital power". [109] There are choices to be made. Are you ready to make them? And to use your coping as a tool, remembering "that Covid-19 has revealed that we are capable of doing things in reality that in theory we thought we couldn't". [110] After all: "Growth happens in many ways and, hopefully this 'unique moment' was yours in which to grow." [111]

CHAPTER 7:

The Pandemic and Climate Change

A CONTEXT THAT BRINGS THE PANDEMIC AND CLIMATE CRISIS TOGETHER

Some readers may now be scratching their heads, and wondering why there is a chapter on the climate crisis in a book which professes to be about the Covid-19 pandemic and reimagining how we work. The reason can be found when we think in terms of *what lessons can we learn from the pandemic,* as there are several significant comparisons that can be drawn, and lessons learnt, between the Covid-19 pandemic response and the climate crisis. The first is: *the climate crisis is here — we are in it and live it.* As Mark Carney writes, "We have created a new era — the Anthropocene — in which our earth's climate is driven, not by the geological rhythm of nature, but by our impacts on the planet." [1] Philosopher A. C. Grayling elaborates: "For the first time in the planet's history the change in the global climate, and the effects this is having, are the result of the activities of a single, numerous, highly active, and highly destructive species: human beings." [2] We are already being confronted by these destructive weather patterns and what is at stake. Grayling advises that in response, "Hope is kept alive by determined and imaginative people and organizations.". [3] Kate Douglas posits that the "growth-based economic model that has delivered unprecedented prosperity and well-being for many over the past few decades is also the driver of environmental problems from climate change to chemical pollution." [4] Greta Thunberg puts it this way: "If economic growth is our only priority, then what we are experiencing now should be exactly what we should be expecting." She adds, "we are never going back to normal again because normal was already a crisis". [5]

Professor Tim Flannery suggests that "the response to the pandemic provides us with a roadmap for dealing with the climate crisis". [6] Thunberg tells us that the lessons include: *"Listen to the science.* Before it's too late … to solve this problem, we need to understand it. Science is a tool, and we all need to learn how to use it." [7] Flannery concurs: "Only careful but resolute action, guided by science, can see us navigate both perils", adding, "with huge changes required in a short time, we are best to listen to the scientists as we prioritise action". [8] Michael Mann in his book *The New Climate War* writes: "Nature had afforded us a unique teaching moment. Watching the pandemic unfold, both the impacts and response, was like watching a time lapse of the climate crisis … [and one of] the important lesson has to do with the role of science and fact-based discourse in decision-making … [and] what can we learn, for example, about the role of science." [9]

David Wallace-Wells articulates the next lesson: *"The longer we wait, the more we lose …* when it comes to climate, we know the problem is the same." [10] Others agree. Professor Grayling writes that "the Covid-19 pandemic so tragically demonstrated that delay is dangerous". [11] Similarly, Tim Flannery concludes: "But delay, even by a few years, could cost us everything." [12] Michael Mann writes: "The coronavirus outbreak also taught some important lessons about the cost of delay. What Covid-19 tells us about tackling the climate crisis: Delay is deadly." [13]

The next lesson is not to get confused by the idea of *"the new normal"*. As Greta Thunberg puts it: "Unfortunately, this is not *'the new normal.'* This crisis will continue to get worse until we manage to halt the constant destruction of our life-supporting systems." [14]

Another lesson is that a *collective approach is needed.* Nick Henry, who is the climate justice lead with not-for-profit Oxfam Aotearoa, says, "The best thing we can do for climate justice as individuals is to find ways to work collectively." [15] New Zealand's climate tsar Dr Rod Carr puts it this way: "Covid-19 has revealed that we are capable of doing things in reality that in theory we thought we couldn't." He adds, "there is a view that the collective response to Covid-19 might offer pointers for climate change …

I think it's revealed there are some things we can only do if we all do our part." [16] Remember, writes Robin Nelson in her article "A microbe proved that individualism is a myth": "Our fates are bound together. Taking care of others is taking care of ourselves." [17] Remember from Chapter 2 the power of the phrase "the team of 5 million" and the editorial from the *NZ Listener* with the message "for now all New Zealanders should ... not look for scapegoats ... but should put their energy and patience into being part of the solution by looking after themselves and looking out for their neighbours". [18] Thunberg articulates the overriding lesson we need to take from this: "Together we can still avoid the worst consequences. We can do the seemingly impossible. But make no mistake — no one else is going to do it for us. This is up to us, here and now. You and me ... the climate and ecological crisis is not happening in some faraway future. It's happening right here and right now." [19]

Another important lesson is that, as Mark Carney puts it, the "Covid crisis has exposed the tragic folly of undervaluing resilience and ignoring systemic risks. As society awakes to these risks, it is beginning to place greater value on sustainability." [20] Thinking first of all about the idea of individual resilience, the question is: *How can, how we coped, with the pandemic teach us how to cope with the climate crisis?* Then broadening our understanding of resilience the question is the design of our cities and our landscapes, and issues about sustainability. What Michael Mann describes in his book *The New Climate War* as an "unexpected lesson of the pandemic" is the "perils of anti-science". "While the Covid-19 pandemic was described as *the invisible* war because the enemy was a virus, we were still familiar with the protests, misinformation and conspiracies that have simply, but quickly and smoothly, slipped from one pandemic to another — the climate crisis." He adds: "the climate crisis exposes the dangers of denial in a much more dramatic fashion ... when people can see in real time on their television screens, their newspaper headlines, their social media feeds, and their backyards". While denial is difficult when you can actually see that we are in a climate crisis, the question remains of how to battle it. [21]

The final lesson is a generational one and explores *our responsibilities to future generations.* Mark Carney writes: "The climate legacy we leave depends on how much we value the future, adding": "once this war against an invisible enemy is over, our ambitions should be bolder. 'A planet fit for our grandchildren.'" [22] The "great hope lies with today's young people

... fighting tooth and nail to save their planet ... There is a moral authority and clarity in their message that none but the most jaded ears can fail to hear." This is emphatically true. "Greta Thunberg, the Extinction Rebellion activists, and all those whom they inspire, rightly refuse to accept that nothing can be done," Mann writes. [23] While we are well aware of the ambitions of Millennials and Generation Zers, more is needed, as Frances Cox-Wright writes: "Young people want to be heard ... not treated merely as spectators in the world they will inherit ... With children and young people asking for a seat at the table for their voices to be heard ... This climate crisis — a children's crisis — needs all of humanity; and all of humanity will benefit from stronger climate action." [24] With school students repeatedly striking over climate change" there is little question of which generation will become the driving force to make radical change. As Caz Sheldon, the spokesperson for Fridays for the Future, says: "[When] we start the year with deadly floods affecting the North Island, it is more important than ever that we act now to prevent even more severe weather events in future." [25]

Reflections

"The Covid-19 pandemic is a stark warning of what the future may hold." [26] Professor Grayling continues, "It is not impossible that the saddest sentiment expressible in any language — 'it's too late' — is already true." [27] Samantha Montano writes of the opportunity on offer: "Some thought the pandemic would be just the sort of focusing event that wakes up the world leaders to the risk of sleeping on the climate crisis ... [and] be able to respond to the all-consuming effects of the climate crisis ... Maybe they would use this 'window of opportunity' to draw obvious parallels, so that one global crisis inspired action on the other." [28] But "the longer we pretend that we can solve the climate and ecological crisis without treating it as such, more invaluable time will be wasted," warns Thunberg. [29] And Mann cautions "will we take away the right lessons?" [30] As Professor Tim Flannery writes, "Despair is not an option. Nor is selfish complacency. Instead, this is the moment to ask what you will do." [31] Perhaps the lessons above can plausibly be viewed as a first attempt to list what could be described as a scheme of *best management practices*, which can then be used as a measure of evaluating our country's progress.

WHAT ACTION IS NEEDED?

But first we build a context by exploring a sample of writers who point to what action is needed and offer solutions, and then explore New Zealand's progress towards its climate goals. First, Professor Grayling offers what he describes as "an ideal solution – that peoples, and their governments act, selflessly and jointly, to address the difficulties and to share the resources, the endeavour, the burdens and benefits. So, *people have to understand clearly what the problems are, and be motivated to act accordingly, chiefly by obliging their primary instrument — their government — to act with other governments to take the necessary steps.*' He adds, "Enabling the positive can be done is what people can oblige their governments to do in circumstances of genuine and effective democracy'" before pointing to how it is the pitfalls, via "the self-interest Law", that get in the way of "genuine and effective democracy." [32] Grayling's arguments are cogent and eloquent, and deserve more space than I am able to offer here.

Mark Carney also begins with a warning: "the combination of the weight of scientific evidence and the dynamics of the financial system suggests that climate change is a major threat to financial resilience and economic prosperity ... it is a risk from which we cannot diversify. Moreover, the window to act is finite and shrinking." He goes on to argue: "There are three technologies needed to solve the climate crisis. The first is engineering ... [and] if allowed sufficient time for the capital stock to turn over, much of the challenge would be met. But given the narrow window, investment must be accelerated [to] a warlike pace ... The second is the 'political technology' to force consensus to break the tragedies of the horizon ... Momentum is building, even if more is required. The third is we need financial markets to work alongside climate policies to maximise their impact ... a sustainable financial system is being built ... it has the potential to amplify the effectiveness of the climate policies of governments and it could accelerate the transition to a low-carbon economy ... But the task is large, the window of opportunity is short, and the risks are existential." [33]

Tim Flannery similarly begins with a warning. "To survive the climate challenge, we need to fight three critical battles, and we can't afford to lose a single one. These three battles bear a striking resemblance to the battles required to prevail against COVID-19." He goes on to explain the three battles. The first "and most urgent involves cutting fossil fuel use, decisively and deeply. The second involves minimising the damage ... our planet will suffer as a result of the greenhouse gases already emitted and those we cannot avoid emitting in future. The third battle is to lay the foundations of a medium- to long-term response to climate change, which will help back our way to climate stability." He ends on a hopeful note, arguing that "the COVID-19 pandemic marks a turning point. Combatting the virus, we have learned how science-based action can lead us out of a crisis ... We are living at a pivotal moment in history, in which the balance of power, both political and in terms of energy, is shifting." [34]

In *The New Climate War*, Michael Mann presents us with a four-themed 'battle plan.' The first theme is *"disregard the doomsayers"*. We simply must "reject the overt doom and gloom that we increasingly encounter in today's climate discourse. The second theme is the *'young generation'*. We should model our actions after theirs and learn their methods and their idealism. The third theme is *'Educate, Educate, Educate.'* There are many honestly confused people ... caught in the crossfire, victims of the climate-change disinformation campaign. We must help them out. Then they will be in a position to join us in battle. The final theme is *'Changing the system requires systemic change'*". [35] Grayling reduces the solution to a single sentence: "The greatest part of the solution lies in policy, with government and international action." [36]

The final plan of action also has policy at its heart. Bill Gates writes: "when we focus on all three things at once — technology, policies, and markets — we can encourage innovation, spark new companies, and get products into the market fast. [Phase one] is classic research and development where ... scientists and engineers dream up the technologies we need. Although we have a number of cost-competitive low-carbon solutions today, we still don't have all the technologies we need to get to 'zero emissions globally', explaining why [this phase is described as] *'Expanding the supply of innovation.'* The second phase is *'Accelerating the demand of innovation.'* It is a little more complicated than the supply phase. It actually involves two steps: the proof phase and the scale-up phase ... Governments (as well as big companies) can help energy start-ups ... because they're massive consumers. If they prioritize buying green, they'll help bring more products to market by creating, certainty and reducing costs. Someone will invent these technologies. It's just a question of who and how soon." [37]

Reflections

A quick piece of content analysis suggests that three lessons could become the driving force of what could be the basis of policy. The first is the need to recognise that we are living in a climate crisis: it is here and now — you only need to witness or live through the extremes of weather, floods, coastal erosion, slips and damage to our roads and highways, livelihoods, homes and properties, not forgetting "rising sea levels, more extreme rain, storm surges damaging property, and a managed retreat from coastal areas". [38] The second is governments working in tandem with other international governments and bodies to set the context for action and goals; this of course means education, education and education, communications and thinking to the future and the lives of younger generations. The third is being led by science and how that can lead us out of a crisis — remembering that we are already in a transitional phase to meet our 2050 targets. The final one, and perhaps the key issue: the need for urgency — action is required now; delay is at our peril.

NEW ZEALAND'S PROGRESS

While beginning to write this section, *The Dominion Post* was reminding us through headlines — "Summer of cyclones? High sea surface temperatures put NZ on red alert" [39] and "2022 was the hottest year" [40] — that "we are living with the next 'significant crisis of the twenty-first century' ... Covid and climate change." [41] Climate Change Minister James Shaw was once again warning us "of the danger of 'predatory delay' where those forces opposed to cracking on with climate change reform try to use any reason to delay". [42] A warning that immediately reminds us of the Covid-19 pandemic whose threat still lingers. The context for Shaw's concerns is simple: in two days' time, 16 May 2022, the new Emissions Reduction Plan was to be announced by the Climate Commission. Here, we explore three critical moments in New Zealand's journey so far, against climate change. The first significant moment is the Emission Reduction Plan, which *The Dominion Post's* Luke Malpass tells us "will effectively propose a series of short, medium and long term measures the government will put in place to help New Zealand to meet its international and stated obligations of net-zero emissions by 2050". [43]

Then we will look at three other significant moments: COP28, COP27 and COP15.

The chief executive of the Climate Change Commission, Jo Hendy, explains that the Emissions Reduction Plan "is an incredibly important piece of work and will have significant impacts for all New Zealanders ... The plan needs to be able to deliver an immediate change in gears in our national response to climate change ... In a few words [the plan embraces] urgency, decisiveness, cohesion and collaboration." [44] The Minister of Climate Change adds: "if successful the plan would decouple New Zealand's economic growth from its emissions path ... and now we have a plan to do that". [45] "While business calls for bold action ... [it also asks for] urgent action on the government's plan and [calls] for a clear role for the private sector." [46] Described as an "Ambitious plan light on details" [47] with "climate activists unimpressed", [48] judgement should, at this stage, not be made too quickly but made in the years that follow, "as they [will] show how effective the plan is at actually driving down emissions." [49] Discussions with the government were promising that "farm emission levies [will be] at the 'lowest price possible' when farmers are due to pay for them in 2025". [50] The plan must be seen as representing "a critical turning point". [51]

Two other potentially significant moments for New Zealand's strategy on climate change came at two of the United Nations' Conference of Parties: COP27 and COP15. While *The Dominion Post* reports that COP27 "falls short of [a] goal ... [on] actions to avoid and minimize loss and damage ... in those communities whose lives and livelihoods have been ruined by the very worst impacts of climate change", it says that the summit "does retain language to keep alive the global goal of limiting warming 1.5C over preindustrial times". [52] All of the COP members were asked "to revisit and strengthen" their ambition — a move everyone voted for. New Zealand's Climate Change Minister "did not ask Cabinet to consider an upgrade as the reason was, he was waiting for a decision on a Climate Change court case ... [The Minister said,] 'I have held off until I know the lay of the land with that ... I'm feeling a bit frustrated by that.'" [53] In late November 2022, the government welcomed the High Court ruling on the climate case, "confirming the legality of the advice by the Climate Change Commission to inform New Zealand's nationally determined contribution and the first three emissions budget". [54]

The third moment also reflects a significant achievement. At the COP15 conference "a historic deal to halt biodiversity loss by 2030" was reached. [55] New Zealand was one of the 190 countries signatory to the agreement. Minister of Conservation the Hon Poto Williams said: "COP15 comes at a defining moment. Biodiversity is being lost faster now than at any period in human history, with an estimated 1 million species threatened with extinction." [56]

COP 28 can be described in terms of a number of crucial moments. The first: "the failure of COP28 to call for a phase-out of fossil fuels is 'devastating' and 'dangerous' given the urgent need for action to tackle the climate crisis". [57] The second was the COP leader saying there was "no science" behind the demands to phase out fossil fuels. [58] The third was the "landmark Cop28 deal reached to 'transition away' from fossil fuels". *The Guardian* reported that the agreement "reinforced the 1.5C goal and recognised it would require a 43% emission cut by 2030 and 60% by 2035 relative to 2019 levels. It implied a major increase in targets and policies when countries submit new commitments in 2025." [59] However, this moment was coloured by the view that the deal "was 'grossly insufficient' ... and will not stop the world facing dangerous climate breakdown". [60] The fourth was the deal reached to help poor countries cope with the impact of the climate crisis. [61] The fifth moment was the "deal to revive hope of 1.5C target 'within reach'". [62]

The Post announced in February 2023: "Earth was for the first time 1.5C warmer over the past 12 months than before the Industrial Revolution. Experts said the milestone was a reminder of the urgent need to cut the carbon emissions that cause climate change." [63] The author of the study being reported described his reaction as "the clock of climate change has been brought forward by about a decade by our findings. So, things that we're thinking would have happened 10 years hence are actually happening now." [64] The challenge is fundamental and complex, because, as economist Thomas Piketty explains, "inequality and class are at the heart of the climate crisis." [65]

Reflections

The overwhelming feeling is, as summed up by Michael Mann, one of, "preserving the well-being of present and future generations. This is what the young people want to achieve. They deserve our respect and full support." [66] Grayling warns: "Our actions have to stand the scrutiny" of did we do our best. [67] Mann suggests that one of the tests we should apply is whether "we come away from [the pandemic] having learned the right lessons". [68] But questions still remain, as described by Carney: "What's at stake if we don't manage a timely transition? What are the potential costs of climate change? And what value would be preserved if we were to achieve net zero? ... How feasible is the transition to net zero? How economic are existing technologies? What is the role of scale? How reliant is net zero on future innovation? To what extent will we have to change our lifestyles." [69]

CLIMATE CRISIS: CYCLONE GABRIELLE

"The huge cyclone devastation across the country is potentially moving the dial on climate change action in Parliament," announced *The Dominion Post* on 15 February 2023. [70] We are now being taught another pandemic vocabulary: learning to distinguish between an emergency response and an adaptation response, reading the words "be ready" and "resilience" frequently, coming against the phrase like "red stickered" — all a subset of "adaptation", making "adaptation no longer climate's poor cousin", [71] along with "slash" as in "inquiry ordered into slash in wake of storm", [72] phrases like "a rethink", "a horrible wake-up call" [73] and "probably the most severe climate related event of its time". [74] Not forgetting "our planners' climate failure", [75] "catastrophic floods" [76] and "second-wettest summer in North island, [77] leading to "how climate change is powering cyclones", [78] "does cyclone Gabrielle have you thinking about climate change? You're not the only one." [79] *The Post* looked back 12 months later: "A year on, the emotion has dulled, but the water has left its mark ... [yet] slowly across the region, both land and lives are being restored and reimagined." The article goes on to sum up the remarkable resilience and fortitude of those battling the devastation, using their own words: "devastated, but not defeated". [80] Hamish Barwick, writing in *The Listener*, says of Tairāwhiti: "We, as a community, always find a way to stay positive. The word 'resilience' is thrown about these days but that sums up this region: self-reliant people who are used to fending for themselves." [81]

Also writing in *The Post* in February 2024, Dr Richard Smith, the director of the Resilience National Science Challenge, echoes these sentiments: "We've seen communities come together in adversity, building connections that will serve them well in future events ... It's been heartening to hear of communities developing plans, storing equipment and supplies, and developing databases of skills and resources." [82] But Dr Smith has another important issue to explore: "how to make disaster recovery less painful … It's easy to imagine a future in which we are constantly in clean-up and costly recovery mode, with the disruption, stress and misery that entails. But with the right investment in our infrastructure, communities, and emergency management system, we could lessen the scale of disruption, thereby making recovery faster and ultimately cheaper."

Following the Auckland anniversary weekend floods, Dr Smith had written an opinion piece in which he had detailed what a more resilient Aotearoa could look like. In this article a year later, he revisits the topic. When explaining it, the key focus is, as you would imagine, on resilience and how that can be supported, managed and operated. Its reach is broad and moves from 'well built' houses 'out of harm's way' and particularly those houses located 'in dangerous locations' requiring 'planned retreat.' Then the focus shifts to 'investing in resilient infrastructure' and how they perform in a climate crisis and how they can be 'quickly restored' in a crisis. Then it moves to the design of urban areas that have the capacity through 'porous surfaces to soak up excess water.' The next shift of focus is on a 'well-resourced emergency management system' that has the capacity to 'receive timely' and crucial warnings that can be used to make prompt up-to-date decisions for planning and preparation purposes." Dr Smith then moves to how communities working together would be supported to shape their resilience 'ahead of a big event.' This would include giving help to those who are "most vulnerable to reduce their risks … Given our exposure to multiple damaging hazards, preparing our people, our systems, and our 'lifeline' services must be a priority for any government. By making risk reduction a priority, we can save money and reduce disruption and suffering. Let's choose that future." [83]

The director of the National Emergency Management Agency, John Price, warns: "Our research shows a concerning trend of complacency … People wait until after an emergency happens before getting prepared … The survey also showed that while 89% agreed it was their responsibility to look after themselves and family or whanau in a disaster only 47% actually had a household emergency plan." [84] As climate change is here and we are experiencing its effects, now is the time to prepare.

Professor John Tookey of AUT's School of Future Environments writes that, although all of those across the political spectrum have agreed to addressing climate change — and in ratifying the Paris Accord have made legally enforceable and time-bound commitments to cut the country's emissions — more is still needed. However, Professor Tookey also argues that "New Zealand's infrastructure planning, investments and commitments remain vague." He points to how now is the time to decide to "what degree the country wants to reduce the impact of the climate crises." If the answer is yes, then it comes at a cost, as it will first need to be, a national priority, because such a commitment requires planning, budgeting, and sequencing that will result in "hundreds of billions of dollars … needed over a multi-decade programme calling for planning, compulsory purchase, and infrastructure construction."   Alongside this is the infrastructural investment needed to facilitate growth and sustainability. With planning, procurement and implementation being time-consuming and costly, Tookey says it is crucial that there is across-the-aisle commitment to prioritise it, concluding that "Failure to do so will inhibit future growth and housing provision, reduce cost-effectiveness, as well threaten the sustainability of communities in vulnerable areas. Cyclone Gabrielle made it clear that kicking this particular can down the road is not acceptable." [85]

THE RELATIONSHIP BETWEEN CLIMATE CHANGE AND CYCLONES — THE SCIENCE

Let's explore some of the ideas hidden in these headlines, beginning with the relationship between climate change and cyclones. Kirsty Johnston, writing in *Stuff*, says: "If the reality of the climate crisis hadn't sunk in for you until this summer, you're probably not alone … but with yet another cyclone hitting the North Island — [and] as fears of drought escalate in parts of the South Island — the impact climate change will have on our lives is becoming harder to ignore." [86] *The Dominion Post*'s climate reporter says there is scientific backing for this concern: "Scientists have cautiously concluded climate change is partly responsible for Cyclone Gabrielle's damage. The February disaster featured many of the effects of a heating atmosphere — souped up storms, extreme rain, flooding, and intense winds." [87] Johnston reports that scientific consensus is building around the interrelationship between cyclones and climate change: "Climate change doesn't cause cyclones, but it does make them more intense. Tropical cyclones get their energy from the sea and the warmer water, the more energy they have to work with. This makes for more powerful storms that grow faster. Sea surface temperatures in New Zealand have been recording records level this summer." [88]

She continues: "Equally, the warming atmosphere also helps to fuel storms. Hot air holds more moisture causing heavier rainfall, like the recent downpours in Auckland that led to widespread flooding. Researchers found climate change was likely responsible for 10 to 20% of that rain." [89] Andrea Thompson, writing in the *Scientific American*, informs us that while global warming causes fewer tropical cyclones, their threat remains as those that do form have a greater chance of becoming intense storms, with global warming "making the atmosphere more hostile to the formation of tropical cyclones". However, the historical data only goes back to the 1970s, "which is not long enough to pick out trends driven by global warming." [90] In March 2023 Agriculture Minister Damien O'Connor was "warning the rural sector to expect more disruption as a result of climate change", adding, "Things are going to change; disruption will be upon us. Nothing is certain in this world and as you travel around climate change is affecting every country, the monetary situation has upset every economic theory we can think of." Matters have not been helped, he says by social media "exacerbating divisions and differences in opinions as well. We have a divide and more finger-pointing now than we ever had." [91] And yet the science is clear: global warming has progressed to a stage that sea levels rising is inevitable, and "will remain elevated for thousands of years even if the world starts cutting emissions now". [92]

Following on from the above, *The Dominion Post* in 2023 reports that the latest report of the IPCC (Intergovernmental Panel on Climate Change) reveals this decade provides "the critical moment for making rapid cuts to emissions from dangerous climate impacts we can no longer avoid". With the world now about 1.1C warmer than in pre-industrial times, there is already "more frequent and more intense extreme weather, causing complex disruption and suffering for communities worldwide". The article continues: "the report stresses our current pace and scale of action are insufficient to reduce rising global temperatures and secure a liveable future for all. But it also highlights that we have many feasible and effective options to cut emissions and better protect communities if we act now ... but the choices we make need to be locally relevant and socially acceptable. And they have to be made urgently, because our options for being resilient are progressively reduced with ever increment of warming above 1.5C." [93]

A TEST OF RESILIENCE

"After 28 days in a national state of emergency, Hawke's Bay and Tairawhiti will enter the recovery phase today," Minister of Emergency Management Kieran McAnulty announced on 14 March 2023, meaning "these eastern regions will join other regions hit by Cyclone Gabrielle in a national transition period". [94] "We have seen what can unfold. Severe weather events that had previously seemed unthinkable, even only a few years ago, are now happening at a pace and intensity we have never experienced before," [Minister of Climate Change James Shaw said as he introduced New Zealand's first ever Climate Adaptation Plan, which] "lays foundations for resilient communities" and provides "a joined-up approach that will support community-based adaptation with national policies and legislation". [95] The communities affected by Cyclone Gabrielle, and those who live in them, will still be faced with making distressing and heart-breaking decisions about what to do in the cyclone's aftermath, even as they enter the transition period or adaptation and recovery mode. Their "lives have been turned upside down", [96] so they will need to harness their resilience as they work out what the situation they now face means for their sense of community, their identity, their networks and friends, and their livelihoods.

While there are still tough calls to make by those caught up in the aftermath the government tried to streamline the recovery and rebuild process with the Severe Weather Emergency Legislation Bill, which would remove any unnecessary red tape. Finance Minister Grant Robertson also announced a taskforce led by Sir Brian Roche to "work alongside communities as we respond to this major event ... [to] ensure the recovery is also locally led and supported by central government. We have also established a Cyclone Recovery Unit in the Department of the Prime Minister and Cabinet to coordinate the work at a central government level." [97] The government offered further cyclone emergency support with Robertson saying: "I have been clear that we have the fiscal headroom to support our people and we do that as we have done through all the other disasters, we have guided this country through." [98]

While the rain continued to fall, Covid-19 showed its hand, with the Hawke's Bay seeing a spike in Covid-19, [99] "an added curveball infecting emergency responder with 14 staff testing positive". [100]

A TEST OF RESILIENCE FOR THOSE COPING WITH CLIMATE CRISIS

Cyclone Gabrielle is indelibly etched in our minds, with how it ravaged provinces, cities, towns, settlements, homes, pastures, roads, highways, and livelihoods. Coping with the aftermath was at a time when, although the regulations might have gone, we were still in the grips of the Covid-19 pandemic. In looking at how best to tackle what at times seemed an overwhelming situation, it seemed plausible to harness the lesson from the pandemic of "working collectively". Doing so could, as Nick Henry suggests, offers the best way to achieve climate justice. Working collectively neatly describes what is generally known as "communal coping", which is defined as "a cooperative problem-solving process ... [which] involves the appraisal of a stressor as 'our' problem and [offers] cooperative action to address it". [101] Communal coping is perfectly captured in the words of a person facing the devastation left by the cyclone: "we are just all coming together and making this work", [102] and in the words of then Prime Minister Christopher Hipkins: "as we've repeatedly seen in recent times, adversity brings out the best in Kiwis ... New Zealand's resilience is being tested like never before." [103]

Other comments of those surveying the cyclone's devastation also capture the meaning of communal coping: "events like this showed the good and the bad in people ... the level of support? — 'Mind Blowing'"; [104] "we came out as a family of six which is a blessing, because it was pretty harrowing ... It was humbling that people would still be turning up, almost two weeks later ... You can't save this, but they are still coming to save the people's spirit, because it is pretty broken right now." [105] The government also recognised the communal work of maraes, and was willing to offer funding, "as an investment in our collective civil defence infrastructure", realising that "the more support they can access, the better-prepared we'll all be when the next disaster strikes". The headline atop this report encapsulates communal coping: "Marae are an integral part of our civil defence infrastructure." [106]

Renee Lyons and colleagues explain what is at the heart of communal coping: "Beyond its important role in coping, communal coping [expresses] notions of social integration, interdependence, and close relationships and may underlie the resilience of families and communities dealing with stressful life events ... [It involves] the pooling of resources of several individuals [or communities] to confront adversity ... Many benefits accrue when people are able to confront a stressor together — mutual awareness and disclosures, shared appraisals, shared resources, and cooperative action and mutual support, practical motives to expand resources and capacity for coping ... As a long term investment... it is owned jointly by all ... but Communal coping is often less a matter of deliberate choice than certain conditions conducive to it having been met." [107]

What Dr Steve Taylor wrote about coping in the Covid-19 pandemic could well apply to living through the cyclone and its aftermath: "in the midst of the suffering and challenges of our predicament, we may develop a heightened sense of appreciation, more authentic relationships, and a new sense of resilience and confidence. We may slow down and learn to live in the present rather than constantly rushing into the future." He goes on to say that a crisis such as a pandemic [or a cyclone] "reminds us that ... we are all in this together, and we will overcome the crisis only through cooperation. Conflict and competition will only lead to more suffering and discord ... we may find that we are stronger and closer to one another than before." [108]

Gawrylewski offers a perspective of coping through resilience: "It takes perseverance and determination, to be sure, but an array of tools can help us build our resilience ... These tools offer hope in even the most trying times that although stress cannot be vanquished it can be managed." [109] Steven Southwick and Dennis Charney describe these tools in detail: "forg[ing] close friendships, exercise, maintaining a close and supportive network, adopting a positive but realistic outlook, bolstering positive emotions — a 'glass half full' — realistic optimism, and reaching out for support from those who care about you and enhancing attitudes like perseverance and endurance" [110] and hope. Just imagine the trauma and the heart-break when people lose everything, houses, livelihoods, and their sense of identity and connection, and don't even own the clothes they are wearing. But difficult as it might seem to find anything positive about such experiences, people still carry a sense of hope and are "buoyed by the unfettered support of the community, strangers and families who [come] to help". [111]

WE ARE ALREADY "LOCKED IN" TO CLIMATE CHANGE

Tom Hunt, writing in *The Post*, "We are [already] locked into the effects of climate change — rising sea levels, more extreme rain, droughts, wildfires, flooding, to name some." With this come some confronting choices and challenges. "[T]he reality is many people in coastal areas will have to leave and it is hoped the Government, as it [rethinks] the Resource Management Act will take a good look at 'managed retreat'." [112] Insurers are "heading down a path of greater risk-based pricing, where the owners of homes at higher risk of things like floods and landslips would pay more for their cover." [113] Climate scientists did not take long to adopt the pandemic's language to explain climate change: "intense rain has once more put people's lives at risk, flooded homes, caused traffic chaos and closed schools – is this the *'new normal?'* [114]

K. Gurunathan writes in *The Post*: "[T]he stark lesson of Cyclone Gabrielle to politicians is not just about food prices in our supermarkets. The real engine room of the cost-of-living crisis is the impact of our consumer capitalist lifestyles and its destruction of our environment." [115] Tim Jones, talking about his book *Emergency Weather*, also offers us a challenge: "Climate Change isn't a thing of the future anymore, something for your grandchildren to worry about. It's here, it's real, and it's coming for all of us ... Take a look along your street and around your neighbourhood. Perhaps you live on a flood plain, perhaps on a hill or an eroding shore. How might climate breakdown come for you: as a flash flood in the night, as a fire through the treetops, as a tornado that strikes without warning? Or relentless summer heat that is too much, at last, to bear ... That's where we're headed if we don't act, as a society, to change the path we're on ... In action lies our only hope of survival. When emergency weather strikes, be ready." [116]

In his book *Under the Weather: A future forecast for New Zealand* Professor James Renwick also paints a picture of the climate challenges that are now all "about our own backyard. Because, just like the rest of the world, we are feeling the effects of climate change. Increasingly intense extreme weather events are damaging the things that we rely on — our homes, our roads, our livelihoods, every one of us personally." He focuses our attention by asking pointed questions, asking the reader to reflect on the ways in which unpredictable weather events have affected them: unprecedented floods, eroded streets, flooded homes, stinking-hot days that buckle train tracks and hamper commutes, or heavy downpours causing land slips. He concludes that " all of these things are real. We see them with our own eyes. Our home turf is changing as the global climate shifts. Coping with this change is challenging, because it means accepting that the land we grew up with is gone. Everything is different now ...". [117]

Our seasons are being tossed about as they oscillate between the extremes of El Niño and La Niña weather patterns. "If last week's predicted El Nino-like pattern is any indication, then that dry summer could come to pass." [118] Again, "By the end of this month or by mid-October, I think we'll really have our first taste of this El Nino event and what's to come for the rest of 2023". [119] Once again the headlines capture the message, this one in *The Post*: "2023 on track to be the hottest year on record", with the article beneath it saying: "This year is increasingly likely to become the hottest year on record, due to a rapidly strengthening El Nino weather pattern and unprecedentedly hot summer." [120] Climate change is a truly global challenge, with researchers saying, "that the heatwaves that has baked much of southern Europe would have been virtually impossible without climate change". [121]

News of climate change and its effects seem as inescapable as the heat. "NZ's hottest ever summer could be ahead — with fire, drought, and sharks" introduces an article where climate scientists explore the "darker side to record temperatures". We are told that "Hot dry weather could spark droughts, impacting farmers, food supply and prices". A meteorologist from NIWA says the weather is down to "a combination of climate drivers", with the main one being El Niño. The increased fire risk comes from not just the dry weather, but also the accompanying winds. With wildfire experts anticipating "our worst season yet", they are gearing up by bringing over firefighters and tanker planes from Australia. There are also predictions of "an invasion of ants and cockroaches inside, ... while the summer heat would initially bring an influx of flies and mosquitos outside, without much rain, they might decrease". And it seems that not even the beach can provide the usual summer solace, as "you may encounter more sharks this summer, with record marine temperatures in New Zealand". [122]

On a similar theme Sally Blundell writes in the Listener: "Climate change means alien invaders are more likely to wreak havoc on our wildlife, farms, and economy. Those charged with repelling the threat say our isolation is no longer enough. ... Responsibility for biosecurity has to be shared, ... online shoppers checking a new parcel for unwelcome insect passengers ... a farmer reporting unusual illness in their livestock, or a traveller returning from overseas and declaring any risky goods in their luggage [says Biosecurity NZ chief biosecurity officer Stu Hutchings]. There is a need for a global approach as well where biosecurity priorities extend across countries and across areas of expertise." [123] As Nathalia Tocci says in *The Guardian Weekly*: "All of a sudden, climate was no longer an abstract threat that could be batted into a distant future; it was already here, causing shocking weather events, destroying lives and leaving people homeless." [124]

BUILDING A BROADER REVIEW OF RESILIENCE: WHAT ARE THE OPTIONS, AND DO THEY MEET OUR CLIMATE OBLIGATIONS AND AID ADAPTION AND SUSTAINABILITY?

In a climate crisis, resilience assumes a broader meaning. Its initial focus is, of course, on the individual and the trauma and heightened level of stress experienced, but then it broadens out to consider the resilience of our cities and communities, before moving on to consider land and infrastructure, including communications, transport and logistics. The Secretary for the Environment James Palmer says, "[C]limate change is accelerating; it is having an adverse effect on our communities ... and predicted to get more severe ... there was no time to lose on adaption ... We are getting a major flood event somewhere in Aotearoa/New Zealand about every eight months at the moment [and] we need to develop consistent approaches for that." [125]

With James Palmer's words ringing in our ears — "that there was no time to lose on adaption" — there is little room to doubt that the issues are significant, as are the decisions to be made: "increasing flood protection, so communities could stay put, or relocation ... difficult decisions will need to be taken around rebuilding locations", [126] although "we have built — and in some regions continue to consent — homes and even communities that cannot be protected from extreme weather events", [127] while "landscapes and geological features are poorly served by current planning, at our own peril", [128] and there is "the potentially destructive impact of the vast amounts of forestry slash generated in New Zealand". [129] Alternatively, "building homes for more climate-resilience can help us be calmer, healthier, safer — and richer". [130]

WHAT ARE SOME OF THE OPTIONS?

Reducing farming emissions

The agriculture sector has undertaken a number of initiatives in an effort to reduce farming emissions, including the following. In August 2023, in an effort to meet New Zealand's international obligations regarding climate change mitigation, the Environment Protection Authority (EPA) approved a feed additive that reduces methane emissions in livestock, but still needed sign-off from the hazardous chemicals regulator. There was a degree of caution about the product's efficacy, given that its use overseas is mostly in housed feeding situations. However, that the EPA was working closely with MPI on the regulation of methane inhibitors was an example of an effort to streamline the EPA's application and assessment process for these substances. [131] Another initiative reported in 2023 in its early stages is that of Waikato-based Ruminant Bio Tech, which "is working on a slow-release pills used to deliver medicines to livestock ... [T]he start-up said its goal now was to deliver a commercially viable product that can cut methane by 70% over six months." [132] Another interesting solution involves feeding cattle seaweed, which looks to reduces their greenhouse gas emissions by 82%. Researchers at the University of California, Davis, reported that: "Cattle that consumed doses of about 80 grams (3 ounces) of seaweed gained as much weight as their herd mates while burping out 82 percent less methane into the atmosphere." [133]

In August 2024, the *New Scientist* reported on a vaccine that cuts methane emissions from cow's burps currently being developed by US start-up ArkeaBio that is looking to launch it commercially within three years. When the prototype of the vaccine, which targets the "methane-producing bacteria that live in cow's digestive systems" was administered in a trial in 2023, the cows produced 12.9 percent less methane over 105 days with no adverse side effects or disruption to growth rate". The results were described as promising, given that a 15 to 20% reduction in methane emissions would be considered substantial, the developers said that that they needed "to be sure that it works, delivers consistent results, is economically feasible and has no side effects". [134]

So all of these efforts are promising, but do they reflect what farmers want? When an article in *The Post* asked farmers just that question, it received a consistent response. Farmers want input, communication, structure and planning. Their need to be consulted and listened to encapsulates many of the ideas of good leadership we explored earlier in the chapter — empathy, trust and social connection. "The over-riding feeling [is] farmers want to be part of the solution, put plans into place and have the right governance and working groups that will drive them." Co-chairperson of Future Farmers Aimee Blake expands on this: "Establishing good feedback loops with rural communities is important. Rather than a top-down approach to telling [farmers what to do], it really needs to start with listening ... [C]atchment groups were the perfect example of how national issues could be taken to a regional scale. There are amazing case studies of what those communities are achieving. We need more support for community-led approaches." She also believed "a domestic food strategy was desperately needed". What is wanted, says 2023 Young Farmer of the Year Emma Poole, "is to get agreement in the sector and a plan in place to achieve the intended outcomes". [135]

Our climate responsibilities have also been rocketed into space, with New Zealand's first government-funded space mission. "MethaneSAT uses satellite technology to pinpoint methane emissions from agriculture — sheep and cows here in New Zealand ... The aim is to verify the accuracy of both satellite and Earth-based measurements and more accurately pinpoint the source of the emissions." [136] The principal scientist from NIWA on this mission, Dr Sara Mikaloff-Fletcher says that "this is the first time we will be able to monitor the kind of pastoral agriculture we have in New Zealand at the kind of spatial resolution we need to support regional climate action ... We won't necessarily be pinpointing individual farms as emissions sources, but we'll be able to detect and quantify methane emissions over New Zealand's agricultural areas; get a general picture and spatial mapping. She points out that methane accounts for more than 43% of total greenhouse gas emissions, and mostly comes from belching livestock. "A lot of the value of this work is not just for understanding New Zealand's emissions but for giving others around the world confidence in how good that data is." These ties in a global methane pledge that New Zealand signed in 2021, undertaking to cut our gas emissions from 2020 levels by 2030. Mikaloff-Fletchers explains that "partnering on the MethaneSAT mission is one of New Zealand's initiatives toward this goal", and is optimistic that gathering and delivering the data will help maintain "hope that we can tackle what sometimes feels like an insurmountable problem". [137]

So technology's role in tackling climate change is increasing, with Madeleine Cuff reporting in the *New Scientist* another initiative, which is the developing of machines that suck up atmospheric carbon. "Removing CO2, in a process called direct air capture (DAC) has been on the cards for some time, but finally, after years of research and small-scale pilot projects, giant carbon-sucking facilities are becoming a reality. The question is, will the industry grow large enough, fast enough?" [138] Remember in Chapter 4, when thinking about climate action, Bill Gates was exploring the role technology could play, saying "someone will invent these technologies. It's just a question of who and how soon." [139]

NZTech clearly supports technology playing a role in climate change mitigation, publishing a report in April 2024 that calls for a "climate technology roadmap which would encourage more investment in carbon-abating technologies but would need both industry and political support to be a success. ... NZTech's chief executive Graeme Muller acknowledges that it can be "more tempting to talk-up the potential of new technologies to abate emissions than to accept sacrifices had to be made". However, he believes: "A bit more of a co-ordinated 'signalling' approach will help with international investment and private investment. NZTech's study listed a number of 'quick wins' that the technology industry could help deliver. In a foreword to the report, Climate Change Minister Simon Watts said that "the scale of transformation required to meet the country's targets meant they could only be achieved by the public and private sectors working hand in hand". [140]

Renewable energy

In 2023, *Stuff*'s climate reporter Olivia Wannan felt the outlook was cautious but positive, citing the belief of climate experts that New Zealand could achieve 95% renewable electricity by 2030. She continued: "Aotearoa reached that climate goal last December — almost. In the last quarter of 2022, hydro dams, geothermal plants, wind, and solar farms provided 94.7% of all power — the highest since records began in 1974 ... Experts, including the Climate Change Commission, stress the national grid will get progressively cleaner ... To consistently achieve 95% renewable power, generators would need to build even more geothermal, wind and solar to supplement hydro when rain doesn't fall." [141] The tongue-in-cheek headline in *The Economist* says it all: "Hug Pylons not trees". [142]

Remember, too, the positive public health outcomes that come with tackling climate change, as articulated by the Director-General of the World Health Organization, Dr Tedros Adhanom Ghebreyesus: "[C]limate mitigation and adaption ... also offering health co-benefits, such as reduced exposure to air pollution, local cooling effects, stress relief and increased recreational space for social interaction and physical activity ... The public health benefits resulting from ambitious mitigation efforts would far outweigh their cost." [143]

There are also words of caution regarding promoting renewable energy. For example, *The Guardian* reports "climate scientists have cautioned against placing too much optimism in the decrease [of emissions] driven by hydropower, given the sector's dependence on high volumes of rain that may reverse with dry conditions borne by El Nino pattern forecast for summer 2023." [144] *The Dominion Post* also reports mixed results: "New Zealand's share of renewable electricity generation (such as hydro, wind and solar) is already high by global standards ... But when all energy is counted — including petrol for non-electric cars, gas for heating, and coal and gas for manufacturing — the share of the country's energy supply coming from low or no-emissions renewable sources is only 40%." [145]

Solar farms

While not necessarily the genesis of solar farming, a significant stimulus in their development came in April 2023 with the Labour-led Government's decision to refer solar energy projects for fast-track consenting. A press release that accompanied Prime Minister Chris Hipkins's announcement explains the situation: "Nearly half a million solar panels across two Waikato solar farm projects that could reduce over 200 million kilograms of carbon pollution each year have been referred for fast-track consenting, creating up to 280 jobs..., the Prime Minister Chris Hipkins announced [in April 2023].

"Referring the Rangiriri Solar Farm Project and Waerenga Solar Farm Project will mean that five significant renewable energy projects [have been fast-tracked], speeding up the transition to a clean energy future." Environment Minister David Parker said: "These projects are examples of the type of renewable energy development needed to meet our environmental goals, and increasing generation and supply improves our national energy resilience." [146] This was followed up in June of the same year when fast-track referrals were agreed for Harmony Energy Solar Ltd's projects near Marton, Opunake and Carterton, and Energy Farms Ltd's projects near Rangitikei and Taranaki. This signalled "large-scale solar investment in five North Island regions, adding power from about 829,000 solar panels to the national grid". [147]

These actions go some way to explaining the following view: "As of 2021, a dynamic change is taking place on farms throughout New Zealand ... Solar farms are now economically viable and are able to sell solar-generated electricity to the grid for mass consumption. Many solar farms are due to be installed in the coming months and years, so expect to see them dotted throughout farmlands nationwide ... [with] over 1900 MW of solar farms planned around New Zealand." [148] Matt Rowe in *The Post* reveals another reason for the enthusiasm that surrounds solar farms: "the cost of building utility scale solar has dropped to the point it is cheaper than wind power and the ability to gain resource consents for solar parks is decidedly easier than consenting a wind farm or hydro scheme. [149] This enthusiasm was not entirely unqualified, however, as we see in an article by Diane McCarthy in *The New Zealand Herald,* where she reports farmers raising concerns surrounding the loss of productive land to solar farms: "[We're] not saying we don't agree with green energy. That's the future. But it's got to be done sensibly." [150]

In his article, Matt Rowe also sounds a qualifier of needing to establish a workforce alongside the solar development: "If solar generation is to make up a significant portion of new renewable electricity generation in this country, it will be vital to build up local expertise, particularly in solar farm engineering and installation ... there is no shortage of local talent. All we need to do is to build experience in the end-to-end designing and installing of solar farms. Now, with the commitment to treble renewable energy generation, growing the local workforce is integral to our success." [151]

Other challenges may curb this enthusiasm, too. One such is that detailed by *The Post*'s senior business reporter Tom Pullar-Strecker, who says that the adding of additional demand to the grid will come with a cost: "a lot of the existing grid was built in the 1960s and 1970s and was at the end of life and needs to be refurbished. About \$30b to \$40b would need to be spent on new generation by 2050." [152]

Wind farms

By the end of 2023, New Zealand will have 19 on shore wind farms operating, with a total installed capacity of 1045 MW. They represent around 10% of New Zealand's total installed generation capacity with additional projects in various stages of investigation, planning and consenting. The vision of NZ Wind Energy Association is that wind power will account for around 20% of our electricity by 2035 ... The time frame for achieving the vision was changed in 2017 from 2030 to 2035 to reflect the lack of recent new development following "a period of reducing electricity demand and high reserves margins." [153] [154] In the move to renewable generation, we need to "retire some of our old, fossil fuel plant and build more wind farms, commission more geothermal power stations, and erect more solar panels". In doing this we can "take advantage of the leaps in technology that make renewable energy more cost-effective than running gas or coal fired generation and recognise its key role in reducing carbon emissions". It concludes: "New Zealand's wind has the potential to be used to generate over three times New Zealand's current annual electricity demand." [155]

The Energy Efficiency and Conservation Authority explains the factors New Zealand's renewable energy relies on: "Our large share of renewable electricity is largely due to favourable geography, including being an island nation with mountains, lakes, relatively consistent wind, and rainfall, plus access to geothermal resources. The percentage of New Zealand's electricity generated from renewable energy sources varies each year depending on the amount of rainfall, and to a lesser extent, the amount of wind." [156] These natural factors need to be carefully harnessed and developed. So when the government released the first Emissions Reduction Plan in May 2022, it "committed to developing regulatory settings to enable investment in offshore renewable energy and innovation. This was alongside other actions to accelerate the development of new renewable electricity generation across the economy." [157] "But it is worth keeping in mind that there's a lot of variability in wind generation that still needs to be managed ... We're working to increase coordination and information sharing to allow participants to react to variations in intermittent generation to better meet the demands of our power system". [158]

Tree planting

Neil Cullen, the president of the New Zealand Farm Forestry Association, describes the many advantages of planting trees: "From ecological benefits to income diversity, planting forest blocks made up of alternative species can be a 'win, win, win' for farmers." He says that the association is a strong advocate for "right tree, right place", and illustrates this with the example of poplar, which are "already being used to stabilise hillsides, and when widely spaced, farmers could still get grazing underneath and claim credits under the emissions trading scheme". Another case of "win, win, win". The association also strongly encourages farmers to plant forest on their least productive land. "It's going to improve viability in the long term," Cullen says. [159]

However, Michael Le Page, writing in the *New Scientist*, discusses a new study that calls into question the idea of tree planting being the quick-fix golden bullet in countering climate change. "Planting forests to absorb more carbon dioxide is seen as key in slowing climate change, but the impact of new trees seems to be lower than expected ... Growing trees will help limit further warming of the planet by soaking up carbon dioxide — but not quite as much as we thought." Indeed, the climate benefits on a global level could be 15 to 30% smaller than previously estimated, because of other factors, such as trees absorbing sunlight. He quotes the study's lead author, the University of Sheffield's Dr James Weber, who says "We are not saying don't plant trees", just cautioning that "the climate benefits aren't as big as we thought". [160] Nevertheless, Dr Weber says "that even with these findings, forests are still essential to solving climate change: We're very much *not* saying that trees are bad." [161]

Le Page's article continues: "The impact that trees have depends in part on what other actions are taken to tackle climate change. The more that is done, the greater the benefits of planting forests, Weber and his colleagues have shown. It's more positive and more efficient if we also do other things as well." Even so "forestation has numerous other benefits for people and wildlife, including reducing erosion, maintaining water supplies and water quality, providing foods and jobs, and reducing local heat extremes. Forestation, and specifically reforestation in forest biomes with native species, is absolutely worth pursuing." Dr Stephanie Roe, co-author of the study, says: "What this study shows is that the overwhelming net effect of forests is a cooling one ... But most importantly, even if they didn't have such a cooling impact, we would still need to save natural forests to support Earth's biodiversity, and the billions of people who depend on them." [162] Dr Roe concludes: "Importantly, the study finds that preventing forests getting cut down, when compared to efforts to plant new forests, is a far more efficient way to mitigate climate change." [163]

Support about the potency of trees comes from the *New Scientist* heading: "Trees are even better for the climate than we thought". Madeleine Cuff's accompanying article discusses the findings of a recent study, which supports Dr Roe's valuing of existing forests. Cuff writes: "Microbes living in the bark of trees are absorbing methane from the air, adding to the climate benefits that we knew trees give us." Methane-eating microbes — called methanotrophs — live on tree bark, and the study has found that methanotrophs are "removing methane from the atmosphere at a large scale, across temperate, boreal and tropical environments". The lead researcher concludes: "Existing forests are that much more important than we thought, and we should preserve them." [164]

Kelp forests

We broadened our horizons when thinking about resilience, sustainability and mitigation in terms of climate change by harnessing space technology to accomplish our climate goals. So there is some complementarity in exploring what lies at the other end of our planet, and investigate what's under our seas that can be harnessed to help battle climate change, especially given the centrality of warming waters to the problem.

The potential helper, we find, are kelp forests. Dr Caitlin Blain, from the University of Auckland's Marine Laboratory is conducting research into where kelp fits into coastal carbon cycles, and looking at the role it might play in slowing down or stopping climate change. Blain's research has revealed that kelp forests are equal to on-land forests in sequestering carbon from the atmosphere. Her next line of inquiry is about just how well they perform.

She explains: "We're obviously trying as a community and across the world to reduce our carbon dioxide emissions. One of the simplest ways to help mitigate the emissions that we've already put out there is by enhancing our natural environment and enhancing those ecosystems that naturally remove carbon dioxide."

Sapeer Mayron writes about Dr Blain's work in the *Sunday News* under a headline that captures the challenge: "Our underwater forests are key to fighting climate change, but the kelp needs our help". Mayron cuts straight to the chase: "Whether it's our warming climate heating the ocean, or extreme weather events sending tonnes of silt into the sea — or a host of other stressors — kelp needs our help to survive." In Auckland's Hauraki Gulf a key problem for kelp "is sediment clouding the water and blocking its sunlight; that essential ingredient that keeps our plants photosynthesising". Blain explains the problem: "We need kelp to photosynthesise and convert carbon dioxide from atmosphere into oxygen, so the ocean darkening above it should worry us." She attributes the growing problem to several causes: one culprit is extremes in the weather resulting in flooding and erosion, which has "dumped [material] into coastal marine areas, blocking the light from the life beneath it; another culprit is overfishing. Together, they "will decimate the kelp", she says.

Dr Blain puts it this way: "The land we live on is connected to the sea, so any little things that we do might seem arbitrary to people, but they can make a big difference when we add them up; whether it's taking care of your rubbish or your recycling, helping plant trees or getting involved in community initiatives that are set out to kind of enhance the environment." She advises: "I think people just need to get involved in ways that they can and that work with their life." [165]

Remember the mantra: "the best thing we can do for climate justice as individuals is to find ways to work collectively". [166] It is the overriding lesson from the pandemic and now the climate crisis. We should heed Greta Thunberg's rallying cry: "Together, we can do the seemingly impossible. But make no mistake — no one else is going to do it for us. This is up to us, here and now. You and me ... It's happening right here and right now." [167] As Professor James Renwick writes: "We really are all in this together. It is going to take effort from all of us, in countries and communities large and small. The best thing we can do is to cooperate, to help and support each other, to be empathetic. To love one another, basically." Remember, helping others is helping ourselves. [168]

Immediate challenges being faced – all evidencing that we are already grappling with a climate crisis

The immediacy of the climate crisis is expressed in several challenges all pointing to the fact that the climate crisis is here, and we need to deal with it. Following are a couple of examples that prevail. The first is when on 7 February 2024 Southland District Mayor Rob Scott signed a declaration for a local state of emergency for the Bluecliffs area. Increased erosion of the banks at the Bluecliffs township, due to heavy rain and sea swells, was putting the homes at risk. As the declaration was announced, Emergency Management controller Simon Mapp said, "At this stage we're building our technical understanding of the risks in the area and what might be possible to provide this community with some more time to manage their retreat." [169] Writing for RNZ a month later, Matthew Rosenberg said the heavy toll on Bluecliffs' permanent residents was evident, reporting they were "very stressed", having "been living under a state of emergency for four weeks ... and evacuation orders ... in the wake of ongoing erosion problems accelerated by the nearby river". [170] Coastal erosion has made its presence felt elsewhere, too, sending a threatening message to other coastal communities in the country. Greta Thunberg points to its urgency: "Sea-level rise will not remain a question of milli-, centi- or decimetres for very long. Even if the change takes time, we must realize that this is not something we can adapt to." [171]

Another example is the extremes of weather we have been experiencing. Converse to the lashing Bluecliffs was taking with constant heavy rain, "parts of the Wairarapa are so dry farmers have resorted to feeding trees to stock. With less than 50mm of rain all year, east coast sheep and cattle farmers were worried if they don't get some soon, they won't have enough feed going into winter." On 27 March 2024, Federated Farmers Wairarapa branch president David Hayes admitted they were on the brink of "declaring a special adverse event". [172]

Another issue is the importance of the sea and its role in climate change. In New Zealand one way this is showing itself is in the spreading of Caulerpa, a fast-growing and invasive seaweed that is "the rapidly spreading ... along parts of our coast". It thrives in warm, clear, shallow waters, growing up to 3 centimetres a day, soon "creating a green carpet across the seafloor and enveloping [everything] in its path. It competes with native seaweeds and sea grasses, smothers shellfish and can shrink the diversity of marine life." While New Zealand's nine native species of Caulerpa are kept under control by local ecosystems, it is two new non-indigenous species of the algae — *Caulerpa brachypus*, and *Caulerpa parvifolia* — that are creating havoc, having been carried into New Zealand's waters on the hulls of boats. [173] Ridding our waters of it is a matter of urgency. Accordingly, on 23 February 2024 Biosecurity Minister Andrew Hoggard announced that the battle to contain the fast-spreading exotic Caulerpa was receiving a $5 million boost to help accelerate the development of removal techniques." [174]

There is also a debate brewing over the Emissions Trading Scheme, as revealed by Climate Change Commission's chair Dr Rod Carr, speaking on RNZ's *Morning Report* on 13 March 2024. While the government had clearly indicated that it plans to rely on the Emissions Trading Scheme to meet New Zealand's climate targets, he said the scheme would not be sufficient to do this in its current form. An over-supply of units "means that large polluters — which buy the units to allow the release of planet-heating gases — often find it is cheaper to buy them than invest in ways to cut pollution". [175] Independent climate change policy expert Christina Hood followed up Dr Carr's comments with an opinion piece in *The Post*, in which she said that "a robust accountability process would mean ministers assess the emissions impact of all major decisions, liaise with the Climate Change Minister to understand the degree to which the ETS is likely to compensate or not, and make Cabinet aware of any resulting emissions shortfall and its cost". [176] A piece published in *The Guardian Weekly* a month later said that new figures were showing that New Zealand's "ambitious plan to reach net zero emissions by 2050 is at risk of being derailed, as the government backslides on climate policies". The commitment to reduce the nation's carbon emissions to net zero by 2050, and meeting its commitments under the Paris climate accords, had been made in 2019 by the Labour-led Government. *The Guardian Weekly* reported that a new draft emissions reduction plan released two days earlier by the New Zealand coalition government, which had been elected at the end of 2023, "has been criticised for putting too much stock in undeveloped technology and offsetting, rather than stopping, emissions". [177] The debate continues.

A snippet in *The Post*, on 14 August 2024, signalled another once hotly-debated topic was being brought back to the table": "Genetic engineering 'ban' to be gone by end of 2025". The twist here was that it would seem that Science, Innovation and Technology Minister Judith Collins was intending to unleash GE as a weapon in fighting climate change, using the example of modified grasses developed to reduce methane emissions from cows. She said that our current ban on GE meant that where there were break-throughs in studies at New Zealand labs, the studies were having to relocate to the United States to do the field testing. [178] With headings announcing "methane emissions rising at fastest rate in decades", [179] you are left wondering how long such a break-through will take before it is available commercially, and how strong the will to get our methane emissions down to our target level really is. Surely when we are confronted with news that "the growth rate of methane is accelerating ... [and] worrisome," and "require[s] immediate action to help avert a dangerous escalation in the climate crisis", [180] it is timely to remember that one of the pandemic's lessons is: delay is deadly.

Elbowing for attention, too, is the issue of wildfires. Under the heading "Climate change is fanning the flames of New Zealand's wildfires future", on 25 February 2024 Senior Research Fellow at Victoria University of Wellington Dr Nathanael Melia addressed how wildfires had burnt through 650 hectares of forest and scrub in Christchurch's Port Hills the previous week. Noting that this was not the first time the area had faced a "terrifying wildfire event", he concluded: "It is clear New Zealand stands at a pivotal juncture. And our once relatively 'safe' regions are now under threat." This fact should instigate all levels of government to evaluate whether the current investment in combating fires would be sufficient to meet the needs in the coming decades. "Our research integrating detailed climate simulations with daily observations reveals a stark forecast: an uptick in both the frequency and intensity of wildfires, particularly in the inland areas of the South Island. It is time to consider what this will mean for Fire and Emergency New Zealand (FENZ), and how a strategic calibration of resources, tactics, and technologies will help New Zealand confront this emerging threat." [181]

Explaining "the climate drivers of wildfires", Dr Melia pointed to the two weather systems that had laid the groundwork for the wildfire. First the wet, warm conditions of the La Niña system had nurtured and nourished the abundance of vegetation in the Port Hills. The following El Niña system created hot, dry conditions that had left the Port Hills' scrub and grass vegetation tinder-dry, driving the "flammability of the region". When the last fires ignited on 13 February, this fuel pile was literally fanned by "a gusty northwesterly … blowing 40–50kph with exceptionally dry relative humidity values". [182] This combination meant it was 66 days before the fires were fully extinguished". [183]

Seabed mining is another flashpoint. An environment debate, wrote Newsroom's Jonathan Milne, has broken out over the "new coalition government's backing of Taranaki seabed mining, which is built around National and New Zealand First's coalition agreement to "investigate the strategic opportunities in NZ's mineral resources, specifically vanadium, and develop these opportunities". The mineral vanadium has increased in value lately with its expanded use in creating the new generation utility-scaled batteries, which Trans-Tasman Resources boss Alan Eggers says "are needed to underpin a transition to renewable power". [184] Jack McDonald, a campaigner and a political commentator, in his opinion piece in *The Post*, "Seabed mining shaping up as early 'fast-track' assault on environment laws", recounted the history of opposing seabed mining in the South Taranaki area, which has lasted "for more than 10 years". Until the coalition government's recent announcement, protesters thought the case had finally been put to bed in 2022, when "the dispute made its way to the highest court in the land, the Supreme Court, which unanimously upheld previous high court and appeal court decisions revoking TTR's permission to mine". [185]

He went on to describe what this recent government announcement signified: "While the fate of seabed mining in South Taranaki remains unknown" its fate now lies with "the Government's controversial Fast-track Approvals Bill, which would allow **then** just three ministers to approve or deny development projects without them having to go through any of the checks and balances set out in environmental law. *At the time of writing* the bill is currently before the environment select committee, which is calling for submissions from the public." This timeline for the Bill entering the House for consent thus was unclear. What was clear was that as the protests continued to grow "we may yet again see people taking to the seas". [186]

The protests have indeed been growing, and the government is now facing battles on two fronts: mining and the fast-track legislation. The first is "linked to the fact that New Zealand is one of the 190 countries as a signatory to the agreement at the COP15 conference to halt biodiversity loss by 2023", [187] not forgetting the endangering of the lives of sealions. [188] The fast-track legislation is also contentious because the legislation *presently* gives the three ministers at the time of writing the power to "override existing environmental laws" with an expert panel to be set up to advise them. [189] Parliamentary Commissioner for the Environment Simon Upton described the proposed fast-track system "as not credible and would lead to disasters," [190] which, along with other opposition, led to the government making some concessions. These included, for example, "giving the ultimate say on whether to approve projects and under what conditions to the expert panel, rather than ministers, exclude mining projects from the regime altogether and, exclude previously-rejected projects." [191] The outcome seems to be that the three ministers are no longer solely responsible for selecting the projects to be fast-tracked, but draw up a long-list that is then submitted to the advisory expert panel. This has not quelled many misgivings, however, as the public and interested parties still have no opportunity to make submissions at any stage in the process: whether in the drawing up of the long-list or the considerations of the expert panel. And who selects the members of the expert panel has been a further matter of disquiet. And the fact remains that there has been a significant shift in the weighting of resource consenting, with economic considerations arguably being given more weight that environmental ones, with the Minister for the Environment not involved, and the three key ministers being those for infrastructure, regional development, and RMA reform. The debate continues as do the protests.

The final issue garnering attention is the melting of ice due to the effects of climate change. In March 2024, the World Meteorological Organization (WMO), the United Nations' weather agency, sounded a red alert on climate change after 2023 saw numerous records set by unprecedented heat and melting Antarctic ice. From Geneva, the WMO released a statement in which the UN agency's secretary-general said: "Never have we been so close ... to 1.5C lower limit of the Paris agreement on climate change (in 2015). Dr Till Kuhlbrodt, of the University of Reading in England, said that "some of the climate extremes we have seen in 2023 are markedly beyond anything seen before". "However, the WMO State of Climate report said that the growth in renewable energy capacity, which last year increased almost 505 compared with 2022 offered a 'glimmer of hope'." [192]

CONCLUSIONS

There has been no shortage of warnings. This first from from the chair of the Climate Change Commission Dr Rod Carr: "Climate-action delay is climate denial because the effect is the same." [193] Professor Tim Flannery would concur: "delay, even by a few years, could cost us everything", adding: "An even greater misconception is [for those who argue] for an 'orderly transition'... The trouble with an orderly transition ... is that it completely ignores the extreme urgency we now face in the climate emergency. In short, the cost of such an orderly transition will be chaotic disorder in the climate system." [194]

In this regard, remember what we learnt from the pandemic: follow the science and the research, not the politics. Flannery would again concur: "A similarly resolute and scientifically informed approach can do the same for the climate emergency." [195] Russell Brown writes in *The New Zealand Listener*: "In the surge in climate change denial is an exaggerated means of coping with the unthinkable." [196]

To get to this point in the conversation the need is to emphasise that climate change is, as Greta Thurnberg points out, "not happening in some faraway future. It's happening right here and right now ... our main challenge, however, is that all these events are happening at the same time, and at maximum speed." [197] She adds: "The longer we pretend that we can solve the climate and ecological crises without treating it as such, [the] more precious time we will lose. [So,] start treating this crisis like a crisis." [198] Lily Duval offers a local perspective in *The New Zealand Listener*: "Conservation holds some of the solutions to the present and future crisis — investing in te taiao (natural world) now will likely save us money. Conservation work is *'an act of hope and resistance'*. It dares to believe that we can help heal our beleaguered environments and it resists the creeping cynicism of a world constantly in crises." [199]

We began this section describing it as climate change, but ended it by describing it as a climate crisis. However, Octavia Cade reassures us: "The future ... does not have to be indifference and abandonment." [200] There is a certain amount of irony when those who argue that the swing has gone too much to favour the environment, when of course the reason for the swing is that we are trying to save the environment.

CHAPTER 8:

Conclusions and Reflections

As a new year beckoned, and "with one week of Parliament to go", at the end of 2022 Luke Malpass is writing in *The Dominion Post*: "it pays to cast the mind back to just how much has changed over the [past] crazy year or two ... a couple of years that most people would rather forget ... [A]nd even writing all this down, it seems like a dystopian fever dream ... [While] not necessarily a criticism of the measures, but a reminder of the truly abnormal times we have lived in. It is also a reminder of the collective trauma the country has been through over these past few years ... and while life may be close to normal again, [it] is now dominated by a cost-of-living crunch ... so we'll see what 2023 brings." [1]

We didn't have long to wait. On 25 January Chris Hipkins was sworn in to become New Zealand's forty-first prime minister, [2] with the Deputy Prime Minister Carmel Sepuloni "making history as the first Pasifika Deputy Prime Minister and the third woman to hold the role", [3] formally completing the handover of power from Jacinda Ardern.

Then on the heels of the new prime minister and deputy prime minister taking office from 12 to 16 February a severe tropical cyclone, Cyclone Gabrielle, hit New Zealand with devastating effect, resulting in a national state of emergency being declared on 14 February 2023. It was to prove "the deadliest and costliest system to hit New Zealand", [4] with the scale of the disaster being attributed to climate change. [5]

This was to be an election year, too, and year-end saw a change of government. Six weeks after the general election on 14 October–, on 27 November the new three-way coalition government — of National, New Zealand First and ACT parties — is sworn in, after which the Cabinet meets for the first time, with Christopher Luxon the forty-second prime minister of New Zealand. The first 100 days from the swearing-in of the new government arrives on 6 March 2024. [6]

With this context in mind, this chapter begins by looking back a year to March 2023 and the former director-general of health Sir Ashley Bloomfield declaring "we're out the other side ...the worst of the Covid-19 pandemic appear[s] to be over — three years on today from Aotearoa's first lockdown [25 March 2020]". Clearly, this is something to celebrate; but he tempers this by emphasising that being over the worst does not mean that it is over. He cautions that "lockdowns 'may have a place' still in the future. He said it has been 'a pretty bumpy journey' but recent travel overseas had shown him everyone's sort of life's getting almost back to completely normal. So that's a good thing." The *Stuff* report continues: "he was proud of the collective efforts New Zealanders had made as well as compliance ... Sir Ashley has also welcomed the Royal Commission of Inquiry into Aotearoa's pandemic response." [7] Endorsing Sir Ashley Bloomfield's comments, on 5 May 2023 World Health Organization Director-General Dr Tedros Adhanom Ghebreyesus declared that Covid-19 no longer represented a "global health emergency," [adding,] "that the decision had been considered carefully for some time and made on the basis of careful analysis of data ... It did not mean the danger was over and said the emergency status could be restated if the situation changed." [8] The threat still lingers.

Covid-19 work continues, of course, but we are now at the point where we should acknowledge that the Covid-19 pandemic has many faces. Naturally, we are drawn almost immediately to thinking of it in terms of regulations, mandates, lockdown, protests, and sadly the deaths and grief. But we have also now been given an opportunity to move on and begin to view the pandemic in every sense as the vehicle which is giving us the chance to reimagine our working lives, and reflect on our lifestyles, our priorities and what we value and what changes we are prepared to make. This is our "unique instructive moment" [9] about the choices that may lie ahead for us.

Also, in this milieu we turn to "stress and mental health issues (often work-related) [which] can be viewed as a modern pandemic". [10] While strictly speaking it is not technically a pandemic, proponent of the four-day week Andrew Barnes has a point in drawing this parallel, as it certainly seems to bear all the hallmarks of one, and is often described in terms of levels. The disruptive possibilities presented by the Covid-19 pandemic also gives us the opportunity to address the scourge of out-of-control stress, allowing us to begin reimagining our working lives, and the future structure of work itself. In doing so we consider contemporary working lives and why there is such an urgent need to make changes, and then go on to explore what progress is being made when thinking about the changes that have been mooted around hybrid working.

Then, just when you were beginning to think surely that must be enough, the chapter turns to the continuing battle the government has been fighting surrounding misinformation, conspiracies, the manipulation of reality, which "seem to be common themes in today's current events". As Andrea Gawrylewski continues, in her piece in the *Scientific American,* "never has it been more important to understand the science of how we humans determine what is true". [11] and how this misinformation manages to seamlessly glide from one pandemic into another. Together, discussion of these themes allows us to end this chapter with a number of mainstream reflections that offer a framework with which, in your own time, you can initiate your own process of reflecting.

THE COVID-19 PANDEMIC: THE SCIENCE AND RESEARCH CONTINUES

Even in this last phase of the pandemic the science that has driven policy and management continues. In *The Dominion Post* Gianina Schwanecke reports that researchers are "investigating the effectiveness of a single, combined vaccine to prevent both influenza and Covid-19 in people between 50 and 80 years old", with the aim of help reducing vaccination fatigue. The study is looking at what would be the best doses of each vaccine to make up a combined vaccine. [12] Work has also advanced our knowledge of how many Covid-19 infections are out there: [13] "by comparing the presence of Covid in our wastewater with the daily reported cases, scientists [can] estimate the true number of infections". [14] Professor Baker is reported as saying that "a well-designed and ongoing infection prevalence survey ... could probe reinfections rates and how many infected people suffer long Covid symptoms". [15]

Reinfections have caught the eye of researchers, and Professor Fuhrer of Monash University "has developed a 'hazard ratio' — it's an indication of how much less likely someone previously infected is to get infected now, compared to someone who has not been infected ... But despite being so widely studied for more than two years, there is still considerable uncertainty around what happens next with the virus", [16] as many of its longer-term effects, including for those living with long Covid, remain unclear.

The Post has reported the same concerning findings of a new study "that suggest Long Covid may have longer term effects on cognition and memory — and that these lead to measurable differences in cognitive performance". However, the researchers have also stressed that "the greater cognitive decline may not be permanent, as participants in this category who had recovered by the time they took part in the study were found to have cognitive deficits comparable to those who recovered quickly". The study's lead author concludes: "It gives us a little bit of hope that those who are struggling with long Covid at the moment — when their symptoms eventually resolve — may experience some cognitive recovery." [17]

THE MANAGEMENT OF THE PANDEMIC REFLECTS THE SCIENCE

Just as the science gave us a better understanding of how to set policy around the pandemic, it has also driven how we manage the pandemic. And management of the pandemic continues. Early in 2023, the Minister for Covid-19 Response Hon Ayesha Verrall had announced that from April all New Zealanders aged 30 years and over would be able to access the new Covid bivalent booster, "as part of the Government's plan to keep Kiwis safe and take pressure off our health system. This new bivalent vaccine would be replacing the existing Pfizer booster, as it "is considered likely to be more effective against Omicron subvariants". She explained that bivalent vaccines work "by combining two strains of a virus, which prompts the body to create antibodies against both strains, providing a greater level of protection". [18]

In line with this management theme, late in 2022 the government had announced that "a major public inquiry into [the government] response to Covid-19", which would be led by Australian-based epidemiologist Tony

Blakely, and would get under way in February 2023 and be completed by June 2024. However, while Professor Michael Baker considered that the information and analysis of such an inquiry would be helpful for the next pandemic, opposition parties protested that the inquiry's scope was too narrow. Nevertheless, "Professor Baker said that its focus on finding lessons for the next pandemic would make a difference." [19] The chair of the Royal Commission of Inquiry into Covid-19, Professor Tony Blakely, writing in *The Post* in June 2023, outlined the Commission's strategy: "We'll be conducting the inquiry in a non-adversarial way that supports identifying key lessons, by making it easy for people to share their experience ... Our focus is on what we can learn to ensure New Zealand is prepared for the future, not on assigning blame or finding fault ... The unfortunate reality is that there will be another pandemic. While it might be uncomfortable, for us to be best prepared we really do need to talk about what has happened and how we responded. Our goal is to distil the lessons we identify to help ensure Aotearoa can respond as well as possible to the next pandemic, safeguarding the health and wellbeing of all New Zealanders in the most effective and fair way possible." [20]

Staying with the management theme, in late 2022 Minister of Research, Science and Innovation Dr Ayesha Verrall announced "a new research platform ... to better prepare New Zealand to fight infection diseases", acknowledging the "strong link between science and action". Hosted by the Institute of Environmental Science and Research and the University of Otago, such a platform would enable better expertise and readiness when new threats arise, explaining: "a network of experts would work together on set research questions but in collaboration with health services and the community". [21]

But, as well as looking to the future, we shouldn't forget to acknowledge that there have already been some remarkable scientific stories emerging during the pandemic. Here, we explore one of them, as reported in the *Scientific American*: how for researchers "the emergence of the disease was an all-hands-on-deck moment". In order to develop an effective vaccine to halt the viruses spread, and diminish its effects, the focus was on finding the virus's genome sequence. "Scientists formed a high-speed scientific hive mind and delivered a super effective vaccine faster than anyone thought possible ... Researchers and clinicians spontaneously organized into focused teams and working groups to solve issues quickly," as well as adapting the ways in which they communicated and how they published their findings. [22]

This was the topic of another *Scientific American* piece, this one by Britt Glaunsinger, in which she explored the implications of the collaborative nature of the coronavirus research, saying that scientists could now "leverage all this effort to better understand other viruses and disease". She suggested that the positive experience of such collaborative research could well be the way of the future: "It will make future work pay off more than if all those individuals went back to just their own niches." This is an important lesson to take forward, given that "this is not going to be the last spillover pandemic we [will] see. It is not going to be the last public health crisis." The lessons learnt from the effectiveness of the Covid research is acknowledged outside of the lab, too, having "given the public a sense of how important it is to have sustained investment in science", she says. [23]

In early April 2023 it was announced that the payoff has arrived. *The Guardian* captures the moment in the headline "A silver lining: how Covid ushered in a vaccine's golden era" followed by the lead-in line "Pandemic accelerated advances in vaccine technology, opening up possibilities for combating array of diseases". [24] Five months later the Nobel Prize in Physiology or Medicine was awarded to the two scientists who created the technology behind mRNA Covid vaccines. The New Zealand Herald explained the significance of their work: "Katalin Kariko and Drew Weissman worked together at the University of Pennsylvania to modify the building blocks of RNA to elicit a positive immune response from the genetic material. The work laid the groundwork for Pfizer and Moderna's Covid-19 mRNA jabs which saved millions of lives." [25]

In May 2024 *The Guardian*'s science editor Ian Sample reported that a vaccine had been created with the potential to protect against a broad range of coronaviruses, including those not yet known. This enabled "a change in strategy towards 'proactive vaccinology', where vaccines are designed and readied for manufacture before a potentially pandemic virus emerges." The work was the result of a collaboration between the universities of Cambridge and Oxford in England, and the California Institute of Technology in America. He quoted the senior author of the study in question, Professor Mark Howarth, as saying the work would be ongoing: "Scientists did a great job in quickly producing an extremely effective Covid vaccine during the last pandemic, but the world still had a massive crisis with a huge number of deaths. We need to work out how we can do even better than that in the future, and a powerful component of that is starting to build the vaccines in advance." Nevertheless, the report's lead author, graduate researcher Rory Hills, said, "it takes us one step forward towards our goal of creating vaccines before a pandemic has even started". (26)

The constant need to understand the nature of the virus has led scientists to explore what *The Post* has described as "the mystery of why the coronavirus left some victims in intensive care and others with no symptoms at all". The article goes on to say that this mystery is now a step closer to being solved, thanks to a study led by Imperial College London: "Scientists at British institutions have uncovered a process through which people can defeat the virus before infection can take hold ... [This] could lead to new treatments for diseases, and to vaccines that copy the body's immune system response." In an effort to understand how immune systems responded to the virus, a sample of healthy volunteers who had never tested positive for the coronavirus were exposed to the virus. The researchers monitored the lining of the volunteers' noses as well as their immune responses. "Some rapidly cleared the virus and showed increased activity in mucosal immune cells without evidence of a widespread immune response. This suggests that they managed to beat the virus before it had a chance to enter their system. [Other] participants later developed full-blown Covid-19, and these volunteers were found to have had a slower immune response in the nose, which scientists believe allowed the virus to establish itself there." (27)

REFLECTING

The preceding section on Covid-19 is intended to set the context which now provides time for us to once more think of the pandemic in another way: how it has given us this singular opportunity to reflect on our own lives and values, what we want, what our priorities will be, and the choices we want to make. This is our unique instructive moment (28) if we choose to make it so. This is not to say that we are done with the Covid virus, or it with us. Certainly more work needs to be undertaken "to become better prepared for new variants — as well as whatever novel virus emerges next". (29) Even so, things look promising, with recent advances in proactive vaccines neatly capturing the way that teams of scientists can now quickly change the face of scientific research to be ready when new threats emerge. Perhaps we can adopt the scientists' mindset in transitioning, so that we, too, can make changes and transition. This means to taking steps to reframe and reappraise how we live with Covid-19", as psychologist Dr Sarb Johal had suggested in a Radio New Zealand interview that was subsequently reported in *The New Zealand Herald*. [30] In doing so, the question remains: are we ready to take on the opportunity that we have been given and begin to reflect on our lifestyles and make those choices to change for the good?

REIMAGINING OUR WORKING LIVES

There are two aims when considering the pandemic as a vehicle for exploring how we may reimagine our working lives as we reflect on the question of *why we work in the way that we do*. Remember that the energy that fuelled the pandemic as a vehicle for change comes from the idea that this is a "uniquely instructional moment" where we will "gain a better sense of the opportunities that await [us]". [31] Our first aim is to consider contemporary working lives and identify why there is such an urgent need to make changes, and then to explore what progress has been made when thinking about the research surrounding the changes mooted surrounding hybrid working.

We begin by acknowledging the claim by 4 Day Week Global's Andrew Barnes : "It comes as no surprise that stress and mental health issues (often work-related) can be viewed as a modern pandemic." [32] We then explore the role that our contemporary working lives play in this, again deferring to Barnes: "The way we're working isn't working for us, our employers or for our families." [33] Professor Julia Hobsbawm writes that the "world of work was already quite sick before the coronavirus took hold", with reported levels of work-related stress being extremely high, and overwork common with devastating consequences. She concludes that "working life has been due for a shake-up for a long time" and while it is not that "questions about work were not being asked before Covid-19 but they were in the background" and largely ignored. "We've known for years that work was not working properly." [34]

Other writers have joined what can now be called a growing consensus. Organisational behaviourist, consultant and business advisor Professor

Lynda Gratton writes: "Long before the arrival of the [Covid-19] pandemic, we knew we'd got into bad working habits: scheduling too many meetings, putting up with long commutes, not spending enough time with our families and feeling the pressure to be 'aways on' ... The wear and tear on our mental health and our increasing carbon footprint warned us our way of working was wrong." [35] Cognitive neuroscientist Dr Sara Mednick makes the following points: "It takes an extraordinary amount of time, energy, and other resources to respond to the pressures bearing down on you from work ... or what is described as 'the daily grind' ... And it's not just the long hours of unrelenting paper pushing that can bring on burnout ... [there is also] the expectation that work should take priority over personal physical and mental health". [36]

Jeff Schwartz and colleagues assert that the defining ethic in the modern workplace is "more, bigger, faster". They explain: "More information than ever is available to us, and the speed of every transaction has increased exponentially, prompting a sense of permanent urgency and endless distraction. We have more customers and clients to please, more e-mails to answer, more phone calls to return, more tasks to juggle, more meetings to attend, more places to go, and more hours we feel we must work to avoid falling further behind." They then ask us to consider our own experience, and then ask: "What's the cost to you of the way that you are working? How truly engaged are you? What's the impact on those you supervise and those you love?" [37] It is Barnes who answers: "[w]hen punishing work schedules become the norm, workers pay the price with their physical and mental health". [38]

It doesn't need to be like this. The desire for change was making its presence felt, as Julia Hobsbawm writes, "before Covid-19 happened: technology and its relationship to humans, flexible working — what we now call 'hybrid working' — but there were also bigger philosophical arguments about the meaning of work itself ... The pandemic lifted the lid on a desire to work differently, or less or with more life balance ... The pandemic brought workplaces centre-stage in the debate about the future of work." [39]

Others echo these themes. Professor Gratton writes, "the pandemic has presented the unique opportunity to 'raise the bar' and 'really lift up' in part because it removed institutional lag, or the delay between institutions and businesses implementing the changes that individuals want and need." She says that another change is that leaders "experienced these tensions first-hand" during lockdown, giving them a new sense of understanding and empathy. The pandemic not only "taught them a great deal", it also gave them an opportunity "to create a stronger alignment between rhetoric and reality ... our collective experiences of the pandemic has created a once-in-a lifetime opportunity to rethink what the workers among us want from work and our working lives and what those of us who are leaders want to encourage and institute within our organizations." She concludes: "the time is now". [40]

Barnes explains that as the pressure for work to change has mounted, "work as a social and economic construct is becoming less stable ... [and so] business leaders, policymakers, workers' unions and climate and equal pay campaigners will collectively ... put their energy into bringing our work practices into the twenty-first century". [41] It is the pandemic that has given us the nudge and a once-in-a-lifetime opportunity to make change and, for those of us who can, to reimagine our working lives. This is a context in which the need for change was brought centre-stage and increased in urgency. Even so, as Julia Hobsbawm says: "No one anticipated ... a global pandemic, let alone prepared for it. Far from it. This made 2019 the last year of modern working life as it had been known since 1945." [42]

PROGRESS TOWARDS HYBRID WORKING

With this context in mind, we now turn to exploring what progress has been made with the changes that have been mooted surrounding hybrid working. Initially, as organisations grappled with the practicalities and implications of flexible working driven by the pandemic and the requirement to work from home, this change frequently led to speculation on what work might look like in the future. This quickly led to an expectation that "a hybrid model of working from both office and home" would become more common. As Richard Walker posits in *The Dominion Post* in 2021: "It's the promise of technology that has been talked about for a long time ... this forced experiment through Covid-19 is going to allow us to do that a lot more." [43] Bear in mind, however, that the flexibility of hybrid working is limited to office-based ("white-collar") workers, leading it to being described by Professor Julia Hobsbawm as "a new era for professional work which blows away the cobwebs of a stale working model". She concludes: "the degree of agency to choose your place and hours of work will come to define us far more than the old classifications. Being a 'white collar' or a 'blue collar' could be replaced by being a 'hybrid have' or a 'hybrid have-not' worker instead." [44]

Research by Professor Jarrod Haar, has shown that hybrid workers are the happiest of the various work groups. He puts this down to the hybrid model offering worker more freedom as well as indicating that their employers trust them: "If my boss says, 'Yes, you can work from home for a couple of days of the week', the signal you're receiving from your boss is 'I trust you to do your job.'" [45] Professor Haar adds that "the evidence shows the hybrid workforce is the new normal — and that is to be welcomed". [46]

Commentators, like Peter Griffin in *The New Zealand Listener*, have been quick to point that "the work from home movement in New Zealand faces logistical challenges but the benefits are compelling". [47] The challenges generally identified concerned the ratio of days worked in the office to those worked at home. For a time the model generally debated suggested three days in the office and two days from home, which gained a level of popularity with a growing consensus to support it. Professor Haas describes this model as "the sweet spot", being ideal for both employers and employees. He adds: "as terrible as the pandemic has been, it has pushed the opportunity of working from home to a new reality for many". [48]

But remember, hybrid working has been described as a work in progress and a great experiment. So it is entirely understandable that, as Andrew Barnes and Stephanie Jones put it, "work as a social and economic construct is becoming less stable", [49] and therefore that there is also a sense that there is still work to do. Researchers are continuing to debate the degree to which "the hybrid patterns being introduced today are far from fixed or settled". Julia Hobsbawn thinks the form hybrid working takes is not important in the long run: "What matters is where things end up — and they do so in a way that acknowledges changes that have been building up for decades waiting, perhaps, for this extraordinary time." [50] Communications and management expert Christine Armstrong argues: "Ultimately, the future of work will be experimental — we will need to work it out and it will be messy, and we will make mistakes ... While there is no clear roadmap, what we do have is an opportunity to reset how we work: This is a moment to change, reset and rethink it. It's ours for the taking, but we have to make some decisions." [51]

Professor Lynda Gratton asks us to "reimagine place and time". In doing so, she argues: "There is no one-size-fits-all solutions, no silver bullet, no list of best practices to copy. Rather it is the design process that begins ... with [the] understanding that [it] will become the basic canvas from you to reimagine work." In her view: "whilst looking at 'best practice' it is useful to broaden your imagination; ultimately each one of us and our organizations has to find a way that uniquely reflects [your] own purpose, context and capabilities ... The time is now — we are faced with some significant choices — do we go back to our old ways of working or do we use this as an opportunity to completely redesign work and make it more purposeful, productive and fulfilling for all?" [52] Let's not forget, Professor Gratton reminds us, that "the pandemic has created a chance to create a stronger alignment between the rhetoric and reality". [53]

The research shows what the reality is, and that now is the moment to seize this extraordinary time and the opportunity it offers — and take it in such a way that harnesses the benefits that are described so compellingly.

HAVE NEW WAYS OF WORKING PREVAILED?

Now, with the 'great experiment' settling, it is time to consider not only whether that moment was grasped, but also, more importantly, whether it has prevailed. As Professor Gratton expresses it: "the pandemic created a chance to create a stronger alignment between rhetoric and reality", whereas prior to the pandemic, organisations "found it hard to move from the rhetoric of flexibility to the reality of putting into practice". [54]

As Virginia Fallon reports it, in an item in *The Post*: "When people were ordered in the early days of the pandemic to pack up and go home, it became a social change that's unlikely ever to be entirely undone. And really, it doesn't have to be. Both during and after that initial lockdown, office workers found that not only could they manage their job just as effectively, if not better from home, but it was cheaper, healthier, and all-round nicer to do so." She adds: "Because as bosses and business associations try to guilt-trip workers into supporting their cities by getting back to the office, they know full well what they're asking them to sacrifice ... Mainly though, there's life outside work, even when you're working from home. Instead of this continued focus on what has cost the country, perhaps it's time to look at what it's saved." [55]

A team of researchers at Massey University put it this way: "more than two years after the first COVID-19 lockdowns, employers are calling their employees back to the office — but are also having to respond to employee push back. Employees are expecting and asking for more flexibility in where they work — they aren't just quietly accepting the 'old ways' of working. Workers have had a taste of work-life flexibility and are demanding this more frequently and with more confidence." [56] Two headlines in 2023 in *The Post* say it all when reporting on hybrid working: "NZ companies embrace hybrid working trends" and "Kiwis embrace flexiwork". [57]

In the piece under the first headline, a CBRE-NZ survey "uncovered a surprising shift in the workplace dynamics of New Zealand businesses ... New Zealand companies are not only keeping the office alive but also leading the way in adapting to hybrid working models ... According to the survey, 52% of New Zealand organizations in the survey have revamped their work-place designs to accommodate new working methods. Almost 90% of survey respondents have reduced or plan to reduce desk or workstation numbers." [58] Shannon Williams, in *ITBrief*, finds: "Offsetting these changes there is increased focus on providing more communal and collaborative spaces alongside more private quiet spaces and focus rooms." [59] *The Post* article explains: "Defining a hybrid working strategy is crucial to getting this right ... the primary challenge is maintaining and building a strong culture when employees spend less time in the office ... The survey provides a valuable counter argument to the 'office is dead' mantra that is so often rolled out ... The office is not an endangered species; it is evolving as organisations start to implement workspace design changes that reflect the new ways of working alongside evolving location and building-specific requirements for amenities." [60]

The second *Post* headline captures the same issues in its "Kiwis embrace flexiwork". *Here*, the 2023 Office Sentiment Survey-JLL showed that "90% of employees say they're happy with the flexible working arrangements offered by their employer ... This shows [that employers] are thinking more about the wellbeing of their staff and how they can best attract and retain top talent with a strategic modern workplace that caters to a wide range of needs ... [However, many organisations] are yet to start the journey of providing the optimum space for their employees and understanding the importance of getting this right and attract staff." [61] For Richard Kauntze, writing in

The Guardian, the message is clear: "The purpose of the office [is being] transformed and is evolving alongside the role of 'office work' and it should benefit both the workforce and local community." [62] In the *Waikato Times*, Luke Malpass recounts how Ron Hennin, the CEO of NIB Health Insurance, "came in on the thesis that we could challenge a market that was incredibly staid, incredibly static". He has endeavoured to introduce a new culture of "not that many desks, lots of collaborative places. Flexibility." Malpass quotes Hennin as saying: "We're completely flexible here … and it's the kind of the office where you just wander around and you get a feel of what people are doing … By design, there are fewer desks than employees. We've tried to create spaces where people don't have to leave the office to relax." [63]

It is interesting to note how managers in New Zealand have been incredibly enterprising in the ways they have tackled the long-felt demand for flexibility. They have gone beyond the boundaries of hybrid models to express flexibility while at the same time offering more enterprising solutions. Under the headline "Boss sees value in gentle start to week", the Post's Jonny Mahon-Heap explains a work model called "bare minimum Mondays" that encourages "employees to take it easy at the start of the working week as a way of preventing burnout". He continues: "Fans of the trend point out how the practice can help employees set their own pace, catch up on chores, and ease into the working week … [Commentators suggest] it's better to reframe it and say, 'What is the best way to make sure you are set up for the rest of the week' … [while as well] it's a matter of building trust between employer and employee and understanding that this is the best way to address potential burnout." [64] Chereè Kinnear writes in *The New Zealand Herald* of another enterprising way to capture the notion of flexibility with Actionstep, a New Zealand software company, offering its employees unlimited annual leave. Vice-president of engineering Stevie "describes it as a "high-trust model", explaining: "It allows people to take leave they need and then come in and do their best work for us … The people are the business and this way we can ensure we have happy and healthy staff who can do their best in their jobs." [65]

The thinking behind flexibility is clear. It sets up satisfied and happy workers. Research also points to workers being more productive and efficient when offered flexible working. This means that leadership also needs to change if flexible arrangements are to be successful. Remember that empathy, trust and social connection are the key for success rather than traditional top-down management. As Hobsbawm points out, employees want to "choose how to manage the time [they] spend working in a way that suits [them] rather than the traditional nine to five, Monday to Friday", [66] and the new twenty-first-century leadership style based on empathy, trust and social connection gives managers the capacity to manage the new patterns of working.

Will these changes — flexible and hybrid working, and the four-day week — prevail? The answer appears to be affirmative. Since 2021, Professor Haar has been tracking workplace trends. Talking on RNZ's *Morning Report* he revealed that even though the overall number of people working from home has dropped, "a hybrid of working in and out of the office has become the new normal". [67] Similarly, BusinessNZ advocacy director Catherine Beard, speaking on *One News* in January 2024, says that while "employers are talking about the pros and cons of the flexible approach to where you work", "the hybrid work model — where people split their time between working from home and working at the office — is still firmly bedded in. She explained that this is especially the case "in the current tighter job market … Offering flexible work arrangements is still key to recruiting staff in that environment." [68] Other experts agree, with *One News* reporting: "Whatever happens in the future, [they] think the way people work has likely changed permanently, [and they] can't see the country heading back to what work life looked like prior to the pandemic." [69]

Hobsbawm sums it up thus: "Covid forced the world into an experiment on remote work as a viable replacement for in-office work for a lot of groups that would never have thought to test the hypothesis. And what they discovered … is that it was certainly plausible. [70] Paraphrasing the view of the chair of the Climate Change Commission, Dr Rod Carr, we were doing in reality what in theory we thought was not possible. Looking at the results of various local and international surveys "also shows that New Zealand's experience throughout the pandemic and subsequent 'return to office' has been significantly different from our global counterparts, … 65% of NZ organizations surveyed have embraced a hybrid working model, combining in-office work with regular remote work". [71] *The Guardian* reports that organisations are now thinking about what is described as a structured in-person work pattern with employees "expected to be in at least twice a week". [72] So, what is the answer to the question raised: will hybrid working prevail? The answer lies in the survey data and the research, which shows how flexibility has been driven by the pandemic from the shadows of academic journals, and now is focused on the redesign of workplaces to accommodate new patterns of working and building a culture that ensures hybrid working will be successful. As one executive surveyed said: "we want to enshrine new working patterns so that they outlast the pandemic". [73]

THE FINAL PANDEMIC: DISINFORMATION AND PROTEST

"Head to Parliament today to marvel at the greenness of the lawn. Ride the slide. It would have been unimaginable just one year and many dollars ago." [74] The occupation of Parliament's grounds began on 7 February 2022 and ended on 2 March, following violent behaviours. Yet while the wild behaviours and the senseless destruction were in plain sight, the "machinery that drives disinformation is often well-hidden and operated by sophisticated software". [75] It may be less obvious to see, but it is easy to read and disseminate, and is given a credence that is not warranted but is afforded it simply because it is the written word. As Andrea Gawrylewski writes in *Scientific American*: "Lies, extremism and the manipulation of reality seem to be common themes in today's current events." [76]

So while the government was battling the Covid-19 pandemic, it was also fighting against the newly arrived wave of rife disinformation. More recently, there has been dismay at how quickly disinformation and conspiracy theories can seamlessly glide from one pandemic to another — from coronavirus to the climate crisis. As Andrea Gawrylewski's *Scientific American* article "Truth Under Attack" points out, this simply illustrates how fundamental and central the science message is: "Never has it been more important to understand the science of how we humans determine what is truth." She continues: "Civic life suffers because of these malevolent forces. Turmoil, anxiety and a sense that society is in jeopardy lead to the kind[s] of polarization that makes winning an argument more important than understanding opponent's viewpoints." [77] In this way, the denial of truth, expertise and sound data has become a hallmark of a post-truth era.

Also writing in the *Scientific American*, Tanya Lewis recounts that because "the science [for Covid-19] was evolving daily [and] there was no expert consensus or body of established research to draw on ... there were plenty of people willing to exploit this information vacuum, creating a secondary epidemic of misinformation ... It didn't take long for bad actors to weaponize the confusion to spread misinformation ... There has been no more consequential or bitter battleground ... than vaccines" [78] and the mandates. In *Nature*, Kathleen Higgins considers that the battle is made more difficult because "Ralph Keyes's 2004 declaration that we have arrived in a post-truth era seems distressingly plausible". [79] Another example of how disinformation can seamlessly glide between topics came with the warning from experts in 2023 "that Artificial Intelligence is likely to be used to spread misinformation and disinformation in the lead-up" to New Zealand's general election in October 2023. [80]

What can be done in the battle for truth? We know about the battle that surrounds Facebook, X (formerly Twitter) and now the Tik Tok app, and "the growing concerns ... within Western governments". [81] We also know the battles around disinformation's nature: "it spreads faster than true information because of its social and emotional qualities". What's more, "Research shows that misinformation can be 'sticky' if it's frequently liked, commented, or shared — or if it evokes feelings of fear. Our cognitive biases also play a role — confirmation bias means we're less likely to doubt or verify information if it aligns with our worldview. In the illusory truth effect repeated exposure to false information makes us more likely to believe it." [82]

On the other hand, Higgins says: "Scientists must keep reminding society of the importance of the social mission of science — to provide the best information possible as the basis for public policy. And they should publicly affirm the intellectual virtues that they so effectively model: critical thinking, sustained inquiry, and revision of beliefs on the basis of evidence." [83] Melinda Wenner Moyer counsels: "Conspiracy theories are a human reaction to confusing times ... So, if we look out for suspicious signatures and ask thoughtful questions about the stories we encounter, it is still possible to separate truth from lies. It may not always be an easy task, but it is a crucial one for all of us." [84] Former prime ministerial science advisor Sir Peter Gluckman sums it up in this question: "Once we can no longer discriminate what is real from what is not real, what does that do to us as human beings?" [85] We leave the last word to George Monbiot, who writing in *The Guardian Weekly* posed the question: "Why do people invent false conspiracies when there are so many real ones to worry about?" [86]

CONCLUSIONS

Three themes emerge for this section. They are: *never has it been more important to understand the science of how we humans determine the truth.* The second reflects *the nature of misinformation and conspiracy theories, and how easily they can slide from one issue to another.* And, thirdly: *how do we battle misinformation?* This is a crucial question to ask, but a difficult one to answer, primarily because the way the messages are conveyed, with the absence of an editorial process giving the consumer the freedom and opportunity to interpret the messages as they please or how it suits them to. But, as Moyer says, the hope is that it is still possible "to separate truth from lies. It may not always be an easy task, but it is a crucial one for all of us." [87]

A key first 'rule' is to be vigilant so that you avoid being fooled. To be able to do this, we need to learn more about the ways in which we fall for fake news. "This entails looking for 'the red flags' — such as identifying people impersonating an expert, or discrediting or trolling opponents — and then, just as importantly, responding to them. This is because "inoculating people before they are exposed to false information, rather than debunking it after the fact, is more effective". So we are told: "Rather than simply correcting facts it's important to address the social and emotional factors at play by discrediting the motives underlying a piece of misinformation. Repeat factual information and use social engagement for good." [88]

To end this chapter and this book, I have listed a number of my reflections after writing each chapter. You may wish to go through the list and choose the ones you think are relevant for you to reflect on, using them as a prompt and framework to help you think things through. All they do is give you a broad structure to prompt your thoughts. The book has covered a range of issues, and these simply represent my attempt to capture some of the key ones.

MAINSTREAM REFLECTIONS

1

The first is essentially one about reappraisal coping. As I have noted many times, the Covid-19 pandemic has many faces, and when we reflect on it we are naturally almost immediately drawn to thinking of it in terms of illness, lockdowns, regulations, mandates, alert levels, trauma and anxiety, protests, and of course grief and death. But now we have also been given an opportunity to move beyond that phase and think of the pandemic as an opportunity to harness growth and reassurance through its other faces. It is clear that for some it has been a vehicle of transition and learning and even awakening. So now is the time, argues Jeff Schwartz, where we can think of the pandemic in terms of moving "from 'disruption to innovation to creation' ... as our 'uniquely instructive moment'." (Think about the number of times I have used the words opportunity, growth, well-being, and hope!) We should, argues Schwartz, "take the view of the future as a broad set of opportunities that will reflect whatever we think is possible". [89]

2

When thinking about how you cope, four issues may give help you understand the stress process. The first is the significance of *how the encounter is appraised* — the assessment you make about how confronting the stressor is. This is the key to understanding the stress process, as this appraisal sets a personal context for you that shapes how you cope, colouring and driving the coping strategies you will use. The second issue is about *how effective your coping* is gauged to be. Remember, figuring out how effective your coping is can be a complex business. One way you can think about it is whether it is a good fit with the context that has prompted the coping strategy. *Negative and positive emotions* are all part of the coping process: positive emotions may emerge and give you a moment of respite and a means to replenish your resources and sustain future coping. The final issue is that *coping requires effort,* and this is key to sustaining your coping and to building your resilience, perseverance and endurance.

3

The overriding theme that emerges from the pandemic and the climate crisis is that *we are all in this together*. Perhaps, the most powerful expression of this theme comes from the phrase *"the team of 5 million"*, as it immediately expresses that collaboration and working together is the most powerful tool we have in any crisis. Although of course there were some who wished to remain on the reserve bench. However the theme of working together is expressed in much of the writing that has been cited, and appears throughout the work of those commenting about the pandemic or the climate crisis. The theme is simply expressed by Robin Nelson: "Our fates are bound together.

Taking care of others is taking care of ourselves." [90] It is a sentiment that Sir Ashley Bloomfield would endorse when he says "the one big lesson I take away is we tend to underestimate the capability and capacity and resourcefulness of our communities". [91]

In the climate crisis it is explained in this way: "the best thing we can do for climate justice as individuals is to find ways to work collectively." [92] Greta Thunberg sets out the overriding lesson in no uncertain terms: "Together, we can do the seemingly impossible. But make no mistake — no one else is going to do it for us. This is up to us, here and now. You and me ... It's happening right here and right now." [93] It is as Professor James Renwick writes: "We really are all in this together. It is going to take effort from all of us, in countries and communities large and small. The best thing we can do is to cooperate, to help and support each other, to be empathetic. To love one another, basically." [94] Although the symbols of the pandemic are no longer present in our lives, although the virus lingers, we are in a climate crisis, so supporting each other and working together should not be taken lightly or quickly forgotten or ignored. As David Runciman tells us in *The Guardian Weekly,* this theme is an expression and "a reminder of what we all have in common. An acute awareness of our shared vulnerability [that just] might create the conditions for a renewed sense of purpose in tackling global problems." [95] In his, valedictory speech to the House in May 2024, the then Minister for Climate Change James Shaw, when reflecting on his role, left us with this message: "The only true legacy we can leave is to cherish the world we've been given and to bequeath a better one for our descendants." [96]

4

We need to acknowledge the way that technology has changed our lives. It has not only changed the way we live, "but shaped our discipline — *cyberpsychology.* [97] Let's reflect on, and explore, this growing body of knowledge; for example, there is technostress [98] and problematic internet use, [99] dependency and addiction, [100] cyberslacking and cyberloafing, [101] and cyberbullying. [102] These are a reflection of the role of technology in our lives, and the point here is to reflect on these topics, as they could well be describing the "emerging realities of contemporary work". [103] Do you get a sense that some of these topics have captured your lifestyle? And, more importantly, what it is doing to your lifestyle — and what are you going to do about it? In her opinion piece in *The Guardian Weekly*, Martha Gill looks at "the personality changes the internet brings out in us: Tribalism, bullying, the wildfire spread of 'crazes', 'instant gratification culture', the triumph of the temper tantrum: future anthropologists may observe that the behaviour of adults online very much resembles that of children offline." [(104)]

5

In the first decades of the new millennium we witnessed the growth of the positive psychology movement. This new movement, now defined as "positive psychology 2.0", seeks to explore a balanced approach that will promote well-being and decrease mental illness by addressing both the positive and negative aspects in life, managing the negatives and enhancing the positives. Psychologist Paul Wong explains that this approach "depicts the complex interactions in living a full life ... and embrace[s] life in totality" — the good and the bad. "To fully experience life, to feel keenly alive, is to embrace life in totality." [(105)] So, we need to explore the positive in the same rigorous way as we have traditionally pursued the negative to "embrace life in totality". [(106)] When we read the title of an article expressing the aims of positive psychology, "Positive organizational behaviour in the workplace: The impact of hope, optimism, and resilience", [(107)] the aims are well set out. Perhaps we can use that as our mantra, as a context to order and balance our thoughts, to embrace the good and the bad. As Wong reminds us, positive psychology provides "a hopeful framework for developing good and fully functioning human beings and psychologically institutions in spite of the negative and finitude in human existence". [(108)] Perhaps, the positive psychology movement is being endorsed when Prime Minister Jacinda Ardern talks about "an economics of kindness". [(109)]

Positive psychology is all about exploring how people flourish; giving it the same empirical emphasis as we have traditionally given to the negative. But we need to be careful to not fall into what Conor Feehly calls the "happiness trap". "We know that a positive attitude can be good for us ... and it isn't surprising that we want to believe things will turn out better for us if we have a positive attitude", [(110)] [but being positive all the time or substituting with being happy all the time — the happiness trap] "can be 'a form of denial a 'head in the sand' ... to the reality of life's problem. It can also suffocate real feelings" [(111)] Research by Professor Maya Tamir at the Hebrew University of Jerusalem has found that, "regardless of culture, greater mental well-being is linked with feeling emotions that we believe are appropriate to our situation, rather than just having positive emotions regardless of context — 'feeling right' as opposed to 'feeling good'." [112] Remember, as Karen Nimmo reminds us: "Optimism is a good thing, it can uplift and inspire. It can nurture hope in others. And in a world that keeps throwing down challenges, it's becoming increasingly rare. So, hold onto your positivity. But don't leak it all over every[thing] else." [113] Russ Harris and Bev Aisbett also warn us that "trying to be perpetually positive can be downright STRESSFUL". [114] The last word goes to Conor Feehly: "The right amount of it [positivity] in the right place and at the right time can work wonders. But we also need to allow space for people to accept the adversity that comes with life. Resilience and growth are attained when we fight through difficult situations." [115]

6

When thinking about sustained working, Tony Schwartz and Catherine McCarthy remind us that it is "about managing your energy, not your time". It is not taking for granted what fuels your capacity to work: your energy. So you need to think about energy-depleting behaviours, avoiding the constant distractions that accompany technology and taking responsibility for coping with them in ways that restores your energy. Schwartz and McCarthy explain: "The core problem with working longer hours is that time is a finite resource. Energy is a different story." There are many ways to systematically expand and renew energy, a key one being pausing and taking breaks. They reveal that taking "intermittent breaks for renewal is associated with higher and more sustainable performance. It is possible to get a great deal of recovery in a short time – if it involves a ritual that allows you to disengage from work and truly change channels." [116]

7

It is Yuval Noah Harari who reminds us that "humans were always far better at inventing tools than using them wisely". [117] Our lives seem to be designed around a requirement to be constantly 'switched on and plugged in', making us increasingly more oblivious to the life that this is creating for us. But Cal Newport informs us that a counter culture is emerging, where there are calls for *digital minimalism*, simply because "new technologies seem to invade [our] cognitive landscape". [118] Sherry Turkle tells us that the risk becomes that "we expect more from the technology and less from each other". She questions: "Technology reshapes the landscape of our emotional lives, but is it offering us the lives we want to lead? It is not what [technology does] for us but what [it does] to us, to our ways of thinking about ourselves, our relationships, our sense of being human." [119] The ideas outlined above are directed at all of us. They give us the opportunity to reflect on the lifestyles that technology creates instead of focusing on "having to have" the technology itself. This timely rebalancing has got to the stage, Sarah Catherall tells us, that European countries "are taking employee's well-being a step further by-passing legislation giving them a right to switch off after work hours". [120]

8

This leads us to reflect on what work–life balance means for us. The BBC's Kate Morgan has done just this, as she explains: "Amid the vast uncertainty of the pandemic era, one thing is clear, more than ever — and more than everything — people want a healthy work–life balance." We now have to thank hybrid working and the four-day work week, as they have introduced for some the reality of flexibility, something that organisations have been grappling with for some time, and is now at the centre of our working lives. Work–life balance is "now broader, deeper and more nuanced — and it is no longer a one-size-fits all". Morgan asks what has changed, and discover that now it is workers, not the companies they work for, who are defining and designing what constitutes "balance" for their individual circumstances. Morgan speaks with Associate Professor Lupu of Paris's ESSEC Business School, who tells her that workers no longer define work–life "as equal time spent in each place, or equilibrium between personal and professional pursuits. Instead, they began to embrace a kind of work–life integration that acknowledges the two are inextricably entwined, and endeavours to make the relationship between the two a healthy one. It is 'Employee-defined balance'." Lupu suggests: "It's not exactly accurate to call it work–life balance, or even work–life *integration*. For me, it's more like a work–life navigation." [121] On reflection, work–life navigation is a thoughtful way to describe it. It gives an immediate sense of freedom and, control, and, more importantly, it offers you the chance to navigate the journey yourself.

9

The future of work appears to be shaping up as a model that is built around different levels of what Alison Maitland and Peter Thomson call "individual autonomy and a culture of trust and responsibility". [(122)] They explain that "careers will no longer be linear or ladder-shaped, but will become more fluid, with people having "more jobs during their careers, and more careers during their working lives". We will see fewer instances of employees having "lifelong loyalty to a single employer", but instead "individuals will rely more heavily on marketing their unique skills, reputation and 'personal brand'". [(123)] It is important to think about your career and how it is shaped. Careers can also be built on serendipitous moments: if you take up these opportunities that present themselves, they are likely to take you in a different direction or offer a different opportunity for you to use your skills. It is important to recognise, too, that careers are not always as formal as they are presented, and it is in these informal serendipitous moments that offer personal levels of satisfaction. So, the message is: don't ignore these moments when they occur.

10

Leadership must also change as these other aspects of our lives change, since leadership is fundamentally contextual. Harold Hillman puts it succinctly: "the biggest lesson of all from COVID-19 pandemic is that we often consciously underplay the importance of social connection, taking it for granted more than we ever care to think". Instead, we should "make empathy real and to make it right, for leaders who believe that connection truly matters". [(124)] Reflecting back on the pandemic and the dramatic changes it has made to working lives, he is absolutely right to position empathy at the core of leadership. It is the "human moments" that are important and need to be at the heart of leadership in times of uncertainty — it is being authentic, empathetic and trusting. So, reflecting on your leadership, you may want to think about where in your leadership style you place empathy.

11

Many of the changes we have mentioned — like reimagining our working lives, our careers and the future of work, the climate crisis, and the pandemic — are already being driven by Millennials and Generation Zers. Their fingerprints are all over the demand for flexibility at work, and they are taking a lead role in building a global movement to stimulate action to mitigate the climate crisis. The presence of Generation Zers in the workforce is being felt in many ways. They have now turned their attention to refining what good work means, which, the BBC's Meredith Turits tells us, it involves "enabling a worker to live the lifestyle they want ... in an industry that aligns with their values and passion and allowing them to build their own personal brand". [125]

12

When thinking about good work, Diane Mulcahy points out that it is also important to recognise that "working lives will be made up of a variety of diverse work and work experiences". [126] James Suzman says this raises questions "about the nature of work and our relationship with it ... and what does this tell us about the way we work?" [127] Lisa Leong and Monique Ross suggest that "it's less about *what* you want to do, and more about *who* you want to be". They explain: "Who are you and what that can tell you about what you should do next ... that's why we need to think about who we are, beyond our identity at work." [128] Simone Stolzoff says it is a matter of defining our relationship to our work "without letting it define you". It boils down to, she says, "how to balance the pursuit of meaningful work with the risk of letting your job subsume who you are". [129] She acknowledges that "work does give meaning to your life", [130] but there needs to be balance so you don't fall prey to what Derek Thompson calls *workism*: "the belief that work is not only necessary to economic production, but also the centrepiece of one's identity and life's purpose". [131] Stolzoff says there need to be the realisation that work is not the only source of meaning, [132] which opens us up for our *unique instructive moment* to reflect and "examine your own relationship with your job". [133]

13

Think back to before the pandemic and reflect on the way you worked. Why? Because, as Karin Reed and Joseph Allen say: "The workplace today, has totally different expectations than it did pre-pandemic." [134] This makes it a good time to think about your habits, and patterns of working and behaviours, comparing what they were before the pandemic and what they are now. If there has been little change, then is there anything that you think is worth changing or arguing for? If there has been change, which working style gives you the most satisfaction — pre- or post-pandemic? What are the features of your job that keep you in your present employment, and what would you like to see changed to give you more satisfaction? If you can't think of what you would like to change, what is that telling you?

14

This should be thought of as a final postscript, thereby giving it a significance that should not be forgotten. In October 2023, the *New Zealand Medical Journal* reported published a call for – "continued mitigation needed to minimise the health burden from COVID-19" by "sixteen of New Zealand's leading scientists and doctors — many regular commentators during the pandemic response" that Covid and its mitigation still be on our radar. [135] Lead author, epidemiologist Professor Michael Baker said that Covid-19 was now "like an unwanted guest that no one wants to talk about any more". But it was still our leading infectious disease killer, followed by influenza, he said. The fact that at the time Prime Minister Chris Hipkins was infected with the virus was a "very sad and poignant" reminder that Covid hadn't gone away. Baker explained: "What we're really arguing is building on the momentum of the pandemic response and what we've learned from that." [136] The call received a lot of publicity, including a piece in *The New Zealand Herald* by Jamie Morton who described the call as asking "for a rethink about how the country manages all respiratory infections". At its core: "They propose a new national strategy that includes measures like raising vaccination rates for at-risk people, supporting those who are self-isolated, improving indoor air quality, encouraging masks in crowded and poorly ventilated spaces and continuing infection control across the healthcare sector." [137] The long tail of Covid-19 lingers on. Soon after the experts' plea we would learn about a sixth wave of Covid-19 sweeping through New Zealand, with the University of Canterbury's Michael Plank saying that while "the wave is likely close to its peak ... a tricky new variant already accounting for a third of cases could see it roll onto winter". [138] It is fitting that we end this book as we started — following the science — with the view of epidemiologists and scientists.

ENDNOTE

During the writing of this book, I was able to reflect on why I was fashioning an idea or an argument in a particular way. I came to the conclusion that all I was trying to do was to simply give a sense of hope and encourage the reader to feel that way as well. It has made me appreciate how powerful a tool reflection is and how much can be gained by engaging in it. This may be explained here because we — you and I — are reflecting on other people's ideas, research and experiences, which offers such fertile ground that you become inspired to rework and develop it further. That is why you should reflect on what I have written and take the same journey I have. Hopefully, by taking the time to reflect you will have the same experiences I have had, and will come away with a pocket full of fresh ways to see things and more importantly reasons to make some changes; another reason why I wrote this book.

I finish with something that Dr Rod Carr, New Zealand's climate tsar, said in an interview with *Stuff* that I was instantly drawn to. To me, it neatly sums up much of what this book is trying to achieve and, in a way, it has become my mantra: "Covid-19 has revealed that we are capable of doing things in reality that in theory we thought we couldn't." [139]

Endnotes

Preface

1   Schwartz, J., with Riss, R. (2021) *Work Disrupted: Opportunity, Resilience, and Growth in the Accelerated Future of Work*, Hoboken, New Jersey: John Wiley & Sons. p. xix.

Chapter 1: New Zealand and the Pandemic

1   https://shorthand.radionz.co.nz/coronavirus-timeline p. 2/42

2   https://shorthand.radionz.co.nz/coronavirus-timeline p. 3/42

3   https://shorthand.radionz.co.nz/coronavirus-timeline p. 3/42

4   https://www.who.int/news/item/27-04-2020-who-timeline-covid-19 p. 2/5

5   https://www.who.int/news/item/27-04-2020-who-timeline-covid-19 p. 3/5

6   https://shorthand.radionz.co.nz/coronavirus-timeline p. 3/42

7   https://www.who.int/news/item/27-04-2020-who-timeline-covid-19 p. 3/5

8   https://shorthand.radionz.co.nz/coronavirus-timeline p. 5/42

9   https://www.who.int/news/item/27-04-2020-who-timeline-covid-19 p. 5/5

10   https://shorthand.radionz.co.nz/coronavirus-timeline p. 4/42

11   https://shorthand.radionz.co.nz/coronavirus-timeline p. 8/42

12   https://shorthand.radionz.co.nz/coronavirus-timeline p. 8/42

13   https://shorthand.radionz.co.nz/coronavirus-timeline p. 11/42

14   https://shorthand.radionz.co.nz/coronavirus-timeline p. 15.42

15   https://shorthand.radionz.co.nz/coronavirus-timeline p. 16/42

16   Coughlan, T. (2020) Health workers urge level 4 alert "now" *The Dominion Post*, Monday March 23, p. 2

17   https://www.beehive.govt.nz/release/new-zealand-moves-covid-alert-level-3-then-level-4-48hours#/ p. 1/3

18   Anon (2020) 'Capital under lock and key.' *The Dominion Post*, Wednesday, March 25, p. 1

19   https://shorthand.radionz.co.nz/coronavirus-timeline p. 19/42

20   Williams, K. (2020) Coronavirus. *The Dominion Post*, Wednesday, March 25, p. 1

21   Ibid (Williams, 2020) p. 1

22   Cooke, H., & Malpass, L. (2020) Sombre mood on NZ's outlook. *The Dominion Post*, Wednesday, March 25 p. 2

23   Hobsbawm, (2022) *The Nowhere Office: Reinventing Work and the Workplace of the Future.* London: Basic Books, pp. x; 3, 4, 7

24   Gratton, L. (2022) *Redesigning Work: How to Transform Your Organization & Make Hybrid Work for Everyone.* UK: Penguin Random House UK, p. 6

25   Thompson, M. (2023) Forward to the book: *Where Is My Office? Reimagining the Workplace for the 21st Century,* (Kane, C., & Anastassiou, E) London: Bloomsbury Business, pp. 8-9

26   Malpass, L. (2020) Simple, just stay at home. *The Dominion Post*, Tuesday, March 24, p. 3

27   Ibid (Malpass) p. 3

28   Ibid (Malpass) p. 3

29   Ardern, J. (2020) We must go hard and we must go early. https://newsroom.co.nz/we-must-go-hard-and-we-must-go-early/ (Hicky, B.) p. 1. Also cited in: Jamieson, T (2020) *American Review of Public Administration*, 50 (6-7), p. 598

30   Carroll, M. (2020) Today a new normal for at-home employees. *The Dominion Post*, Monday, March 23, p. 2

31   Williams, C. (2021) *The future of work. Economist: Special Report*. April 10th p. 3

32   Ibid (Williams) p. 2

33   Ibid (Williams) p. 2

34   Ibid (Williams) p. 2

35   Cooke, H., & Malpass, L. (2020) Sombre mood on NZ's outlook. *The Dominion Post*, Wednesday, March 25, p. 2

36   Williams, K. (2020) Capital under lock and key. *The Dominion Post*, Wednesday March 25, p. 1

37   Cooke, H., & Malpass, L. (2020) Sombre mood on NZ's outlook. *The Dominion Post* Wednesday, March 25, p. 2

38   Zhong, R. (2022) Generation Covid: Roaring Twenties. *NZ Listener*, June 4, p. 16

39   Mangia, K. (2020) *Making the new normal work for you: Working from Home.* New Jersey: John Wiley & Sons. pp. 6-7

40   Schwartz, J. (2021) *Work Disrupted: Opportunity, Resilience, and Growth in the accelerated Future of Work.* New Jersey: John Wiley & Sons. pp. xix-xx

41   Warzel, C., & Petersen, A. H. (2022) *Out of Office: the big problem and bigger promise of working from home.* Melbourne & London: Scribe p. 9

42   Mangia, K. (2020) *Making the new normal work for you: Working from Home.* New Jersey: John Wiley & Sons p. 7

43   Williams, K. (2020) Capital under lock and key. *The Dominion Post*, Wednesday, March 25, p. 1

44   Anon (2020) Quiet War: (Headline on the front page) *The Dominion Post*, Friday, March 27, p. 1

45   Cooke, H. (2020) Level 4 saves 80,000 lives. *The Dominion Post*, Friday, March 27, p. 1

46   https://shorthand.radionz.co.nz/coronavirus-timeline/ p. 21/42

47   Anon. (2020) We celebrate the people essential to keeping New Zealand going through the Covid-19. (Headline on frontpage) *The Dominion Post* Thursday, Aril 9, p. 1

48   Devlin, C. (2020) Tools to aid home learning. *The Dominion Post*, Thursday, April 9, p. 2

49   Devlin C. (2020) Gluckman wants border quarantine. *The Dominion Post*, Thursday, April 9, p. 2

50   Fallon, V. (2020) Call for return to normal life. *The Dominion Post*, Tuesday, April 14, p. 1

51   Coughlan, T. (2020) PM reaffirms border controls, four-week. *The Dominion Post*, Tuesday, April 14, p. 2

52   Gray, M. (2020) https://washingpost.com/outlook/2020/11/03/abundance-caution-cliche-language-pandemic/

53   Anon (2022) PMs share plans. *The Dominion Post*, Thursday, April 16, p. 2

54   Cooke, H. (2020) Pandemic rules get blurrier. *The Dominion Post*, Friday, April 17, p. 1

55   Coughlan, T. (2020) Ardern's decision of a lifetime. *The Dominion Post*, Monday 20, p. 1

56   Cooke, H. (2020) 'Let's finish what we have started.' *The Dominion Post*, Tuesday, April 21, p. 1

57   Anon (2020) ANZAC Day at Home. *The Dominion Post*, Friday April 24, p. 1

58   Devlin, C. (2020) Call to keep up the vigilance. *The Dominion Post*, Monday, April 27, p. 4

59   Cooke, H. (2020) Pandemic: Level 3 is here. *The Dominion Post*, Tuesday, April 28, p. 1

60   Anon (2020) Taste of freedom. *The Dominion Post*, Wednesday, April 29, p. 1

61   https://shorthand.radionz/coronavirus-timeline/ p. 29/42

62   Williams, K. (2022) Bloomfield clears up 'elimination' claims. *The Dominion Post*, Wednesday, April 29, pp. 2-3

63   Martin, H. (2022) No new Covid cases-what happens now? *The Dominion Post,* Tuesday, May 5, pp. 2-3

64   Cooke, H. (2020) Coronavirus: Level 2 on Thursday sees restrictions ease. *The Dominion Post*, Tuesday, May 12, pp. 2-3

65   Earley, M. (2020) 'Play it safe' call from PM. *The Dominion Post*, Tuesday, May 12, p. 3

66   Malpass, L. (2020) Comment: 'Labour's back-to-basics Budget ...' *The Dominion Post*, Friday, May 15, p. 1

67   Martin, H. (2020) Health: Disability services, DHBs win. *The Dominion Post*, Friday, May 15, p. 4

68   Kenny, K. (2020) Covid-19: PM reveals new 'digital diary' app for tracing. *The Dominion Post*, Tuesday, May 19, pp. 3-3

69   https://www.beehive.govt.nz/release/new-zealand-joins-global-search-covid-19-vaccine/ p. 1/3

70   Devlin, C. (2020) $37m for Covid-19 vaccine. *The Dominion Post*, Wednesday, May 27, p. 3

71   https://www.beehive.govt.nz/release/new-zealand-joins-global-search-covid-19-vaccine p. 1/3

72   Coughlan, T. (2020) Coronavirus: Level 1 move: life as 'normal' as it can be. *The Dominion Post*, Tuesday, June 9, pp. 2-3

73   Bathgate, B. (2020) PM's Covid-19 epiphany on bridge. *The Dominion Post*, Wednesday, June 10, pp. 2-3

74   Cooke, H. (2020) Covid confidence is shaken by two new cases. *The Dominion Post*, Wednesday, June 17, pp. 2-3

75   Devlin, C. (2020) Covid shambles: Will person to blame step up? *The Dominion Post* Thursday, June 18, pp. 2-3

76   https://shorthand.radionz.con.nz/coronavirus-timeline/ p. 42

77   https://dpmc.govt.nz/news/new-covid-19-business-unit-dpmc/ p 1/2

78   https://www.dia.govt.nz/COVID-19Response-Update-Wednesday-12-August-2020/ p 1/3

79   https://COVID-19.govt.nz/assets/Proactive-Release/Alert-levels-and-restrictions/

80   https://www.parliament.nz/get-involved/features/looking-back-at-delayed-elections-in-new-zealands-history/ p. 1/4

81   https://www.rnz.co.nz/news/national/437359/timeline-the-year-of-covid-19-in-new-zealand/ p. 1/8

82   https://www.rnz.co.nz/news/national/425228/covid-19-auckland-to-remain-at-alert-level-2-point-5-untl-at-least-16-september-ardern/ p. 1/4

83   https://covid19.govt.nz/news/-and-data/latest-news/new-zealand-will-move-alert-level-1-auckland-will-move-to-alert-level-2-with-no-extra-restrictions/

84   https://www.dia.govt.co.nz/COVID-19-Response-Update-Monday-5-October-2020/ p. 1/4

85 Coughlan, T. (2020) Analysis: Was lockdown on the level? *The Dominion Post*, Thursday, August 20, p. 1

86 https://www.beehive.govt.nz/release/first.covid-19-vaccine-purchase-agreement-signed/ p. 1/3

87 Anon. (2020) Headline on page 1. *The Sunday Star Times*, October 18, p. 1

88 Malpass, L. (2020) Labour wins big but now the real work starts. *The Sunday Star Times*, October 18, p. 2

89 https://www.beehive.govt.nz/release/new-cabinet-covid-19-recovery/ p. 1/3

90 https://www.rnz.co.nz/political/429648/jacinda-ardern-reveals-new-cabinet-line-up-robertson-named-as-deputy-pm-live-updates/ p. 1/11

91 https://www.rnz.co.nz/news/national/437359/timeline-the-year-of-covid-19-in-new-zealand/ p. 18/32

92 https://www.rnz.co.nz/news/national/437359/timeline-the-year-of-covid-19-in-new-zealand/ p. 19/32

93 https://www.beehive.govt.nz/release/masks-be-worn-auckland-public-transport-and-all-domestic-flights/ p. 1/3

94 https://www.beehive.govt.nz/news/national/437359/timeline-the-year-of-covid-19-in-new-zealand/ p. 20/32

95 https://covid19.govt.nz/news-and-data/latest-news/new-zealands-plan-to-manage-covid19-over-summer/ p. 1

96 https://www.rnz.co.nz/news/national/437359/timeline-the-year-of-covid-19-in-new-zealand/ p. 20/32

Chapter 2: New Zealand and the pandemic 2021–2024

1 Ball, J. (2023) The Other Pandemic: *How Qanon Contaminated the World* London: Bloomsbury Publishing, pp. 6: 12

2 Harari, Y, N. (2018) 21 *Lessons for the 21st Century*. Jonathan Cape, p. 7

3 https://www.rnz.co.nz/news/national/437359/timeline-the-year-of-covid-19-in-new-zealand/ p. 22/32

4 https://www.rnz.co.nz/news/national/435107/government-grants-vaccine-suppliers-indemnity-against-claims/ p. 1/3

5 https://covid.immune.org.nz/covid-19-vaccines-nz/vaccine-safety/vaccine-approval-process-nz/ p. 1/3

6 https://www.rnz.co.nz/news/covid-19/covid-19-pfizer-biotech-vaccine-new-zealand-government-gives-formal-approval/ p. 1/5

7 https://www.beehive.govt.nz/release/new-covid-19-payment-supports-businesses/ p. 1/3

8 https://www.rnz.co.nz/news/national/436414/what-you-need-to-know-auckland-moves-to-alert-level-3-rest-of-new-zealand-to-level-2/ p. 1/5

9 https://www.rnz.co.nz/news/national/437359/timeline-the-year-of-covid-19-in-new-zealand/ p. 24/32

10 https://www.rnz.co.nz/news/national/436599/auckland-to-drop-alert-level-2-rest-of-nz-to-level-1-at-midnight/ p. 1/4

11 https://www.rnz.co.nz/news/national/436569/frontline-staff-prepare-to-get-dose-of-covid-19-pfizer-vaccine/ p. 1/4

12 https://www.rnz.co.nz/news/national/437359/timeline-the-year-of-covid-19-in-new-zealand/ p. 25/32

13   https://www.dcnz.org.nz/resources-and-publications/updates/2021/auckland-moves-to-covid-19-alert-level-1-from-11-59pm-monday-22-february/ p. 1/1

14   https://www.rnz.co.nz/news/national/437359/timeline-the-year-of-covid-19-new-zealand/ p. 26/32

15   https://www.rnz.co.nz/news/national/437067/covid-19-first-south-island-border-workers-get-vaccine-as-second-batch-of-pfizer-biotech-arrives/ p. 1/6

16   https://www.rnz.co.nz/news/national/437359/timeline-the-year-of-covid-19-in-new-zealand/ p. 27/32

17   https://www.dia.govt.nz/Local-Goverment-COVID-19-Response-Update-Saturday-27-February-2021/ p. 1/2

18   https://www.rnz.co.nz/news/national/437359/timeline-the-year-of-covid-19-in-new-zealand-/ p. 28/32

19   https://www.rnz.co.nz/news/national/437359/timeline-the-year-of-covid-19-in-new-zealand/ p. 29/32 OR https://dia.govt.nz/Update...March-2021/

20   https://www.beehive.govt.nz/release/govt-purchases-enough-pfizer-vaccine-whole-country/ p. 1/3

21   https://www.rnz.co.nz/national/programmes/checkpoint/audio/201786828/first-large-scale-covid-19-vaccination-clinic-opens-in-auckland/ p. 1/1

22   https://covid19.govt.nz/news-and-data/latest-news/independent-group-to-oversee-continual-improvement-in-covid-19-response/ p. 1/3

23   https://covid19.govt.nz/news-and-data/latest-news-COVID-19-vaccine-rollout-plan/ p. 1/4

24   https://beehive.govt.nz/release/auckland-move-alert-level-1-midday/ p. 1/3

25   https://www.stuff.co.nz/national/politics/30027252/covid-19-government-plans-to-hire-army-of-coronavirus-vaccinnators/ p. 1/6

26   https://www.rnz.co.nz/news/political/440019/covid-19-govt-sets-up-scientist-group-to-advise-on-vaccine-rollout-border.changes/ p. 1/3

27   https://legislation.govt.nz/regulation/public/2021/0065/latest/LMS481029.htmI/ p. 1/1

28   https://www.govt.nz/news-items/covid-19-vaccine-background-media-panel-15-april-2021/ p. 1/1

29   https://www.beehive.govt.nz/release/making-border-stronger/ p. 1/4

30   https://www.rnz.co.nz/news/national/441509/mandatory-vaccination-rule-for-border-workers-tocome-into-effect/ p. 1/3

31   https://www.rnz.co.nz/news/national/442778/covid-19-excitment-builds-as-cook-islands-travel-bubble-begins/ p. 1/11

32   https://www.beehive.govt.nz/release/government-guarantees-free-vacines-every-new-zealander/ p. 1/3

33   https://www.nzherald.co.nz/nz/politics/covid-19-coronavirus-revealed-3800-unvaccinated-border-workers-1100-miss-testing-timeline/EFEJDWC.../ p. 1/4

34   https://www.mcguinnessinstitute.org/projects/pandemic-nz/covid-19-timeline/ p. 59/122

35   https://www.beehive.govt.nz/release/1-million-more-pfizer-doses-arrive-july/ p. 1/3

36   https://beehive.govt.nz/release/plan-vaccine-rollout-general-population-announced/ p. 1/3

37   https://www.rnz.co.nz/news/political/4455213/medsafe-gives-pfizer-vaccine-provisional-approval-for-ages-12/ p. 1/7

38   https://www.abc.net.au/news/2021-06-23nz-raises-alert-level-wellington-covid-19-australian-tourist/100015920/ p. 1/3

39 https://tepapa.govt.nz/about/press-and-media/press-releases/2021-media-release/te-papa-closes-after-becoming-location/ p. 4

40 https://www.mcguinnessinstitute.org/projects/pandemic-nz/covid-19-timeline/ p. 57/122

41 https://www.1news.co.nz/2021/06/24/passengers-bound-for-raratonga-removed-from-air-nz-flight/ p. 1/4

42 https://swdc.govt.nz/update-wellington-region-returns-to-covid-19-alert-level-1-at-midnight-on-tuesday-29-june/ p. 1/2

43 https://www.sciencemediacentre.co.nz/2921/06/30/when-will-nz-have-herd-immunity-against-covid-19-expert-reaction/ p. 1/2

44 https://www.rnz.co.nz/news/national/446076/covid-19-new-zealand-ranks-second-in-return-to-normal-ranking/ p. 1/2

45 https://thespinoff.co.nz/politics/07-07-2021/live-updates-july-7-purpose-built-miq-facilities-unfeasible-by-officials/ p.2/19-3/19 OR https://thespinoff.co.nz/politics/07/07/2021/live-updates-july-7-500,000-NZers-fully-vaccinated-roll-out-ramping-up/

46 https://www.beehive.govt.nz/release/early-pfizer-shipment-boosts-vaccine-schedule/ p. 1/2

47 https://www.stuff.co.nz/national/health/coronavirus/3000357211/covid-19-nzs-first-mass-vaccination-event-to-be-held-in-auckland-at-end-of-july/ p. 1/7

48 https://www.nzherald.co.nz/nz/politics/covid-19-coronavirus-the-plan-to-reopen-nz-home- isolation-shorter-miq-for-vaccinated-travellers/MPEMU.../ p. 1/2

49 https://www.dia.govt.nz/COVID-19-Local-Government-response-Unit-Update-Tuesday-17-August-2021/ p. 1/2

50 https://www.beehive.govt.nz/release/level-4-remain-in-place-keep-nzers-safe/ p. 1/2

51 https://www.nzdoctor.co.nz/timeline-coronavirus/ p 73/208 and 76/208

52 https://www.beehive.govt.nz/release/level-4-remain-place-keep-nzers-safe/ p. 1/2

53 https://covid.immune.org.nz/news-insights/covid-19-vaccination-programme-extended-12-15-year-olds/ p. 1/3

54 https://www.beehive.govt.nz/release/record-keeping-mandatory-most-events-and-business/ p. 1/3

55 https://www.spada.co.nz/news-events/covid-19-update-27-aust-2021-alert-levels-to-change/ p. 1/3

56 https://www.nzdoctor.co.nz/timeline-coronavirus/ p. 82/208

57 https://www.rnz.co.nz/news/national/450606/northland-to-move-to-alert-level-3-at-midnight-tonight/ p. 1/3

58 https://www.rnz.co.nz/news/national/450890/delta-2-what's-changed-with-alert-level-2/ p. 1/3

59 https://www.beehive.govt.nz/release/half-million-pfizer-vaccines-denmark/ p. 1/2

60 https://www.auckland.ac.nz/en/news/2021/09/17/better-mask-guidelines-to-stop-covid-19-htmI/ p. 1/6

61 https://www.miq.govt.nz/about/news/update-miq-voucher-release-via-virtual-lobby-2/ p. 1/2

62 https://dia.govt.nz/COVID-19-Response-Update-Monday-20-September-2021/ p. 1/3

63 https://www.stuff.co.nz/national/politics/300413503/covid19-new-zealands-vaccine-rollout-explained-in-13-charts-as-government-talks-up-90-percent/ p. 1-2/20

64 https://www.nzdoctor.co.nz/timeline-coronavirus/ p. 8/208

65 https://www.behive.govt.nz/release/upper-hauraki-move-alert-level-2/ p. 1/3

66 https://www.rnz.co.nz/news/national/452511/covid-19-in-focus-developments-on-28-september/ p. 3/6

67 https://nzdoctor.co.nz/timeline-coronavirus/ p. 89/208

68 https://www.reuters.com/world/asia-pacific/new-zealand-reports-27-covod-19-cases-amin-anti-lockdown-protests-2021-10-02/ p. 1/8

69 https://www.dia.govt.nz/Local-Government-COVID-19-Resonse-Update-Sunday-3-October-2021/ p. 1/2

70 https://www.covid19.govt.nz/news-and-data/latest-news/auckland-restrictions-eased-in-steps/ p. 1/1

71 https://www.health.govt.nz/covid-19-novel-coronavirus/covid-19-vaccines/recommended-timing-gaps-different-covid-19-vaccines/ p. 1-2/4

72 https://www.beehive.govt.nz/release/extension-alert-level-3-boundary-waikato/ p. 1/3

73 https://www.covid19.govt.nz/news-and-data/latest-news/northland-to-move-to-level-3-tonight/ p. 1/1

74 https://www.nzdoctor.co.nz/timeline-coronavirus/ p. 95/208

75 https://www.health.govt.nz/news-media/media-releases/new-zealands-first-ever-vaxathon-launches/ p. 1/2

76 https://www.health.govt.nz./news-media/media-releases/super-saturday-smashes-vaccinathon-records/ p. 1/2

77 https://www.nzherald.co.nz/nz/covid-19-delta-thousands-at-auckland-lockdown-protest-brian-tamaki-speaks-police-keep-distance/NYPJ6ETBX2U.../ p. 1/3

78 https://www.health.govt.nz/news-media/media-releases/new-possibilities-horizon-my-covid-record-website-launches/ p. 1/2

79 https://www.beehive.govt.nz/release/mandatory-vaccination-two-workforces/ p. 1/3

80 https://www.dia.govt.nz/Covid-19-Local-Government-Response-Unit-Update-Monday-18-October-2021/ p. 1/3

81 https://www.beehive.govt.nz/release/restrictions-eased-parts-waikato-alert-level-northland-remain-alert-level-2/ p. 1/3

82 https://www.stuff.co.nz/national/politics/126812971/covid-19-miq-stays-shortened-for-vaccinated-travellers-but-ardern-says-transtasman-bubble.../ p. 1/6

83 https://www.stuff.co.nz/national/health/coronavirus/126617941/covid-19-pfizer-vaccine-granted-provisional-approval-for-two-more-years/ p. 1/4

84 https://www.mbie.govt.nz/about/news/rapid-antigen-tests-now-being-trialed-by-new-zealand-businesses/ p. 1/3

85 https://www.1news.co.nz/2021/10/29/huge-anti-lockdown-crowd-marches-through-auckland-streets/ p. 1/4

86 https://nzdoctors.co.nz/timeline-coronavirus/ p. 100/208

87 https://www.beehive.govt.nz/release/northern-parts-northland-move-alert-level-3/ p. 1/3

88 https://www.beehive.govt.nz/release/covid-19-restrictions-ease-waikato-tomorrow-auckland-move-next-week/ p. 1/3

89 https://www.beehive.govt.nz/release/waikato-move-to-alert-level-2/ p. 1/2

90 https://www.dia.govt.nz/covid-19-Government-Response-Unit-Monday-8-November-2021/ p. 1/3

91 https://www.beehive.govt.nz/release/workplace-vaccination-extended-cover-police-and-nz-defence-force/ p. 1/3

92   https://www.mcguinnessinstitute.org/projects/pandemic-nz/covid-19-timeline/ p. 33/122

93   https://covid19.govt.nz/news-and-data/latest-news/covid-19-media-conference-8-november-2/ p. 2/2

94   https://covid19.govt.nz/news-and-data/latest-news/covid-19-media-conference-8-november-2/ p. 2/2

95   https://beehive.govt.nz/release/vaccine-pass-ready-kiwi-summer/ p. 1/7

96   https://beehive.govt.nz/release/auckland-boundary-change-15-december/ p. 1/4

97   https://www.beehive.govt.nz/release/govt-providing-tools-vaccinate-workforces/ p. 1/3

98   https://www.mcguinnessinstitute.org/projects/pandemic-nz/covid-19-timeline/ p. 27/122

99   https://www.stuff.co.nz/national/health/coronavirus/300462257/covid19-govt-invests-15-billion-in-testing-tracing-and-support-for-cases/ p. 1/8

100   https://www.beehive.govt.nz/release/traffic-light-levels-announced/ p. 1/2

101   https://https://nzdoctor.co.nz/timeline-coronavirus/ p. 114/208

102   https://www.mcguinnessinstitute.org/projects/pandemic-nz/covid-19-timeline/ p. 23/122

103   https://www.mcguinnessinstitute.org/projects/pandemic-nzcovid-19-timeline/ p. 22/122

104   https://www.rnz.co.nz/news/national/457821/prime-minister-jacinda-ardern-announces-any-changes-to-traffic-light-system/ p. 1/4

105   https://www.health.govt.nz/news-media/media-releases/first-omicron-case-detected-new-zealand/ p. 1/3

106   https://www.beehive.govt.nz/release/aotearoa-hits-90-percent-fully-vacinated-milestone/ p. 1/3

107   https://covid19.govt.nz/news-and-data/latest-news/omicron-governments-plan-to-minimise-risk/ p. 1/1

108   https://www.bloomberg.com/news/articles/2021-12-21/new-zealand-delays-phased-border-reopening-due-to-omicron/ p. 1/3

109   https://www.beehive.govt.nz/release/government-confirms-covid-19-vaccinations-protect-tamariki/ p. 1/3

110   https://www.rnz.co.nz/news/national/458777/covid-19-omicron-case-was-active-in-the-community-ministry-of-health-confirms/ p. 1/3

111   https://www.rnz.co.nz/news/national/459786/government-postpones-next-miq-lottery-due-to-spike-of-omicron-cases-at-border/ p. 1/2

112   https://covid19.govt.nz/covid-19-vaccines/covid-19-vaccine-facts-and-advice-covid-19-vaccination-andchildren/ pp. 1-3/3

113   https://www.adhb.health.nz/about-us/latest-stories/book-yourbooster/ p. 1/3

114   https://www.rnz.co.nz/news/national459786/government-postpones-next-miq-lottery-due-to-spike-of-omicron-cases-at-border/ p. 1/2

115   https://www.rnz.co.nz/news/national/459759/covid-19-update-on-18-january-14-new-community-cases-today-30-at-the-border/ p. 1/3

116   https://www.stuff.co.nz/national/health/coronavirus/300499958/covid19-miq-worker-contact-tests-positive-possible-omicron-case-in-palmerston-n.../ p. 5/10

117   https://twitter.com/covid 19nz/status/1494352374462316549/ p. 2/4

118   https://www.beehive.govt.nz/speech/nz-move-red/ p. 1/5

119   https://www.rnz.co.nz/news/political/460181/covid-19-testing-capacity-increased-with-rapid-antigen-and-robots/ p. 1/6

120   https://www.beehive.govt.nz/release/government-announces-three-phase-public-health-response-omicron/ p. 1/5

121   https://www.beehive.govt.nz/release/prime-minister-enters-a-self-isolation-after-being-deemed-close-contact#:-text-Prime-Minister-enters-self-islo.../ p. 1/2

122   https://covid19.govt.nz/news-and-data/latest-news/update-on-covid-19-cases-31-january-2022/ p. 1/1

123   https://www.oecd-library.org/sites/e1a5801d-enhtml?itemid=/component/e1a5801d-en/ p. 2/81

124   https://www.mcguinnessinstitute.org/projects/pandemic-nz/covid-19-timeline/ p. 10/122

125   https://www.mcguinnessinstitute.org/projects/pandemic-nz/covid-19-timeline/ p. 9/122

126   https://www.beehive.govt.nz/release/border-reopens-stages-27-february/ p. 1/5

127   https://www.employsure.co.nz/wp-content/uploads/2022/01/U-FACTSHEET-masks-and-face-coverings.pdf/

128   https://www.mcguinnessinstitute.org/projects/pandemic-nz/covid-19-timeline/ p. 7/122

129   https://www.stuff.co.nz/national/health/coronavirus/127713109/antivaccine-mandate-protesters-at-parliament-pitch-tents-for-the-night/

130   https://www.stuff.co.nz-national/3000516015/live-wet-weather-does-little-to-slow-mandate-protest-at-parliament/ p. 15

131   https://stuff.co.nz/national/127828513/protest-concert-at-parliament-causing-serious-concerns-for-police/ p. 1/13

132   https://www.nzdoctor.co.nz/timeline-coronavirus/ p. 140/208

133   https://www.nzdoctor.co.nz/timeline-coronavirus/ p. 142/208

134   https://www.rnz.co.nz/news/political/461484/new-zealand-to-move-to-phase-2-of-omicron-plan-jacinda-ardern/ p. 1-2/6

135   https://www.rnz.co.nz/news/political/461452/prime-minister-jacinda-ardern-says-parliament-protesters-not-interested-in-engaging/

136   https://www.nzdoctor.co.nz/timeline-coronavirus/ p. 144/208

137   https://www.mcguinnessinstitute.org/projects/pandemic-nz/covid-19-timeline/ p. 124/208

138   https://www.beehive.govt.nz/release/new-financial-support-businesses-affected-omicron/ p. 1/3

139   https://www.nzdoctor.co.nz/timeline-coronavirus/ p. 147/208

140   https://www.rnz.co.nz/political/462175/covid-19-omicron-outbreak-new-zealand-to-move-to-phase-3-of-response/ p. 1-2/6

141   https://www.health.govt.nz/covid-19-novel-coronavirus/covid-19-health-advice-public-covid-19-testing-rapid-antigen-testing-rat/ p. 1/6

142   https://www.beehive.govt.nz/release/self-isolation-requirements-removed-step-2-brought-forward/ p. 1/3

143   https://www.nzdoctor.co.nz/timeline-coronavirus/ p. 151/208

144   https://www.stuff.co.nz/dominion-post/news/wellington/30052929966/full-coverage-police-operation-ends-parliament-occupation/ p. 1-2/17

145   https://www.rnz.co.nz/news/national/462620/protesters-scatter-around-wellington-as-clean-up-continues-from-parliament-protest/ p. 1-2/18

146   https://nzhearld.co.nz/covid-19-wellington-protest-riots-fire-and-violence-as-police-end-occupation/SKASWAE3HBT3GZOY2SNZ.../ p. 1/11

147   Malpass, L., & Witton, B. (2022) Grounds officially reopen after protest. *The Dominion Post*, Friday, June 24, p. 3

148   https://www.stuff.co.nz/the-press/news/127931376/wellington-protesters-heading-to-cranmer-square-christchurch-protesters-claim/ p. 1/7

149   https://www.newshub.co.nz/home/newzealand/2022/03/christchurch-residents-near-anti-mandate-protest-occupied-cranmer-square-say-ongoing-disruption-is-callous-and-selfish-driven-some-out-of-their-homes/html/ p. 1/6

150   https://newsline.ccc.govt.nz/news/story/council-police-welcome-end-to-cranmer-square-protest/ p. 1/6

151   https://www.stuff.co.nz/national/health/coronavirus/127999281/christchurch-anti-mandate-protesters-have-left-cranmer-aquare/ p. 1/6

152   https://www.nzdoctor.co.nz/timeline-coronavirus/ p. 157/208

153   https://www.health.govt.nz/covid-19-novel-coronavirus/covid-19-vaccines-getting-novavax/ p. 1/5

154   https://www.beehive.govt.nz/release/islation-period-reduced-10-7-days-third-vaccine-becomes-available#/ p. 1/3

155   https://www.beehive.govt.nz/release/rapid-antigen-tests-more-widely-available-schools-and-early-learning/ p. 1/3

156   https://www.health.govt.nz/covid-19-novel-coronavirus/covid-19-response-planning/covid-19-epidemic-notice-and-orders/ p. 2/19

157   https://www.dia.govt.nz/Covid-19-Government-Response-Unite-Update-Friday-25-March-2022/ p. 1/3

158   https://www.beehive.govt.nz/more-covid-medicines-most-risk-new-zealanders/ p. 1/3

159   https://www.nzdoctor.co.nz/timeline-coronavirus/ p. 176/208

160   https://www.nzdoctor.co.nz/timeline-coronavirus/ p. 177/208

161   https://www.nzdoctor.co.nz/timeline-coronavirus/ p. 181/208

162   https://www.beehive.govt.nz/release/workplace-vaccination-guidance-updated/ p. 1/3

163   https://www.beehive.govt.nz/release/young-people-16-and-17-eligible-covid-19-boosters/ p. 1/3

164   https://www.rnz.co.nz/political/465198/covid-19-all-nz-to-move-to-orange-setting-from-11-point-59-pm-tonight/ pp. 1-2/3

165   https://www.nzherald.co.nz/nz/ministry-of-health-requested-private-covid-tests-after-just-2-per-cent-of-january-and-february-stock-showed-up/ p. 1/5

166   https://www.medsafe.govt.nz/COVID-19/treatment-applications.asp/ p. 3/4

167   https://www.nzdoctor.co.nz/timeline-coronavirus/ p. 195/208

168   https://www.nzdoctor.co.nz/timeline-coronavirus/ p. 195-196/208

169   https://www.1news.co.nz/2022/05/01/first-case-of-omocron-ba-4-variant-detected-at-nzs-border/ p. 2/4

170   https://www.rnz.co.nz/news/political/466268/new-zealand-reopens-border-to-visa-waiver-countries/ p. 1/4

171   https://www.theguardian.com/world/2022/may10/new-zealand-once-covid-free-tops-1-million-cases-since-pandemic-began/ p. 1/4

172   https://www.stuff.co.nz/national/health/coronavirus/300585200/covid-19-question-of-true-number-of-cases-could-spell-messy-future-for-health/ p. 1/9

173   Leahy, B., & Gabel, J. (2022) At-risk Kiwis warned of Covid repeats. *The Weekend Herald*, Saturday, May 14, p. A3

174   Anon (2022) Omicron could be less deadly than influenza. *The Dominion Post*, Saturday 14 May, p. 2

175   Anon (2022) ill winter tipped. *The Dominion Post*, Saturday, May 14, p. 2

176   https://www.stuff.co.nz/opinion/128670774/covid-19-unprecented-and-unfinished/ p. 1/6

177 Thomas, R. (2022) 'It's not over': Vigilance urged. *The Dominion Post*, Friday, May 13, p. 1

178 https://www.stuff.co.nz/national/health/300590239/covid-19-second-peak-expected-to-hit-as-early-as-june/ p. 1/6

179 Martin, H. (2022) What you need to know as NZ hits 1000 Covid-19 deaths. *The Dominion Post*, Thursday, May 19, pp. 4-5

180 McConnell, G. (2022) Pre-departure tests to go 'soon.' *The Dominion Post*, Thursday, May 19, p. 2

181 Malpass, L. (2022) Finance boss Robertson walks the tightrope. *The Dominion Post*, Friday, May 20, pp. 2-3

182 https://covid19.govt.nz/news-and-data/latest-news/update-my-vaccine-pass-for-those-who-want-it-from-24-may/ p. 1/3

183 Witton, B. (2022) Brakes put on change of traffic light setting. *The Dominion Post*, Wednesday, May 25, p. 3

184 Anon (2022) National News: Covid at a glance. *The Dominion Post*, Wednesday, June 1, p. 9

185 Marton, H. (2022) New subvariants circulating. *The Dominion Post*, Monday, June 6, p. 3

186 https://www.beehive.govt.nz/release/government-outlines-plans-future-covid-19-variants/ p. 1/3.

187 Witton, B. (2022) Major health reforms to become law. *The Dominion Post*, Wednesday, June 8, p. 5

188 Bhatiaw, R. (2022) Renewed call to fix doctor 'bottleneck.' *The Dominion Post*, Saturday, June 4, p. 3

189 Kenny, K. (2022) Dipping vaccination rates leaving NZ vulnerable. *The Dominion Post*, Wednesday, June 15, pp. 10-11

190 https://www.beehive.govt.nz/release/pre-parture-tests-removed-june-20/ p. 1/3

191 Anon. (2022) National News: Covid at a glance. *The Dominion Post*, Wednesday, June 15, p. 9

192 Witton, B. (2022) Flu, staff illness cause new hospital pressures-Little. *The Dominion Post*, Wednesday, June 22, p. 4

193 Bathgate, B. (2022) Dire warning from health front line. *The Dominion Post*, Saturday, June 25, p. A2

194 https://www.rnz.co.nz/news/national/469902/covid-19-weariness-health-officials-pessimistic-on-uptake-of-second-booster/ p. 1/3

195 https://www.health.govt.nz/covid-19-novel-coronavirus/covid-19-health-advice-public/advice-people-covid-19/getting-reinfected-covid-19/ p. 1/4

196 Anon. (2022) Alert Level to be reviewed. *The Dominion Post*, Monday, June 27, p. 3

197 Anon. (2022) National News: Covid at a glance. *The Dominion Post*, Saturday, July 2, p. A2

198 Malpass, L. (2022) Orange setting stays, Covid advice changes. *The Dominion Post*, Friday, July 1, p. 5

199 https://www.tdhb.org.nz/dhb/health-nz.shtmI#/ p. 1/3

200 Williams, K. (2022) Schools in 'survival mode.' *The Dominion Post*, Saturday, July 2, p. A3

201 https://www.health.govt.nz/news-media/media-releases/new-zealands-first-monkey-case-isolation-home/ p. 1/2

202 https://www.reuters.com/world/asia-pacific/new-zealand-announces-free-masks-and-tests-health-system-struggles-with-covid-2022-07-14/ p. 1/8

203 Anon. (2022) 60,000 resident fast tracked and counting. *The Dominion Post*, Saturday, July 2, p. A2

204   https://www.rnz.co.nz/news/national/470282/significant-wave-of-omicron-may-already-be-here/ p. 1/5

205   https://www.rnz.co.nz/news/national/470380/covid-19-update-omicron-subvariant-ba-2-point-75-detected-as-24-further-deaths-9626-new-commu.../ p. 1/2

206   Harris, S. (2022) Worrying signs in Covid wave. *The Dominion Post*, Wednesday, July 13, p. 2

207   Hyde, C. (2022) 'A tough few weeks' ahead as new wave rises. *The Dominion Post*, Monday, July 11, p. 2

208   Martin, H. (2022) Flu rates continue to rise. *The Dominion Post*, Saturday, July 9, p. A2

209   Thomas, R. (2022) 'It will break many': Health crisis. *The Dominion Post*, Tuesday, July 12, p. 2

210   Thomas, R. (2022) 'People are dying from this' – Nurse. *The Dominion Post*, Wednesday, July 20, p. 4

211   Macintosh, C. (2022) Calls to Healthline rise 40%. *The Dominion Post*, Thursday, July 7, p. 3

212   https://www.beehive.govt.nz/release/new-measures-tackle-covid-19-and-flu/ p. 1-2/4

213   McConnell, G. (2022) Bloomfield's plea: Kiwis 'do your bit.' *The Dominion Post*, Friday, July 15, p. 5

214   Martin, H. (2022) NZ changes way it reports Covid deaths. *The Dominion Post*, Wednesday, July 20, p. 5

215   https://www.stuff.co.nz/national/education/3000642391/covid-19-government-changes-position-on-masks-in-schools-again-enforcement-advice-issue.../ p. 1/8

216   Lynch., K & Martin, H. (2022) Why Covid may have peaked. *The Dominion Post*, Saturday, July 30, p. A2

217   Anon (2022) National News: Covid at a glance. *The Dominion Post*, Thursday, Saturday, July 30, p. A2

218   Martin, H. (2022) Bloomfield signs off with upbeat finale. *The Dominion Post*, Thursday, July 28, p. 7

219   https://www.immigration.govt.nz/about-us/border-closres-and-exception/border-entry-requirements/ p. 1/2

220   Schwanecke, G. (2022)'Everyone around me has caught Covid.' *The Dominion Post,* Saturday, July 30, p. A9

221   Keyes, C. (2002) The Mental Health Continuum: From Languishing to Flourishing in Life. *Journal of Health and Social Behavior*, 43 (2), p. 210

222   Grant, A. (2021) There's a Name for the Blah You're Feeling: Its Called Languishing. https://nytimes.com/2021/04/19/well/mind/covid-mental-health-languishing-htmI/ p. 1/2

223   Bowron, J. (2022) When we face patients competing for care, we can't afford to say: 'I'm over it.' https://www.stuff.co.nz/opinion/129331357/when-we-face-patients-competing-for-care-we-can't-afford-to-say-i'm-over-it/ p. 2/18

224   Anon(2022)https://www.healthline.com/health/mental-health/languishing#/what-are-the-signs/ p. 1/14

225   Baker, G. (2022) Running Beyond Empty. *NZ Business*, May, p. 15

226   Burke, J. (2022) Languishing: what to do if you're feeling restless, apathetic or empty. https://theconversation.com/languishing-what-to-do-if-you're-feeling-restless-apathetic-or-empty-174994/ p. 1/3

227   Yuko, E. (2022) That Mental Rut You're Going through Has a Name-and Here's What to do About it. https://realsimle.comhealth/mind-mood/what-is-languishing/ p. 1/7

228   Fielding, S. (2021) Languishing is the Mood of 2021. How to identify it and How to Cope. https://www.wellmind.com/languishing-is-the-mood-of-2021-5180999/ p. 16

229   Grant, A. (2021) There's a Name for the Blah You're Feeling: It's called Languishing. https://www.nytimes.com/2021/04/19/well-mind/covid-mental-health-languishing.htmI/ p. 1/2

230   Young, R., & McMahon, S. (2021) Living, But Not Flourishing: The Pandemic-Fuelled Feeling Known As 'Languishing.' https://wbur.org/hereandnow/2021/05/04/languishing-pandemic-mental-health/ p. 1-2/6

231   Wade, G (2024) How not to languish: Do you feel aimless and numb inside? Is it hard to pinpoint what's wrong? You may be languishing, says Cory Keyes. He tells Grace Wade how to turn this around and flourish. New Scientist 13 April, pp.40-43 AND Keyes, C (2024) *Languishing: How to Feel Alive Again in a world That Wears Us Down*, Transworld Publishers: London, pp. ix; 195

232   Lewandowsky, S., Jacobs, P., & Neil, S. (2022) Conspiracy Theories Made It Harder for Scientists to Seek the Truth. *Scientific American*, 326, 3, p. 68

233   Lewis, T. (2022) Science Journalism Shifts with New Realities. *Scientific American*, 326, 3, p. 34

234   O'Sullivan, and et al., (2021) Impact of the COVID-19 Pandemic on Loneliness and Social Isolation: A Multi-Country Study. International Journal of *Environmental Research and Public Health* 18, p. 1/18

235   https://www.harvardmagazine.com/2020/12/feature-the-loneliness-pandemic/ p. 1/18

236   Johnson, S. (2023) Loneliness is a threat to public health worldwide, warns WHO, *The Guardian*, Friday 12th November, p. 21

237   Banerjee., D. & Rai, M. (2020) Social isolation in Covid-19: The impact of loneliness. *International Journal of Social Psychology*, 66 (6), p. 526

238   O'Sullivan, R. and et al., (2021) Impact of the COVID-19 Pandemic on Loneliness and Social Isolation: A Multi-Country Study, 18, *International Journal of Environment Research and Public Health*, p. 2/18

239   McConnell, G. (2022) Bloomfield's plea: 'Kiwis do your bit' *The Dominion Post*, Friday, July 15, p. 5

240   Watkins, T. (2022) Our day of reckoning with Covid is here, and what have we done? https://www.stuff.co.nz/300638892/our-day-of-reckonong-with-covid-is-here-and-what-have-we-done/ p. 1;3/18

241   Schwartz, J. (2022) How COVID Changed the world. *Scientific American*, 326, 3, p. 26

242   Nelson, R. G. (2022) A Microbe Proved That Individualism is a Myth. *Scientific American*, 326, 3, p. 28

243   Ibid (Nelson) p. 29

244   Martin, H. (2022) Bloomfield signs off with upbeat finale. *The Dominion Post,* Thursday, July 28, p. 7

245   Editorial (2020) Into the void. *New Zealand Listener*, April 4, p. 3

246   Blackburn, C. C. (2022) COVID is Here to Stay: how do we live with it? *Scientific American*, 326, 3, p. 75

247   Watkins, T. (2022) Our day of reckoning with COVID is here, and what have we done? https://www.stuff.co.nz/opinion/300638892/our-day-of-reckoning-with-covid-is-here-and-what-have-we-done/ p. 2; 3/18

248   Reed, K.M. & Allen, J.A. (2022) *Suddenly Hybrid: Managing the Modern Meeting*. Hoboken, New Jersey, John Wiley & Sons, Inc. p. xi

249   https://www.rnz.co.nz/news/political/462175/covid-19-outbreak-new-new-zealand-to-move-to-phase-3-of-response/ p. 1-2/6

250   Reed, K.M. & Allen, J.A. (2022) *Suddenly Hybrid: Managing the Modern Meeting.* Hoboken, New Jersey, John Wiley & Sons, Inc. p. xii

251   https://www.rnz.co.nz/news/national/446076/covid-19-new-zealand-ranks-second-in-return-to-normal-ranking/ p. 1/2

252   Franks, J. (2022) Covid-19: Pandemic measures saved 2750 lives, caused life expectancy to rise. https://www.stuff.co.nz/national/health/coronavirus/127917427/covid-19-pandemic-measures-saved-2750-lives-caused-life-expectancy-to-rise/ pp. 1-2/6

253   Olley, S. (2023) 'We're out the other side': Sir Ashley Bloomfield reflects on Covid three years on. https://www.stuff.co.nz/national/health/coronavirus/300839129/were-out-the-other-side-sir-ashley-bloomfield--reflects-on-covid-three-years-on/ p. 1/8

254   https://covid19.govt.nz/about-our-covid19-response/ pp. 1-2/2

255   Cheng, D. (2023) Covid19: Government ditches all remaining restrictions, as case hospitalisations rise https://www.nzherald.co.nz/nz/covid-19-government-ditches-all-remaing-restrictions-as-case-hospitalisations-rise/OJWFQTIXY5HZHPPBAGD4/ p. 1/6

256   Olley S. (2023) 'We're out the other side': Sir Ashley Bloomfield reflects on Covid three years on. https://www.stuff.co.nz/national/health/coronavirus//300839129/were-out-the-other-side-sir-ashley-bloomfield-reflects-on-covid-three-years-on/ p. 1/8

257   https://95bfm.com/news/aotearoa-needs-to-prioritise-covid-19-response-says-epidemiologist-professor-michael-baker/ 28 April, 2023, p. 1/3

258   https://nzhearld.co.nz/nzmichael-baker-world-health-organization-covid-19-status-change-makes-no-practical-difference-to-management/ 7 May, 2023, p. 1/3

259   https://odt.co.nz/news/national/enormous-amount--covid-around/ 18 December 2023, p. 2/5

260   Lourens, M. (2023) Covid could yet ruin Christmas, New Year. *The Post* Thursday, December 21, 2023. p. 3

261   Brownlie, K. https://newshub.co.nz/home/new-zealand/2024/02/ p. 1-2

262   Anon (2024) Covid-19: Free rapid antigen tests to be available until end of June. *The Post* Thursday, February 1, 2024, p. 3

263   Thomas, R. (2024) Covid Booster supported. *The Post*, Friday, January 5, 2024, p. 1

264   Morton, J. (2023) https://www.nzherald.co.nz/nz/fifth-covid-19-wave-looks-to-be-driving-biggest-bump-since-january-michael-baker/ 21 November 2023, pp. 1/3-2/3

265   Martin, H. (2023) https://www.stuff.co.nz/national/health/301007808/whats-going-on-with-covid19-is-this-how-its-always-going-to-be/ November 18, 2023, pp. 3/7-4/7

266   Watson, M. (2023) https://newshub.co.nz/home/new-zealand/2023/12/professor-michael-bakers-predictions-as-fifth-covid-wave-sweeps-nz/ December 18, p. 2

267   Wade, G. (2023) Covid-19 crisis phase ended but virus still lingers. *New Scientist* 260, 16-23 December, 2023, p. 19

268   Royal Commission (2024) You can now give your feedback in expanding the terms of reference of the Royal Commission into the COVID-19 response. *The Post* Friday, February 9, 2024, p. 4

269   https://www.rnz.co.nz/news/national/517948/covid-19-update-6636-new-cases-and-7-further-deaths/ pp. 1/2-2/2

270   Reed, K.M., & Allen, J.A. (2022) *Suddenly Hybrid: Managing the Modern Office.* Hoboken: New Jersey: John Wiley & Sons, p. xi

271   Hobsbawm, J. (2022) *The Nowhere Office: Reinventing Work and the Workplace of the Future.* London: Basic Books UK, p. xi; x

272   Reed, K.M., & Allen, J.A. (2022) *Suddenly Hybrid: Managing the Modern Office*. Hoboken: New Jersey: John Wiley & Sons, p. xii

273   Hobsbawm, J. (2022) *The Nowhere Office: Reinventing Work and the Workplace of the Future*. London: Basic Book UK, pp. 2-3

274   Barnes, A., with Jones, S. (2020) *The 4 Day Week: How the Flexible Work Revolution Can Increase Productivity, Profitability and Well-Being And Create A Sustainable Future*. London: Piatkus, p. 11

275   Schwartz, J., with Riss, S. (2021) *Work Disrupted: Opportunity, Resilience, and Growth in the Accelerated Future of Work*. Hoboken: New Jersey: John Wiley & Sons Inc, pp. xix; xx

276   Ibid (Schwartz) p. v

Chapter 3: Reimagining our working lives

1   Ashford, S. J., George, E. & Blatt, R. (2007) Old Assumptions, New Work. *The Academy of Management Annals*, 1;1, p. 67. **AND** Baruch, Y., & Hind, P. (1999) Perpetual Motion in Organizations: Effective Management and the Impact of the New Psychological Contracts on "Survivor Syndrome" *European Journal of Work and Organizational Psychology*, 8:2, pp. 295-306

2   Maitland, A., & Thomson, P. (2011) *Future Work: How Businesses Can Adapt and Thrive in the New World of Work*. Houndmills, Basingstoke: Palgrave Macmillan, p. 29

3   Spreitzer, G. M., Cameron, L., & Garrett, L. (2017) Alternative Work Arrangements: Two Images of the New world of Work. *Annual Review of Organizational Psychology and Organizational Behavour*, 4, p. 475

4   Marler, J. H., Barringer, M. W., & Milkovich, G.T. (2002) Boundary and Traditional Contingent Employees: Worlds Apart. *Journal of Organizational Behavior*, 23, p. 425

5   Mulcahy, D. (2017) *The Gig Economy: Getting Better Work, Taking More Time Off, and Financing the Life You Want*. New York: AMACOM

6   Gephart, R. P. (2002) Introduction to the Brave New Workplace: Organizational Behavior in the Electronic Age. *Journal Of Organizational Behavior*, 23, p. 327

7   Spreitzer, G. M., Cameron, L., & Garrett, L. (2017) Alternative Work Arrangements: Two Images of the New World of Work. *Annual Review of Organizational Psychology and Organizational Behavior*, 4, p. 493

8   Maitland, A., & Thomson, P. (2011) *Future Work: How Businesses Can Adapt and Thrive in the New World of Work*. Houndmills, Basingstoke: Palgrave Macmillan, p. 149

9   Donkin, R. (2010) *The future of work*. Houndmills, Basingstoke: Palgrave Macmillan, p. 249

10   Mulcahy, D. (2017) *The Gig Economy: Getting Better Work, Taking More Time Off, and Financing the Life You Want*. New York: AMACOM p. 2.

11   Suzman, J. (2020) *Work: A History of How We Spend Our Time*. London: Bloomsbury Circus, p. 10

12   Valintine, F. (2022) *Future you*. Auckland: HarperCollins (New Zealand) Ltd. p. 27

13   Ibid (Valintine 2022) p. 29

14   Gherini, A. (2022). https://blog.asana.com/2022/05/gen-z-workers/ p. 1/8

15   Colbert, A., Yee, N., & George, G. (2016) The Digital Workforce and the Work-place of the Future, *Academy of Management Journal*, 59, p 731

16   Donkin, R. (2010) *The Future of Work*. Houndmills, Basingstoke: Palgrave Macmillan, p 6

17   Morgan, J. (2014) *The Future of work: Attract New Talent, Build Better Leaders, and Create a Competitive Organization*. Hoboken, New Jersey: John Wiley & Sons. p. 3

18   Ibid (Morgan 2014) p. 14

19   Valintine, F. (2022) *Future You*. Auckland: HarperCollins (New Zealand) Ltd. p. 28

20   Maitland, A., & Thomson, P. (2011) *Future Work: How Businesses Can Adapt and Thrive in the New World of Work*. Houndmills, Basingstoke: Palgrave Macmillan, p. 32

21   Morgan, J. (2014) *The Future of Work: Attract New Talent, Build Better Leaders, and Create a Competitive Organization*. Hoboken, New Jersey: John Wiley & Sons. p. 29

22   Ibid (Morgan 2014) p. 30

23   Valintine, F. (2022) *Future You*. Auckland: HarperCollins (New Zealand) Ltd. p. 138.

24   Ibid (Valintine 2022) p. 145

25   Williams, C. (2021) The future of work is flexible, Agile, Inspired, Evolving, Collaborative. *The Economist*, Special Report, April 10th. p. 4

26   Hill, A., & Hill, D. (2021) *Work from Anywhere*. Milton, Queensland: John Wiley & Sons Australia Ltd. p. xii

27   Leong, L., & Ross, M. (2022). *This Working Life*. Melbourne: Hardie Grant Books. p. 66

28   Gratton, L. (2014) *The shift: The Future of Work is Already Here*. London: William Collins. An imprint of HarperCollins Publishers. p. 197

29   Schwartz, J., with Riss, S. (2021) *Work Disrupted: Opportunity, Resilience, and Growth in the Accelerated Future of Work*. Hoboken, New Jersey: John Wiley & Sons Inc. p. xix

30   Leong, L., & Ross, M. (2022) *This Working Life*. Melbourne: Hardie Grant Books. pp. 279-280

31   Mangia, K. (2020) *Working from Home: Making The New Normal Work For You*. Hoboken, New Jersey: John Wiley & Sons Inc. pp. 6-8

32   Donkin, R. (2010) *The Future of Work*. Houndmills, Basingstoke: Palgrave Macmillan. p. 8

33   Roy, A. (2020) The Pandemic is a portal. https://www.ft.com/content/10d8fSe8-74eb-11ea-95fe-fcd274e920ca/ p. 12/13-13/13. **AND** Roy, A. (2022) AZADI: *Fascism, Fiction and Freedom in the Time of the Virus*. Penguin Random House UK, Chapter 9, The Pandemic is a Portal, p 203 (Chapter first published in the *Financial Times*, 4 April 2020)

34   Carroll, M. (2020) Today a new normal for at-home employees. *The Dominion Post*, Monday 23rd March, p. 2

35   Neeley, T. (2021) *Remote Work revolution: Succeeding from Anywhere*. New York: HarperCollins Publishers. p. xii

36   Fried, J., & Hansson, D. H. (2013) *Remote: Office Not Required*. London: Vermilion. pp. 4-5

37   Warzel, C., & Petersen, A. H. (2022) *Out of Office: the big problem and bigger promise of working from home*. Melbourne & London: SCRIBE Publications. P. 9

38   Gratton, L. (2014) *The Shift: The Future of Work is Already Here*. London: William Collins. An imprint of HarperCollins Publishers. p. 196

39   Katsoudas, F., & Patel, J. (2022) *Hybrid Work-Powered by Choice. HBR's latest thinking on the future of business*. Boston, Massachusetts: Harvard Business Review Press, p. xiii

40   Kropp, B. (2021) *The New World of Work. HBR's latest thinking on the future of business*. Boston, Massachusetts: Harvard Business Review Press, p. xii

41   Carroll, M. (2021) Our year in the future of work. *The Dominion Post*, Wednesday 13th January, p. 14

42   Kropp, B. (2021) *The New World of Work. HBR's latest thinking on the future of business*. Boston, Massachusetts: Harvard Business Review Press, p. xi

43   Burrell, M. (2021) Our year in the future of work. *The Dominion Post*, [Carroll, M.] Wednesday, January 13, p. 14

44   Fried, J., & Hansson, D. H. (2013) *Remote: Office Not Required*. London: Vermilion, p. 4

45   Seal, R. (2020) *Solo: How to Work Alone (and Not Lose Your mind)*. London: Souvenir Press, p. vii

46   Haar, J. (2022) 'Anti-work' movement gains momentum. [Mcilraith, B.] *The Dominion Post*, Saturday, July 2, p. B10

47   Ibid (Mcilraith,2022) p. B10

48   Burrell, M. (2021) Our year in the future of work. [Carroll, M.] *The Dominion Post*, Wednesday, January 13, p. 14

49   Caird, F. (2021) Our year in the future of work. [Carroll, M.] *The Dominion Post*, Wednesday, January 13, p. 14

50   Rosenburg, B. (2021) Our year in the future of work. [Carroll, M.] *The Dominion Post*, Wednesday, January 13, p. 14

51   Kropp, B. (2021) *The New World of Work. HBR's latest thinking on the future of business*. Boston, Massachusetts: Harvard Business Review Press, p. xiv

52   Tso, M. (2022) https://stuff.co.nz/national/12812035/no-hurry-to-get-public-servants-to-return-to-the-office-after-relaxation-of-covid-rules/ March, 28. p. 1/-5/5

53   Starks, J. (2022) Does working from home have a future? *The Dominion Post*, Saturday, June 4th p. B12

54   Cooper, C. (2021) Your Move: Home or Office? (Levy, M.) *The Dominion Post*, Tuesday, December, 28, p. 20

55   Katsoudas, F., & Patel, J. (2022) *Hybrid Work-Powered by Choice. HBR's latest thinking on the future of business*. Boston, Massachusetts: Harvard Business Review Press, p. xv

56   Fonseka, D. (2022) Tight job market will add to future skill shortages. *The Dominion Post*, Wednesday, September 7th p. 21

57   Campbell, D. (2023) Researchers say flexible working can reduce risk of heart attack. *The Guardian*, November 10, 2023, p. 13

58   Catherall, S. (2024) Putting work in its place. *The NZ Listener*, Vol 289, No 4336, February 17, 2024 p. 20

59   Hill, A., & Hill, D. (2021) *Work from Anywhere*. Milton, Melbourne, John Wiley & Sons, Australia, Ltd. p. 4

60   Hill, A., & Hill, D. (2021) *Work from Anywhere*. Milton, Melbourne, John Wiley & Sons, Australia, Ltd. p. 6

61   Minter, H. (2021) *WFH Working From Home*. London, Greenfinch, An imprint of Quercus Editions Ltd. p. 3

62   Ibid (Minter,2021) pp. 3-4

63   Robson, D. (2022) https://www.bbc.com/worklife/article/20220201-how-thinking-about-future-you-can-build-a-happier-life/ pp 1/5;2/5

64   Turits, M. (2021) https://www.bbc.com/worklife/article/20211209-thebiggest-lessons-about-work-from-2021/ p. 6/7

65   Ibid (Turits 2021) p. 2/7

66   Ibid Turits, M. (2022) https://www.bbc.com/worklife/article/20220628-the-six-big-things-weve-learned-about-hybrid-work-so-far/ p. 2/5

67   Ibid (Turits 2022) p. 2/5

68   Ibid (Turits 2022) p. 3/5

69   Gratton, L. (2021) How to Do Hybrid Right. *Harvard Business Review*, May-June, p. 68

70   Turits, M. (2022) https://www.bbc.com/worklife/article/20220628-the-six-big-things-weve-learned-about-hybrid-work-so-far/ p. 3/5

71   Ibid (Turits, 2022) p. 4/5

72   Ibid (Turits, 2022) p. 4/5

73   Gratton, L. (2021) How to Do Hybrid Right. *Harvard Business Review*, May-June, p. 74

74   Leong, L., & Ross, M. (2022) *This Working Life*. Melbourne: Hardie Grant Books. p. 179

75   The Editors (2020) The New Work/Life Balance. *Harvard Business Review*, Special Issue, Winter, p. 2

76   Friedman, S. D. (2020) Be a Better Leader, Have a Richer Life. *Harvard Business Review*, Special Issue, Winter, p. 67

77   Leong, L., & Ross, M. (2022) *This Working Life*. Melbourne: Hardie Grant Books. p. 179

78   Leong, L., & Ross, M. (2022) *This Working Life*. Melbourne: Hardie Grant Books. p. 181

79   Newport, C. (2016) *Deep Work*. Great Britain: Piatkus. (Title of Book)

80   Newport, C. (2016) Deep Work. Great Britain: Piatkus. p. 3

81   Csikszentmihalyi, M. (2002) *Flow*. London: Rider, An imprint of The Random House group.

82   Ibid (Newport, 2016) p. 85

83   Fried, J. & Hansson, D., H. (2013) *REMOTE: Office Not Required*. UK: Vermilion, an imprint of Ebury Publishing. p. 8

84   Ibid (Fried, & Hansson, 2013) pp. 7-8

85   Zorn, J., & Marz, L. (2022) *Golden. The Power of Silence in a World of Noise*. Ebury Edge, an imprint of Ebury Publishing. p. 11

86   Ibid (Zorn & Marz 2022) p. 18

87   Zorn, J., & Marz, L. (2017) The Busier You Are, the More You Need Quiet Time. Store. hbr.org/product/the-busier-you-are-the-more-you-need-quiet-time/HO3JEH (Harvard Business Review March 17, p. 1)

88   Ibid (Zorn & Marz 2022) p. 7

89   Ibid (Zorn & Marz 2022) p. 31

90   Hari, J. (2022) *Stolen Focus: Why you can't pay attention*. London: Bloomsbury Publishing. p. 2

91   Ibid (Hari 2022) p. 7

92   Ibid (Hari 2022) pp. 10-11

93   Ibid (Hari 2022) p. 57

94   Ibid (Hari 2022) p. 51

95   Ibid (Hari 2022) p. 58

96   Ibid (Hari 2022) p. 51

97   Rutherford, D. (2008) Measuring the New Zealand Knowledge Economy. *Labour: Employment and Work in New Zealand*, p. 394

98   Ibid (Rutherford 2008) p. 394

99   Coyle, D., & Quah, D. (2002) *Getting the Measure of the New Economy*. London: The Work Foundation, p. 8

100   Ell, S. (2017) Seeking the knowledge workers. https://nzherald.co.nz/business/seeking-the-knowledge-workers/XRZVMC26N3S16IT7XKEWINT1DM/ p. 2/4

101   Ibid (Ell 2017) p. 2/4

102   Ibid (Ell 2017) p. 3/4

103   Ibid (Ell 2017) p. 3/4

104   Katsoudas, F., & Patel, J. (2022) Hybrid Workplace – Powered By Choice. *Harvard Business Review: HBR's latest thinking on the future of business.* Boston: Massachusetts: Harvard Business Review Press, p. xii

105   Gephart, R. P. (2002) Introduction to the Brave New Workplace: Organizational Behavior in the Electronic Age. *Journal of Organizational Behavior* 23, Special Issue. p. 335

106   Kropp, B. (2021) The New World of Work: your organization must adapt-there is no going back. *Harvard Business Review: HBR's latest thinking on the future of business.* Boston: Massachusetts: Harvard Business Review Press, p. xii

107   Katsoudas, F., & Patel, J. (2022) Hybrid Workplace – Powered by Choice. H*arvard Business Review: HBR's latest thinking on the future of business.* Boston, Massachusetts: Harvard Business Review Press, p. xiii

108   Gratton, L. (2021) How To Do Hybrid Right. *Harvard Business Review*, May-June, p. 74

109   Cotter-Martin, T. (2022) The Future of Work Requires New Mindsets. *NZ Business+Management*, August, p. 13

110   Hillman, H. (2021) *EM-PA-THY: The Human Side of Leadership.* Auckland: Bateman Books, pp. 4-5

111   Jacob, K., Unerman, S., & Edwards, M. (2022) *belonging: The Key to Transforming and Maintaining Diversity, Inclusion and Equality at Work.* London: Bloomsbury Business, pp xiii, xx, xxii

112   Morgan, K. (2021) Remote work is working. So, why do we need a physical space? https://www.bbc.com/worklife/article/20210806-the-case-against-hybrid-work/ pp. 13/18-14/18.

113   Fayard, A-L., Weeks, J., & Khan, M. (2021) Designing the Hybrid Office: From workplace to culture space. *Harvard Business Review*, March-April, p. 117

114   Bell, M. (2022) Modern offices need 'fewer hot desks, more work lounges, in-house café space.' https://www.stuff.co.nz/business/propert/129572321/modern-offices-need-fewer-hot-desks-more-work-lounges-inhouse-cafe-space/ p. 1/14

115   Fayard, A-L., Weeks, J., & Khan, M. (2021) Designing the Hybrid Office: From workplace to culture space. *Harvard Business Review*, March-April, p. 118

116   Ibid (Fayard, Weeks & Khan 2021) p. 120

117   Morgan, K. (2021) Remote work is working. So, why do we need a physical space? https://www.bbc.com/worklife/article/20210806-the-case-against-hybrid-work/ p. 14/18

118   Ibid (Fayard, Weeks & Khan 2021) p. 121

119   Ibid (Fayard, Weeks & Khan 2021) p. 119

120   Kane, C., & Anastassiou, E. (2023) *WHERE IS MY OFFICE? Reimagining the Workplace for the 21st Century.* London: Bloomsbury Business, pp. 7; 105, 128

121   Topsfield, J. (2020) Has the future of the office changed forever. https//:www.smh.com.au/national/the-pandemic-has-fueled-irreversable-growth-in-our-working-lives-20201009-p56314.html/ p. 2/7

122   Valintine, F. (2022) *Future You.* Auckland: HarperCollins Publishers (New Zealand) Ltd, pp. 141-142

123   Ansell, M. (2016) Jobs for life are a thing of the past. Bring on lifelong learning. https://www.thegardian.com/higher-education-network/2016/may/31/jobs-for-life-are-a-thing-of-the-past-bring-on-lifelong-learning/ p. 3/4

124   Selingo, J. J., & Simon, K. (2017) The Future of Your Career Depends on Lifelong Learning. https://www.forbes.com/sites/schoolboard/2017/10/09/the-future-of-your-career-depends-on-lifelong-learning/#1eab447c1bd7 pp. 3/5-4/5

125   Gratton, L. (2014) *The Shift: The Future of Work is Already Here.* London: William Collins, An imprint of HarperCollins Publishers, pp. 200; 198

126   Schwartz, J. with Riss, (2021) *Work Disrupted: Opportunity, Resilience, and Growth in the Accelerated Future of Work.* Hoboken, New Jersey, John Wiley & Sons Inc, pp. 159-160

127   Sloman, M. (2015) *The Changing World of The Trainer: Emerging Good Practice.* Abington, Oxon, Routledge p. 7

128   https://www.careers.govt.nz/courses/find-out-about-study-and-training-options/micro-credentials/#cID_7385 p. 1/4

129   Blazevic, O. (2020) https://www.candlefox.com/blog/a-comprehensive-guide-to-micro-credentials-in-nz/ p. 3/6

130   Selingo, J. J., & Simon, K. (2017) The Future of Your Career Depends on Lifelong Learning. https://www.forbes.com/sites/school-board/2017/10/09/the-future-of-your-career-depends-on-lifelong-learning/#1eab447c1bd7 p. 3/5

131   Ibid (Selingo & Simon 2017) p. 4/5

132   Kivunja, C. (2015) Teaching Students to learn and to Work Well with 21st Century Skills: Unpacking the Career and Life Skills Domain of the New Learning Paradigm. *International Journal of Higher Education,* 4 (1), pp. 3; 5; 7-9

133   Leong, L., & Ross, M. (2022) *This Working Life,* Melbourne: Hardie Grant Books, An imprint of Hardie Grant Publishing. p. 280

134   Cribb, J. (2019) Parents, quit playing the NCEA game. *The Dominion Post,* Thursday, January 31st p. 17

135   Ibid (Leong & Ross 2022) p. 51

136   Maitland, A., & Thomson, P. (2011) *Future Work: How Businesses Can Adapt and Thrive in the New World of Work.* Basingstoke: Palgrave MacMillan pp. 152-153

137   Ibid (Leong & Ross 2022) pp. 52; 62

138   Peek, S. (2021) Communication Technology and Inclusion Will Shape the Future of Remote Work. https://businessnewsdaily.com/8156-future-of-remote-work.ntml pp. 1/8-2/8

139   Ibid (Peek 2021) p. 3/8

140   Ibid (Peek 2021) pp. 3/8-5/8

141   Marr, B. (2021) The 5 Biggest Technology Trends in 2022. https://www.forbes.com/sites/bernardmarr/2021/09/27/the-5-biggest-technology-trends-in-2022/?sh=320e2a9b2414 pp. 1/8-2/8

142   Ibid (Marr, 2021) pp. 2/8-3/8;5/8-6/8

143   https://www.vistaequitypartners.com/insights/an-introduction-to-immersive-technologies/ p. 1/12

144   Haas, M. (2022) Women Face a Double Disadvantage in the Hybrid Workplace. Harvard Business Review March 24 https://hbr.org/2022/03/women-face-a-double-disadvantage-in-the-hybrid-workplace/ p. 5

145   https://www.bbc.com/worklife/article/20210804-hybrid-work-how-proximity-bias-can-lead-to-favourism/ p. 5/13

146   Ibid (Haas 2022) p. 5

147   Ibid (Haas 2022) p. 5

148   Hall, R. (2022) Hybrid working may hold back women's careers, say managers. https://www.theguardian.com/society/2022/sep/25/hybrid-working-may-hold-back-womens-careers-say-managers/ p. 2/5

149   Ibid (Haas 2022) p. 1

150   Ibid (Haas 2022) p. 2

151   Ibid (Hass 2022) pp. 3-5

152   Wardecki, A. (2022) Hybrid working and the proximity bias: what does it mean for women? https://globalwomen.org.nz/news/with-bias-for-women/ pp. 1/6-2/6

153   Ibid (Wardecki (2022) pp. 3/-4/6

154   Turits, M. (2021) The 6 biggest lessons about work from 2021. https://www.bbc.com/article/20211209/the-biggest-lessons-about-work-from-2021/ p. 6/7

155   Katsoudas, F., & Patel, J. (2022) Hybrid Workplace – Powered by Choice. *Harvard Business Review: HBR's latest thinking on the future of business.* Boston: Massachusetts, Harvard Business Review Press, p. xvi

156   Ibid (Katsoudas & Patel 2022) p. xvi

157   Ibid (Katsoudas & Patel 2022) p. xiii

158   Anon (2022) Hybrid Workplace. *Harvard Business Review: HBR's latest thinking on the future of business.* Boston: Massachusetts, Harvard Business Review Press – cited from the book's back cover.

159   Katsoudas, F., & Patel, J. (2022) Hybrid Work – Powered by Choice. *Harvard Business Review: HBR's latest thinking on the future of business.* Boston: Massachusetts, Harvard Business Review Press, p. xiii

160   Roy, A. (2020) The pandemic is a portal https://www.ft.com/content/10d8f5e8-74eb-11ea-95e-fcd274e920ca pp.12/13-13/13. Also see: Roy A. (2022) *AZADI: Fascism, Fiction and Freedom in the Time of the Virus.* Penguin Random House UK, (Chapter 9 The Pandemic is a Portal p. 203)

161   Rashbrooke, M. A portal into opportunity missed? *The Press,* Saturday, October 8, p. B1

162   Hall, R. (2022) Hybrid working may hold back women's careers, say managers. https://theguardian.com/society/2022/sep/25/hybrid-working-may-hold-back-womens-careers-say-managers/ p. 3/5

163   Burrell, M. (2021) The future of work is already here. *The Dominion Post,* Tuesday, January 12, p. 21

164   Fuller, P. (2022) Small city businesses face strong headwinds. *The Dominion Post,* Wednesday September 21st p. 2

165   Government rolls out mental and wellbeing tools to small businesses across New Zealand. https://www.beehive.govt.nz/release/govt-rolls-out-mental-health-and-wellbeing-tools-small-businesses-across-new-zealand/ p. 1/3

166   Hunt, T., & Williams, K. (2020) We're in 'a pile of pain.' *The Dominion Post,,* Monday, 23, p. 1

167   Manson, B. (2022) Hospo workers on the front line. *The Dominion Post,,* Saturday, August 6, p A9

168   Lai., Y-L., & Cai, W. (2022) Enhancing post-COVID-19 work resilience in hospitality: A micro-level crisis management framework. *Tourism and Hospitality Research* 0(0) p. 1

169   Owens, D. (2022) Tourism Trap. *The New Zealand Listener,* May 7-13, p. 20

170   Cropp, A. (2022) Job vacancies attract little interest. *The Dominion Post,* August, Friday 12th p. 11

171   Hubbard, C. (2022) 'Discerning travellers' sought, not those on shoestring, says Minister https://www.stuff.co.nz/travel/129537172/discerning-travellers-sought-not-those-on-shoestring-says-minister/ p. 1/5

172   Schwartz, J., with Riss, S. (2021) *Work Disrupted: Opportunity, Resilience, and Growth in the Accelerated Future of Work.* Hoboken, New Jersey, John Wiley & Sons, p. xix

173 Roy, A. (2020) https://www.ft.com/content/10d8f5e8-74eb11ea95fe-fcd274e920ca/ p. 13/13

174 Katsoudas, F., & Patel, J. (2022) Hybrid Workplace – Powered by Choice. *Harvard Business Review: HBR's latest thinking on the future of Business.* Boston: Massachusetts, Harvard Business Review Press, p. xv

175 Morgan, J. (2014) *The Future of Work.* Hoboken, New Jersey, John Wiley & Sons, p. xiv

Chapter 4: Our working lives and the four-day working week

1 Barnes, A., with Jones, S (2020) *The 4-day week: How the flexible revolution can increase productivity, profitability and well-being, and create a sustainable future.* London: Piatkus, p. 187

2 Baruch, Y., & Hind, P. (1999) Perpetual Motion in Organizations: Effective Management and the impact of the New Psychological Contracts on "Survivor Syndrome" *European Journal of work and organizational Psychology,* 8;2, 295-306.

3 Guardian Weekly, (2021). Global Report: *Government agrees to trial of four-day working week.* 19 March p. 4

4 Smith, D. (2022). 'This is not a crazy idea any more': Are we on the precipice of a four-day working week revolution? https://stuff.co.nz/business/130351527/this-is-not-a-crazy-idea-any-more-are-we-on-the-precipice-of-a-fourday-working-week-revolution/

5 Inman, P. (2021). 'We see huge benefits': firms adopt four-day week in Covid crisis. https://theguardian.com/business/2021/jan/05/four-day-week-covid-crisis/ p. 1/5-4/5

6 Marra, M. (2019). Economics of a four-day working week: research shows it can save businesses money. https://theconversation.com/economics-of-a-four-day-working-week-research-shows-it-can-save-businesses-money-126701/

7 Applied Economist (2020). How do you switch to a four-day week? October 6th. https://applied.economist.com/articles/four-day-week/ pp. 1/7-7/7

8 Barnes, A., with Jones, S. (2020). *The 4-day week: How the flexible work revolution can increase productivity, profitability and well-being, and create a sustainable future.* London: Piatkus, pp. 23; 17

9 Ibid (Barnes 2020) p. 4

10 Ibid (Barnes 2022) p. 1/2

11 https://www.rnz.co.nz/national/programmes/sunday/audio/2018806342/four-day-working-week-plan-picking-up-steam/ p. 1/3 (Interview with Charlotte Lockhart)

12 https://www.rnz.co.nz/news/national/475870/making-the-four-day-week-youve-got-to-move-to-the-future/ p.1/4 (Reporter Rayssa Almeida 2020)

13 Smith, D. (2022) Businesses trial four day working week but expert says employees should go even further. https://www.stuff.co.nz/business/129430957/businesses-trial-four-day-working-week-but-expert-says-employees-should-go-even-further/ p. 1/9

14 Dockrill, P. (2022) Huge 4-day work week experiment begins in the UK: The largest ever conducted. https://www.sciencealert.com/huge-4-day-work-week-experiment-begins-in-the-UK-the-largest-ever-conducted/ p. 1/3

15 Anon: CTU calls for mass pilot four-day work week. *The Dominion Post,* Wednesday, 28, 2022. p. 3

16 Ibid (Barnes, 2020) p. 69

17 Ibid (Barnes, 2020) p. 160

18 Ibid (Barnes, 2020) p. 161

19 Ibid (Barnes, 2020) p. 162

20   Ibid (Barnes, 2020) p. 2

21   Christian, A. (2022). The realities of the four-day workweek. https://www.bbc.com/worklife/article/20220322/-the-realities-of-the-four-day-work-week/ p. 2/5

22   Lufkin, B., & Mudditt, J. (2021). The case for a shorter workweek. https://www.bbc.com/worklife/article/20210819/the-case-for-a-shorter-workweek/ p. 3/5

23   Barnes, A., with Jones, S. (2020). *The 4 Day Week: How the flexible work revolution can increase productivity, profitability and well-being, and create a sustainable future.* London: Piatkus p. 101

24   Ibid (Barnes 2020) p. 190

25   Ibid (Lufkin & Mudditt) 2021, pp. 2/5-3/5

26   Ibid (Lufkin & Mudditt) 2021, pp. 1/5-2/5

27   Ibid (Lufkin & Mudditt) p. 3/5

28   Ibid (Lufkin & Mudditt) 2021 pp. 3/5-4/5

29   Ibid (Barnes, 2020) p. 187

30   Smith, D. (2022). Four-day work week anyone? *The Dominion Post*, December 24, p. B7

31   Christian, A. (2023) Four-day work week trail: The firms where it didn't work https://www.bbc.com/worklife/article/20230319/four-day-work-week-trial-the-firms-where-it-didnt-work/ pp. 1/5-4/5

32   Barnes, A., with Jones, S. (2020) *The 4 Day Week: How the flexible Work Revolution Can increase productivity, profitability and Well-Being, and create a Sustainable Future.* Britain: Piatkus, p. 190

33   Ibid (Barnes) p. 24

34   Ibid (Barnes) pp. 161-162; 193

35   Hope, K. (2024) Business leaders aligning on the big issues. *The Post*, Tuesday, February p. 13

36   Spoonley, P. (2023) cited in Hunt, T. 'A little less colourful.' *The Post*, Saturday, May 13, A10.

37   Susskind, R., & Susskind, D. (2022) *The Future Of The Professions.* Oxford: Oxford University Press. pp. xlvi, lii & xlix, and backcover.

38   Maitland, A., & Thomson, P. (2011) *Future Work: How Businesses Can Adapt and Thrive in the New World of Work* Basingstoke: Palgrave MacMillan, pp. 149; 152

39   Schwartz, with Riss, S. (2021) *Work Disrupted: Opportunity. Resilience, and Growth in the accelerated Future of Work,* Hoboken, New Jersey: John Wiley & Sons, p. 19

40   Spicer, A. (2024) Career ladders may be broken, but a fulfilling job is still within reach. *The Guardian Weekly,* 5 April, p. 17

41   Ibid (Maitland & Thomson) p. 149

42   Valentine, F. ((2022) *Future You.* HarperCollins Publishers (New Zealand) Ltd. p. 141

43   Revenson, T. A., & DeLongis, A. (2011) Couples coping with chronic stress. IN S. Folkman (ed) *The Oxford Handbook of Stress, Health and Coping,* p. 105

44   Hillman, H. (2021) *Em-Pa-Thy: The Human side of Leadership.* Auckland: Bateman Books. pp. 172-173

45   Hobsbawm, J. (2022) *The Nowhere Office: Reinventing Work and the Workplace of the Future.* London; Basic Books, p. 15

46   Suzman, J. (2020) *WORK: A History of How We Spend Our Time.* London: Bloomsbury Circus, p. 407

47   Graeber, D. (2019) *Bullsh*t Jobs: The rise of pointless work and what we can do about it.* UK: Penguin Random House, p. xvi

48   Ibid (Graeber, 2019) p. 196

49   Coats, D., & Lekhi, R. (2008) *'Good Work': Job Quality in a changing economy*. London: The Work Foundation p. 13

50   Ibid (Graeber, 2019) p. 202

51   Ibid (Graeber, (2019) p. 195

52   Ibid (Suzman, 2020) p. 410

53   Ibid (Graeber, 2019) p. 205

54   Brown, A., Charlwood, C., Forde, C., & Spencer, D. (2006) *Changing job quality in Great Britain 1998-2004*. Employment Relations Research Series No 70. London DTI.

55   Maslach, C., Leiter, M. P. (2022) Work Changed Forever: People realized their jobs don't have to be that way. *Scientific American*, 326, March pp. 60-61

56   Spoonley, P. (2023) cited in Hunt, T. 'A little less colourful.' *The Post*, Saturday, May 13th p. A10

57   Ibid (Suzman, 2020) p. 388

58   Ibid (Maslach & Leiter, 2022) p. 61

59   Ibid (Maslach & Leiter, 2022) p. 60

60   https://www.rnz.co.nz/national/programmes/sunday/2018806342/four-day-working-week-plan-picking-up-steam/ (interview with Charlotte Lockhart) pp. 1/3, 2/3, 3/3

61   Barnes, A. with Jones, S. (2020) *The 4-day week: How the Flexible Work Revolution can increase Productivity, Profitability and Well-Being and a Sustainable Future.* London: Piatkus, pp. 187;190

62   Anon (2022) 100- The number of companies now signed up for a permanent ...' *The Guardian Weekly*, 2nd December, p. 9

63   Gratton, L. (2022) *Redesigning Work: How to Transform Your Organization & Make Hybrid Work for Everyone.* UK: Penguin Random House, pp. 13-14

Chapter 5 : The pandemic and other society consequences

1   Anthony, A. (2021) Cities Under Siege. *New Zealand Listener*, February 6-12, p. 16

2   Hill, A., & Hill, D. (2021) *Work from Anywhere.* Melbourne: John Wiley & Sons Australia, Ltd p. xii

3   Evenden, I. (2022) Future Cities: Green, Friendly and Clean: How We Could Reimagine Urban Life After the Pandemic, *BBC Science Focus*, August, p. 63

4   McDonough, W. (2021) How Cities Could Save Us. *Scientific American*, Special Issue, 30, 4, p. 108. **See also**- (2017) McDonough, W. 'Positive Cities' Can Improve Earth as Well as People's Lives https://www.scientificamerican.com/article/positive-cities-can-improve-earth-as-well-asppeoples-lives/ pp. 1/10-10/10

5   Ibid (McDonough, 2021) pp. 108-109; 110-111

6   Manns, J. (2022) Sustainable cities and transport to match. *The Dominion Post*, Saturday, July 2nd p. A8. **See also**- Manns, J. (2024) We need to have better conversations about our cities https://thespinoff.co.nz/wellington/11-03-2024/we-need-to-have-better-conversations-about-our-cities/ pp. 1/11-11/11

7   Evenden, I (2022) Future Cities: Create 15-minute Cities. *BBC Science Focus*, August, pp. 63; 64-65

8   Strang, B. (2022) Why Wellington's transit plans are heading south. *The Dominion Post*, Thursday, June 30th pp. 2-3

9   Evenden, I. (2022) Reimagine the High Street. *BBC Science Focus*, August, p. 68

10   Gourley, E. (2022) S30m Fund for active transport. *The Dominion Post*, Wednesday, September 7th p. 3

11   Evenden, I. (2022) Rewild the City. *BBC Science Focus*, August pp. 66-67

12   Yanes, J. (2022) https://bbvoopenmind.com/en/science/enviroment/green-spaces-sustainable-cities-heathier/ pp. 2/5-3/5

13   Armoudian, M., & Boarin, P. (2024) We need to radically transform our cities for sustainability. *Sunday Star-Times*, February 18, p. 14

14   Haskel, J., & Westlake, S. (2022) *Restarting the Future: How to Fix the Intangible Economy.* Princeton and Oxford: Princeton University Press, p. 22

15   Raworth, K. (2018) *Doughnut Economics: Seven Ways to Think Like a 21st -Century Economist.* London: Random House Business Books, p. 53

16   Ibid (Raworth 2018) p. 31

17   Zorn, J., & Beachy, B. (2021) https://hbr.org/2021/02/a-better-way-to-measure-gdp/ p. 3

18   Suzman, J (2020) *WORK: A History of How We Spend Our Time.* London: Bloomsbury Circus, p. 412

19   Anon (2024) FREE EXCHANGE: Discoveries from the recovery. *The Economist*, January, 20, p. 63

20   Ibid (Suzman 2020) p. 402

21   Henderson, R. (2021) *Reimagining Capitalism: In A World On Fire.* Dublin: Penguin Random House UK: p. 19

22   Carney, M. (2022) *Values: An Economist's Guide to Everything that Matters.* London: William Collins Books. p. 184

23   Inman, P., & Bartholomew, J. (2023) Are young people poised to put the brakes on endless Growth? *The Observer*, December 3, p. 52

24   Ibid (Raworth, 2018) pp. 42-43

25   Ibid (Raworth, 2018) p. 60

26   Zorn, J., & Beachy, B. (2021) A Better way to Measure GDP. https://hbr.org/2021/02/a-better-way-to-measure-gdp/ p. 2

27   Ibid (Zorn & Beachy, 2021) p. 2

28   Ibid (Zorn & Beachy, 2021) pp. 3-4

29   Ibid (Zorn & Beachy, 2021) p. 5

30   Carney, M. (2022) *Values: An Economist's Guide to Everything That Matters.* London: William Collins Books, p. 298

31   Ibid (Carney, 2022) p. xii

32   Dasgupta, Sir P. (2021) *The Economics of Biodiversity: The Dasgupta Review.* (London: HM Treasury) p. 5

33   Elliott, l. (2021) We need to value our natural resources more than we do GDP. *The Guardian Weekly*, February, pp. 28-49

34   Stiglitz, J. E., Sen, A., & Fitoussi, J-P. (2009) Report by the Commission on the Measurement of Economic Performance and Social Progress. p. 21

35   Ibid (Stiglitz et al., 2009) p. 7; 23

36   Dalziel, P., & Saunders, C. (2019) *Wellbeing Economics: Future Directions for New Zealand.* Wellington: BWB, see back cover.

37   Ibid (Dalziel & Saunders, 2019) pp. 40-41

38   Ibid (Dalziel & Saunders, 2019) p. 114

39   Ibid (Dalziel & Saunders, 2019) see back cover

40   Ryan, G. J. (2022) *Comparonomics: Why life is better than you think, and how to make it better*. Oxford: Big Idea Publishing Company. pp. 30-31

41   Ibid (Ryan, 2022) p. 225

42   Ibid (Ryan, 2022) pp. 99-100

43   Ibid (Ryan, 2022) pp. 87-92

44   Ibid (Ryan, 2022) p. 121

45   Malpass, L. (2024) Labour lynchpin's mixed legacy. *The Post*, Wednesday, February 21, p. 1

46   Zorn, J., & Beachy, B. (2021) A Better Way to Measure GDP. https://hbr.org/2021/a-better-way-to-measure-gdp/ p. 3

47   Stiglitz, J. E. (2020) https://scientificamerican.com/article/gdp-is-the-wrong-tool-for-measuring-what-matters/ p. 1

48   Ibid (Stiglitz, 2020) p. 3

49   Ibid (Stiglitz, 2020) pp. 9; 11

50   Grant, A. (2021) *Think Again: The Power of Knowing What you Don't Know*. London: WH Allen. pp. 9;12

51   Hill, A., & Hill, D. (2021) *Work from Everywhere*. Melbourne: John Wiley & Sons Australia Ltd, p. xii

52   Henderson, R. (2021) *Reimagining Capitalism in a World on Fire*. Dublin: Penguin Random House UK, p. xii

53   Ibid (Henderson, 2021) p. 4

54   Ibid (Henderson, 2021) pp. 6; 10-11

55   Myers, D. G. (2007) Costs and Benefits of American corporate capitalism. *Psychological Inquiry* 18, pp. 43-47

56   Stears, M., & Parker, I. (2021) *Responsible Capitalism and Behavioural Change*. Institute for Public Policy Research, London, pp. 5, 7-8

57   Stiglitz, J. E. (2019) Age of upheaval. *New Zealand Listener*, 2026 July, p. 15

58   Gilligan, G. (2022) Inclusive Capitalism – Genuinely Liberation or just a Placatory Siege Response? https://clmr.unsw.edu.au/article/market-conduct-regulation/inclusive-capitalism-genuinely-liberating-or-just-a-placatory-siege-response%3F/ p. 2/4

59   Ibid (Gilligan, 2022) p. 4/4

60   Ibid (Gilligan, 2022) p. 2/4

61   Ibid (Gilligan, 2022) pp. 2/4-3/4

62   Ibid (Gilligan, 2022) p. 4/4

63   Stiglitz, J. E. (2022) Inequality Got Much Worse. *Scientific American* 326, March p. 52.

64   Ibid (Henderson, (2021) p. 12

65   Gostin, L. O. (2022) Global Health Institutions Reached Their Limits. *Scientific American* 326, March, p. 46

66   Ibid (Henderson, 2021) p. 11

67   Ibid (Henderson, 2021) p. 27

68   Ibid (Henderson, 2021) p. xiii

69   Stiglitz, J, E., Sen, A., & Fitoussi, J-P. (2019) *Report by the Commission on the Measurement of Economic Performance and Social Progress*. p. 18

70   Susskind, D. (2024) *Growth: A Reckoning*. Allen Lane, UK: an imprint of Penguin Books. p. 271

Chapter 6: Coping in a challenging and changing world

1 Snyder, C. R., & Pulvers, K. M. (2001) Dr. Seuss, the Coping Machine, and "Oh the Places You'll Go" In C. R. Snyder, (ed.) *Coping with stress: Effective people and processes,* Oxford: Oxford University Press, p. 4

2 Snyder, C. R., & Dinoff, B. L. (1999) Coping: Where have you been? In C. R. Snyder (ed.) *Coping: The psychology of what works,* Oxford: Oxford University Press, p. 5

3 Aldwin, C. M. (2009) *Coping and Development: An integrative perspective.* (2nd ed.) New York: The Guilford Press p. 86

4 Folkman, S., & Moskowitz, J. T. (2004) Coping: Pitfalls and Promise. *Annual Review of Psychology* 55, p. 747

5 Aldwin, C., M. (2009) *Coping, and Development: An Integrative Perspective.* (2nd Edition) New York: The Guilford Press, p. 182

6 Ibid (Aldwin) p. 193

7 Lazarus, R. S. (1993) Coping, theory and research: Past, present and future. *Psychosomatic Medicine,* 55, p. 237

8 Lazarus, R. S. & Folkman, S. (1991) The concept of coping. In A. Monet & R.S. Lazarus (eds.) *Stress and coping: An anthology* (3rd Ed) pp. 198, 199, 201

9 Aldwin, C., M. (2009) *Coping and Development: An Integrative Perspective.* (2nd Edition) New York: The Guilford Press, p. 86

10 Lazarus, R., S. (2000) Toward better research on stress and coping. *American Psychologist* 55, p. 670

11 Lazarus, R., S. (1993) Coping theory and research. Past, present and future. *Psychosomatic Medicine* 55, p. 244

12 Smith, G. (2019) *The Book of Knowing.* New Zealand: Allen & Unwin, p. 38

13 Folkman, S., & Lazarus, Coping and emotion. IN A. Monat & R. S. Lazarus (eds) *Stress and Coping: An Anthology* (3rd Eds.) p. 210

14 Aldwin, C. M. (2009) *Stress, Coping, and Development: An Integrative Perspective.* (2nd Ed.) New York: The Guilford Press. p. 32

15 Ibid (Alwin 2009) p. 32

16 Ibid (Alwin 2009) p. 33

17 Gordon, J. (2021) 4 strategies for coping with pandemic stress https://magazine. medlineplus.gov/article/4-strategies-for-coping-with-pandemic-stress/ pp. 1/8-2/8

18 Magellan Healthcare (2021) https://usf.edu.documents/benefits/magellan/tips-pandemic-coping-adults-covid-19-pdf p. 1

19 Suttie, J. (2020) Five Lessons to Remember When Lockdown Ends https://greatergood. berkeley.edu/article/item/five-lessons-to-remember-when-lockdown-ends/ pp.1/7-6/7.

20 Moyer, M., W. (2021) Coping with Pandemic Stress. *Scientific American,* Special Edition, Spring, pp. 37-39

21 Southwick, S. M., & Charney, D. S. (2021) Ready for Anything. *Scientific American,* Special Edition, Spring, pp. 94; 99, 100 and 103

22 Taylor, S. (2021) The Coronavirus and Post-Traumatic Growth. *Scientific American,* Special Edition, Spring, pp 109; 111

23 Denworth, L. (2021) The Biggest Psychological Experiment: What Can The Pandemic teach Us About How People Respond To Adversity. *Scientific American,* Special Edition, Spring, pp. 42; 44

24 Ibid (Denworth, 2021) p. 45

25   Revenson, T. A., & DeLongis, A. (2011) Couples Coping with Chronic Illness. In S. Folkman (ed) *The Oxford Handbook of Stress, Health, and Coping*. Oxford: Oxford University Press, p. 105

26   Denworth, L. (2021) The Biggest Psychological Experiment: What Can the Pandemic Teach Us About How People Respond to Adversity? *Scientific American*, Spring, p. 45

27   Folkman, S., & Moskowitz, J. T. (2004) Coping: Pitfalls and Promise. *Annual Review of Psychology* 55, pp. 759-758

28   Ibid (Folkman & Moskowitz 2004) p. 759

29   Ibid (Folkman & Moskowitz 2004) p. 766

30   Ibid (Folkman & Moskowitz 2004) p. 767

31   Southwick, S. M., & Charney, D., S. (2021) Ready for Anything. *Scientific American*, Special Edition, Spring, p. 99

32   Walker, P. (2021) *The Miracle Pill: Why a sedentary world is getting it all wrong*. London: Simon & Schuster UK Ltd, pp. 6; 205; 275-276

33   Wilson, M. (2022) Active benefits: Physical exercise not only keeps our bodies in shape, it helps protect brains, too. *The New Zealand Listener*, October 8, p. 45

34   Lazarus, N. (2020) *The Lazarus Strategy: How to Age Well and Wisely*. London: Yellow Kite: An Imprint of Hodder & Stoughton, p. 10

35   Southwick, S., M. & Charney, D., S. (2021) Ready for Anything. *Scientific American*, Special Edition, Spring, pp. 100-101

36   Jabr, F. (2021) Head Strong. *Scientific American*, Special Edition, Spring, p. 71

37   Lineen, J. (2022) The Healing Power of Walking. *The Dominion Post*, Life, January 19, p. 11

38   Shivas, O. (2022) The Whole Truth: You don't need to walk 10,000 steps a day https://pacificmedianetwork.com/articles/the-whole-truth-you-dont-need-to-walk-10000-steps-a-day/ pp. 2/4-3/4

39   Berry, S. (2021) everyone is hooked on the idea but 10,000 steps a day is not the ideal. https://www.smh.com/lifestyle/health-and-wellness/everyone-is-hooked-on-the-idea-but-10-000-steps-a-day-is-not-the-ideal/ p. 1/4

40   Ibid (Berry 2021) p. 4/4

41   Halicioglu, T. (2021) Everyone is Hooked On the Idea But 10,000 Steps A Day Is Not The Ideal https://techilive.in/everyone-is-hooked-on-the-idea-but-10000-steps-a-day-is-not-the-ideal/ p. 3/44

42   Lazarus, N. (2020) *The Lazarus Strategy: How to Age Well and Wisely*. London: Yellow Kite: An imprint of Hodder & Stoughton, pp. 25-26

43   Ibid (Halicioglu 2021) pp. 2/4; 3/4

44   Geddes, L. (2023) Walking just 4,000 steps a day can cut the risk of dying from any cause, analysis finds. https://www.theguardian.com/society/2023/aug/09/revealed-walking-just-4000-steps-a-day-can-reduce-risk-of-dying/ pp. 1-4/6

45   Anon. Walking 10,000 steps a day really can make us healthier. *New Scientist*, 261, No 3482, 16 March 2024, p. 13

46   Blum, D. (2023) Stressed About Your Step Count? Even 4,000 Can Have Big Health Benefits. https://www.nytimes.com/2023/08/09/well/move/steps-walking-health-benefits.html/ pp. 1-2/2

47   Ibid (Geddes 2023) p. 4/6

48   https://www.1news.co.nz/2023/08/10/10/just-4000-steps-per-day-can-lower-your-risk-of-death-study/ p. 3/10

49   Hall, A. (2024) Commentary-Upfront: One Step at a time. *New Zealand Listener,* February 3, p. 4

50   Lu, D. (2023) Prescribed time in nature linked to improvements in anxiety, depression and blood pressure. https://www.theguardian.com/environment/2023/april/04/prescribed-time-in-nature-linked-to-improvements-in-anxiety-depression-and-blood-pressure/ p. 1/5

51   Lu, D. (2023) Prescribing nature: the restorative power of a simple dose of outdoors. https://www.theguardian.com/environment/2023/feb/12/prescribing-nature-the-restorative-power-of-a-simple-dose-of-outdoors/ pp. 1/7-3/7

52   Denworth, L. (2024) Greenery Improves Body and Mind. *Scientific American,* May, pp. 76-77

53   Cox, D. (2024) A better pill to swallow. *The Guardian Weekly,* 5 January, pp. 30-31

54   Gross, T. (2021) Just Move: Scientist Author Debunks Myths About Exercise And Sleep https://www.wbur.org/npr/959140732/just-move-scientist-author-debunks-myths-about-exercise-and-sleep/ p. 2/9

55   Lazarus, N. (2020) *The Lazarus Strategy: How to Age Well and Wisely.* London: Yellow Kite: An Imprint of Hodder & Stoughton, p. 11

56   Nimmo, K. (2022) Get your mind MATCH-Fit. *The Dominion Post,* May 25, p. 11

57   McCallum, H. (2024) Knight and bay. *The Post,* Saturday February 17, (front page)

58   Bezzant, N. (2024) The rest is history: Rest – both sleep and non-sleep – is essential to help our overstressed bodies and minds repair themselves. But many of us remain in a constant state of 'fight, flight or freeze. *The New Zealand Listener* May 4, p. 16

59   Macpherson, G. with Kohler, A. (2024) *Age Less: The new science of slower and healthier ageing.* Auckland: An Upstart Press Book, pp. 234; 238; 180-181

60   Marshall, M. (2024) How much Exercise is Too Much? *New Scientist,* 27 July, p. 34

61   Wade, G. (2024) What Is The Quickest Way To Get Fit? *New Scientist,* 27July, p. 34

62   Ibid (Macpherson 2024) pp. 215; 234

63   Newport, C. (2019) *Digital Minimalism: Choosing a Focused Life in a Noisy World.* Penguin Random House UK, pp. 94-95, 98-99, 109, 120-122

64   Ibid (Newport, 2019) pp. 125-126

65   Anon (2024) Write down thoughts and shred them to relieve anger. *The Guardian Weekly* 19 April, p. 9

66   Taylor, S. (2021) The Coronavirus and Post-Traumatic Growth. *Scientific American,* Special Edition, Spring, p. 111

67   Denworth, L. (2021) The Biggest Psychological Experiment: What Can the Pandemic Teach us About How People Respond to Adversity? *Scientific American,* Special Edition, Spring, p 45

68   Nelson, R., G. (2022) A Microbe Proved That Individualism Is a Myth. *Scientific American,* March, p 29

69   Robson, D. (2024) Better connected. New Scientist, June 1, pp. 40, 42,43

70   Clear, J. (2018) *Atomic Habits: Tiny changes, Remarkable Results, An Easy & Proven Way to build Good Habits & Break Bad Ones.* London: Penguin Random House UK, p. 38, 41, 54, 47-49,62, 65, 111

71   Watson, D. (2023) Up & atom: forget the grand New Year's resolutions. Making little changes that go the distance is how to achieve big. *The New Zealander Listener,* January 3, p. 18

72   Clear, J. (2018) *Atomic Habits: Tiny Changes, Remarkable results, An Easy & Proven Way to Build Good Habits & break Bad Ones.* London: Penguin Random House UK, p. 10

73   Bezzant, N. (2024) The rest is history, *The New Zealand Listener*, May 4th, p. 16

74   Hammond, C. (2020) *The Art of Rest: How to find respite in the modern age*. Edinburgh: Canongate Books Ltd pp. 1; 2; 4; 5; 6

75   Drew, L. (2023) Relax to the max. *New Scientist*, 259, 3454, 2nd September, citing Professor Hamond, p. 33

76   Ibid (Drew, 2023) citing Professor Hammond, p. 33

77   Ibid (Drew, 2023) citing Professor Hammond, p. 32

78   Ibid (Drew, 2023) p. 33

79   Ibid (Drew, 2023) p. 33, also citing Professor Hammond, p. 34

80   Ibid (Drew, 2023) citing Professor Hammond p. 33

81   Ibid (Drew, 2023) citing Professor Hammond p. 33

82   Ibid (Hammond, 2020) p. 100

83   Ibid (Drew, 2023) citing Professor Hammond p. 33

84   Ibid (Hammond, 2020) p. 249

85   Waytz, A. (2023) Beware a culture of busyness. *Harvard Business Review*, March-April, pp. 60;62

86   Lyubykh, Z., & Gulseren, D. B. (2023) How to Take Better Breaks at Work, According to Research. *Harvard Business Review*, May 31st p. 3/10

87   Schwartz, T., & McCarthy, C. (2010) *Manage Your Energy Not Your Time. HBR'S 10 Must Reads On Managing Yourself.* Boston, Massachusetts: Harvard Business Review Press, p. 61-62

88   Ibid (Schwartz & McCarthy, 2010) p. 62

89   Drew, L. (2023) Relax to the max. *New Scientist*, 2nd September, p. 34

90   Loving Life (2023) Microbreaks at work and their impact on employee wellbeing. https://lovinglifeco.com/ p. 3

91   Watson, R. (2018) *Digital Versus Human: how we live, love, and think in the future*. London: Scribe Publications, pp. 1-3

92   Newport, C. (2024) *Slow Productivity: The lost Art of Accomplishment Without Burnout*. UK: Penguin Random House UK, p. 7

93   Newport, C. (2023) An Exhausting year in (And Out Of) The Office. The New Yorker, December 27th, https://www.newyorker.com/an-exhausting-year-in-and-out-of-the-office/

94   Ballesteros, C. (2024) Why We're More Exhausted Than Ever. https://time.com/6694092/exhaustion-increasing-causes-essay/ p. 3/11

95   Arthur, A. (2024) The Other Energy Crisis. *New Scientist*, 20th April, p. 23

96   Ibid (Ballesteros, (2024) pp. 7/11-8/11

97   Ibid (Bezzant 2024) p. 16

98   Anon https://socialscience.international/keynes-possibilities/

99   Feldman, D. (2022) Hope. *Psychology Today*, March/April, p. 52

100 Schwartz, J., with Riss, S. (2021) *Work Disrupted: Opportunity, Resilience, and Growth in the Accelerated Future of Work*. Hoboken, New Jersey: John Wiley & Sons Inc, pp. 7; xix

101 Leong, L., & Ross, M. (2022) *This Working Life: How to Navigate Your Career in Uncertain Times*. Melbourne/London: Hardie Grant Books, pp. 279, 280, 288

102 Mangia, K. (2020) *Working from Home: Making the New Normal Work for You*. Hoboken, New Jersey: John Wiley & Sons Inc, pp. 6-7

103   Gratton, L. (2014) *The Shift: The Future of Work is Already Here*. London: William Collins Publishers, p. 197

104   Snyder, C. R. (1999) *The Psychology of What Works*. New York, Oxford: Oxford University Press, p. 5

105   Snyder, C. R., & Pulvers, K.M. (2001) Dr Seuss, the Coping Machine, and "Oh the Places You'll Go." IN Snyder, C.R. (Ed) *Coping with Stress: Effective People and Processes*, New York, Oxford University Press, pp. 5;4

106   Denworth, L. (2021) The Biggest Psychological Experiment: What can the pandemic teach us about How people respond to adversity? *Scientific American*, Special Edition, Spring, p. 44

107   Gawrylewski, A. (2021) The Pursuit of Resilience. *Scientific American*, Special Edition, Spring, p. 1

108   Schwartz, J., with Riss, S. (2021) *Work Disrupted: Opportunity, Resilience, and Growth in the Accelerated Future of Work*. Hoboken, New Jersey: John Wiley & Sons Inc, p. xix

109   Feldman, D. (2022) Hope. *Psychology Today*, March/April, p. 52

110   Matthews, P. (2021) National Portrait: Rod Carr, climate tsar. https://www.stuff.co.nz/environment/climate-news/124292382/national-portrait-rod-carr-climate-tsar p. 5/8

111   Dewe, P. (2023) Coping in the New World: The Challenges of the 'New Normal' of Work and Life. IN Kinder, A., Hughs, R., and Cooper, C. (Eds) (2023) *Occupational Health and Wellbeing: Challenges and Opportunities in theory and Practice*. London: Routledge (Taylor & Francis Group) p. 177

Chapter 7: The pandemic and climate change

1   Carney, M. (2022) *Values: An Economist's Guide to Everything That Matters*. London: William Collins Books, p. 228

2   Grayling, A. C. (2022) *For the Good of the World: Is Global Agreement on Global Challenges Possible?* London: A Oneworld Book, p. 13

3   Ibid (Grayling 2022) p. 187

4   Douglas, K. (Ed.) (2022) Human Society: How evolution and psychology shaped our world. *New Scientist Essential Guide No 14*. England, p. 81

5   Thunberg, G. (2022) Thunberg urges overthrow of 'oppressive' system. *The Press*, Friday, November 4th p. 17

6   Flannery, T. (2020) *The Climate Cure: Solving the Climate Emergency in the Era of COVID-19*. Melbourne: Text Publishing, p. 6

7   Thunberg, G. (created by) (2022) *The Climate Book*, UK: Allen Lane an imprint of Penguin Books, pp. 1-3

8   Ibid (Flannery, 2020) pp. 6;16

9   Mann, M. E. (2022) *The New Climate War: the fight to take back our planet*. Melbourne, London: Scribe Publications, pp. 238-239

10   Wallace-Wells, D. (2022) Lessons from the pandemic. In G. Thunberg (created by) *The Climate Book*, UK: Allen Lane an imprint of Penguin Books, p. 382

11   Ibid (Grayling 2022). p. 34

12   Ibid (Flannery, 2020) p. 18

13   Watts, J. (2020) Delay is deadly: what Covid-19 tells us about tackling the climate crisis. https://www.theguardian.com/commentisfree/2020/mar/24/covid-19-climate-crisis-governments-coronavirus/ p. 1/6

14   Ibid (Thunberg, G, 2022) p. 49

15   Heeringa, S. (2023) This is climate change, here's what we can do about it. https://www.stuff.co.nz/enviroment/climate-news/131243406/this-climate-change-heres-what-we-can-do-about-it/ p. 4/16

16   Matthews, P. (2021) National Portrait: Rod Carr, climate tsar. https://www.stuff.co.nz/environment/climate-news/124292382/national-portrait-rod-carr-climate-tsar/ p. 5/8

17   Nelson, R. G. (2022) A Microbe Proved That Individualism is a Myth. *Scientific American*, 326, 3, March, p. 29

18   Editorial (2020) Into the void. *New Zealand Listener*, April 4th p. 3

19   Ibid (Thunberg, 2022) pp. 43; 48

20   Carney, M. (2022) *Values: An Economist's Guide to Everything That Matters.* London: William Collins Books, p. 230

21   Mann, M. E. (2022) *The New Climate War: the fight to take back our planet.* Melbourne – London: Scribe Publications, pp. 227; 246

22   Carney, M (2022) *Values: An Economist's Guide to Everything That Matters.* London: William Collins Books. p. 226

23   Mann, M.E. (2022) *The New Climate War: the fight to take back our planet.* Melbourne, London: Scribe Publications, p. 6. **Also see:** Grayling, A. C. (2022) *For the Good of the World: Is Global Agreement on global Challenges?* London: A Oneworld Book pp. 27-28

24   Cox Wright, F. (2023) Seat at climate table no longer optional. *The Post*, Wednesday, August 30, p. 20

25   Armah,M.(2023)https://www.stuff.co.nz/environment.climate-news/131346562/school-strike-4-climate-school-students-get-ready-again-over-climate-change/ pp. 1/8-2/8

26   Grayling, A. C. (2022) *For the Good of the World: Is Global Agreement on Global Challenges Possible?* London: A Oneworld Book, p. 3

27   Ibid (Grayling 2022). p. 10

28   Montano, S. (2022) We Didn't Get Serious about the Climate Crisis. *Scientific American*, 326. March, p. 47

29   Ibid (Thunberg, 2020) p. 157

30   Ibid (Mann, 2022) p. 239

31   Flannery, T. (2020) *The Climate Cure: Solving the Climate Emergency in the Era of COVID-19.* Melbourne, Australia: Text Publishing, p. 2

32   Grayling, A. C. (2022) *For the Good of the World: Is Global Agreement on Global Challenges Possible?* London: A Oneworld Book, pp. 188; 189; 196-199

33   Carney, M. (2022) *Values: An Economist's Guide to Everything That Matters.* London: William Collins Books, pp. 262-263

34   Flannery, T. (2020) *The Climate Cure: Solving the Climate Emergency in the Era of COVID-19.* Melbourne: Text Publishing Company, pp. 12-14

35   Mann, M. E. (2022) *The New Climate War: the fight to take back our planet.* Melbourne, London: Scribe Publications, p. 6

36   Grayling, A. C. (2022) *For the Good of the World: Is Global Agreement on Global Challenges Possible?* London: A Oneworld Book, p. 28 – (citing Mann's final theme 'the solution lies in policy.')

37   Gates, B. (2022) *How to avoid a climate disaster: The Solutions We Have and The Breakthroughs We Need.* UK-USA: Penguin Random House UK, pp. 194; 199; 203; 217

38   Hunt, T. (2023) 'A little less colourful.' *The Post*, Saturday, May 13, p. A10

39 Quill, A. (2023) Summer of cyclones? High sea surface temperatures put NZ on red alert. *The Dominion Post*, Tuesday, January 10th p. 2-3

40 Wannan, O. (2023) 2022 was the hottest year. *The Dominion Post*, Thursday, January 12th p. 1

41 Carney, M. (2022) *Values: An Economist's Guide to Everything That Matters*. London: William Collins Books, p. 5

42 Malpass, L. (2022). Acid test on how much the climate matters. *The Dominion Post*, Saturday, May 14th p. B5

43 Ibid (Malpass 2022) p. B5

44 Hendy, J. (2022) https://www.climate.commission.govt.nz/news/new-zealands-first-emissions-reduction-plan-a-critical-turning-point/ pp. 1/6-2/6

45 Malpass, L. (2022) Reshaping economy, society to drive down carbon emissions *The Dominion Post*, Monday 16th May, pp. 1-2; 3

46 Carroll, M. (2022) Business calls for bold action. *The Dominion Post*, Tuesday, May 17th p. 13

47 Malpass, L. (2022). Ambitious plan light on details. *The Dominion Post*, Tuesday, May 17th p. 9

48 Wannan, O. (2022) Climate activists unimpressed. *The Dominion Post*, Tuesday, May 17th pp. 1-2

49 Ibid (Malpass 2022) p. 9

50 Wannan, O. (20220 Agri emissions: What farmers won and lost in the Government's plan. https://www.stuff.co.nz/enviroment/climate-news/130832361/agri-emissions-what-farmers-won-and-lost-in-the-governments-plan/ p. 1/7

51 Hendy, J. (2022) New Zealand's First Emissions Reduction Plan a Critical turning Point. https://www.climatecommission.govt.nz/news/new-zealand-first-emissions-reduction-plan-a-critical-turning-point/ p. 1/6

52 Anon (2022) COP27 falls short of goal. *The Dominion Post* Monday, November 21, 2022, p. 18

53 Wannan, O. (2022) Climate Goals for COP27. *The Dominion Post* Thursday, November 3rd, p. 18

54 Government welcomes High Court ruling on climate case. https://www.beehive.govt.nz/release/government-welcomes-high-court-ruling-climate-case/ p. 1/3

55 Casey, M. (2022) COP15: Nations reach a historic deal to halt biodiversity loss by 2030. https://www.stuff.co.nz/environment/climate-news/300770056/cop15-nations-reach-a-historic-deal-to-halt-biodiversity-loss-by-2030#:-text-cop1.../ p. 1/7

56 New Zealand to support new global biodiversity targets at COP15. https://www.beehive.govt.nz/release/new-zealand-support-new-global-biodiversity-targets-cop15/ p. 1/3

57 Carrington, D. (2023) 'Devastating': scientists respond to Cop28 failure on fossil fuel phase-out. *The Guardian*, Thursday 14 December 2023, p. 4

58 Carrington, D., & Stockton, B. (2023) 'No science' to phasing out fossil fuels, says Cop leader. *The Guardian*, Monday 4 December, 2023, p. 1

59 Morton, A., Greenfield, P., & Harvey, F. (2023) Landmark Cop28 deal reached to 'transition away' from fossil fuels. *The Guardian*, Thursday 14 December 2023, pp. 1; 4

60 Harvey, F., Greenfield, P. & Lakhani, N. (2023) Climate draft condemned as 'weak' and 'insufficient' *The Guardian*, Tuesday 12 December 2023, pp. 1-2

61 Harvey, F., Lakhani, N. Mason, R. (2023) Deal agreed at Cop28 to help poor countries cope with climate crisis. *The Guardian*, Friday 1 December 2023, pp. 1; 6

62   Harvey, F. Deal to revive hope of 1.5C target 'within reach' at Cop28. *The Guardian*, Wednesday 29 November 2023, p. 2

63   Anon (2023) Global temperature rise reaches 1.5C average. *The Post*, Friday, February 9, p. 14

64   McCulloch, M. (2024) Quips & Quotes. *The NZ Listener*, Vol 289, No 4336, February 17, 2024, p. 8

65   Harvey, F. (2023) Inequality and class are at the heart of the climate crisis, says Piketty. *The Guardian*, Thursday 23 November, 2023, p. 26

66   Mann, M., E. (2022) *The New Climate War: the fight to take back our planet*. Melbourne-London: Scribe Publications, p. 253

67   Grayling, A. C. (2022) *For the Good of the World*. London: A Oneworld Book, p. 44

68   Ibid (Mann 2022) p. 270

69   Carney, M. (2022) *Values: An Economist's Guide to Everything That Matters*. London: William Collins Books, pp. 240; 265

70   Whyte, A. (2023) Devastation may move action on climate change. *The Dominion Post*, Wednesday February 15, p. 14

71   Thomas, B. (2023) Adaption no longer climate's poor cousin. *The Dominion Post* Thursday, March 2nd p. 17

72   McConnell, (2023) Inquiry ordered into slash in wake of storm. *The Dominion Post* Friday February 24, p. 5

73   Pullar-Strecker, T. (2023) Orr calls for 'be ready' approach to resilience. *The Dominion Post*, Thursday, February 23, p. 3

74   Whyte, A. (2023) Shaw pushes for climate alliance. *The Dominion Post*, Wednesday February 1, p. 12

75   Crossen, T. (2023) Our planners' climate failure. *The Dominion Post* Thursday February 16, p. 14

76   Kenny, K. (2023) Cracking the code of catastrophic floods. *The Dominion Post* Monday, February 27, p. 14

77   Tokalau, T. (2023) Second-wettest summer in NI. *The Dominion Post*, Saturday, March 4th p. A2

78   Wannan, O. (2023) How climate change is powering cyclones like Hale. https://www.stuff.co.nz/envronment/climate-news/300805788/how-climate-change-is-powering-cyclones-like hale/ p. 1/6

79   Johnston, K. (2023) Does Cyclone Gabrielle have you thinking about climate change? You're not the only one. https://www.stuff.co.nz/environment/climate-news/300805788/does-cyclone-gabrielle-have-you-thinking-climate-change-youre-not-the-only-ones.../ p. 1/8

80   Macdonald, N. (2024) 'Devastated but not defeated' The Post, Saturday February 10, p. 1

81   Barwick, H. (2024) A summer of Hope. *New Zealand Listener*, January 13th p. 4

82   Smith, R. (2024) How to make disaster recovery less painful. *The Post*, Friday, February 16th p. 15

83   Ibid (Smith, 2024) p. 15

84   Jacobson, J. (2024) Forgetting: Recipe for disaster. *The Post*, Wednesday, February, 7, pp. 1-3

85   Tookey, J. (2024) A year on and big cyclone questions linger. *The Post*, Thursday, February 8, p. 18

86   Ibid (Johnston,2023) p. 1/8

87   Wannan, O. (2023) Climate change partly caused Gabrielle, scientists conclude. *The Dominion Post*, Wednesday, March 15, p. 5

88   Ibid (Johnston,2023) p. 2/8

89   Ibid (Johnston, 2023) p. 2/8

90   Thompson, A. (2022) Global Warming Causes Fewer Tropical Cyclone. *Scientific American*, June 27, pp. 1-2

91   Witton, (2023) Warning of even more climate disruption. *The Dominion Post,* Saturday, March 18, p. A5

92   Anon (2023) Sea levels will stay high for millennia: scientists. *The Dominion Post,* Monday, March 20, p. 15

93   Haywood, B. (2023) IPCC: Critical time in climate change. *The Dominion Post,* Wednesday, March 22, pp. 6-7

94   Anon (2023) Emergency ends. *The Dominion Post*, Tuesday, March 14, p. 3

95   Shaw, J. (Hon) First ever climate adaption plan lays foundations for resilient communities. https://www.beehive.govt.nz/release/first-ever-climate-adaption-plan-lays-foundations-resilent-communities. pp. 1/3-2/3

96   Vance, A. (2023) Two words that could turn lives upside down. *The Dominion Post*, Saturday, March 18, p. B1

97   Robertson, G. (Hon) & Mcanulty, K. (Hon) New legislation to streamline Cyclone recovery. https://www.beehive.govt.nz/release/new-legislation-streamline-cyclone-recovery/ pp. 1/3

98   Robertson, G. (Hon) & Wood, M. (Hon) (2023) Government delivers further cyclone emergency support. https://www.beehive.govt.nz/release/government-delivers-further-cyclone-emergency-support/ p. 1/3

99   Anon (2023) Covid spike adds to woes. *The Dominion Post,* Thursday, March 1, p. 5

100   Thomas, R. (2023) Region 'still vulnerable.' *The Dominion Post*, Wednesday, March 1, p. 5

101   Lyons, R. F., Mickelson, K.D., Sullivan, M., Coyne, J. C. (1998) Coping as a Communal Process. *Journal of Social and Personal Relationships*, 15 (5), p. 579

102   Redstall, S. (2023) Local communities partner with relief effort. *The Dominion Post,* Tuesday, February 21, p. 8

103   Whyte, A. (2023) https://www.stuff.co.nz/national/politics/131272630/cyclone-gabrielle-pm-warns-tough-calls-to-come-as-resilience-tested-like-never-before/ pp. 1/23-2/23

104   Schwanecke, G. (2023) One man, an inflatable boat, and several rescues. *The Dominion Post*, Saturday 25th p. A8

105   Thomas, R. (2023) The last to be rescued. *The Dominion Post*, Monday, February 27, p. 1

106   Godfery, M. (2023) Marae are an integral part of our civil defence infrastructure. https://www.stuff.co.nz/131440655/morgan-godfrey-marae-are-an-integral-part-of-our-civil-defence-infrastructure/ pp. 1/7-5/7

107   Lyons, R.F., Mickelson, K.D., Sullivan, M., Coyne, C. C. (1998) Coping as a Communal Process. *Journal of Social and Personal Relationships*. 15 (5) pp. 579, 580,582,587,588-585

108   Taylor, S. (2021) The Coronavirus and Post-Traumatic Growth. *Scientific American*, Special Edition, Spring, p. 111

109   Gawrylewski, A. (2021) The Pursuit of Resilience. *Scientific American*, Special Edition, Spring, p. 1

110   Southwick, S. M., & Charney, D.S. (2021) Ready for anything. *Scientific American*, Special Edition, Spring, pp. 94;99-100; 102-103

111   Thomas, R. (2023) The last to be rescued. *The Dominion Post*, Monday, February 27, p. 1

112   Hunt, T. (2023) 'A little less colourful:' Climate change and the world we are handing to today's toddlers. *The Post*, Saturday, May 13, p. A10

113   Stock, R (2023) IAG begins insurer 'retreat' from flood-prone homes. *The Post*, Wednesday, September 20, p. 18

114   Wannan, O. (2023) A WET YEAR or a new reality? *The Post* Thursday, May 11, p. 24

115   Gurunathan, K. (2023) Is it time to give up on the false hope? *The Post*, Monday, July 24, p. 14

116   Jones, T. (2023) *Canvas, The NZ Herald*, Saturday, September 30, p. 6

117   Renwick, J. (2023) *Under the Weather: A Future Forecast for New Zealand*. New Zealand: HarperCollins Publishers, pp. 96-97

118   Noll, B. (2023) (cited in) *The NZ Listener*, 287, 4316, September 23-29, p. 8

119   Ibid (Noll, 2023) p. 8

120   Anon (2023) 2023 on track to be the hottest year on record. *The Post*, Thursday, August 10, p. 22

121   Anon (2023) Heatwaves 'impossible without climate change.' *The Post*, Wednesday, July 26, p. 26

122   Quill, A. (2023) NZ's hottest ever summer could be ahead – with fire, drought and sharks. https://www.stuff.co.nz/national/weather-news/300975921/nzs-hottest-ever-summer-could-be-ahead-with-fire-drought-and-shars#/ pp. 1-7/13

123   Blundell, S. (2023) Keep out! *The NZ Listener* 287, 4312, August 26-September 1, pp. 16-21

124   Tocci, N. (2023) After real progress on climate, Europe now faces a 'greenlash.' *The Guardian Weekly*, 209, 3, July 21, p. 17

125   Whyte, A. (2023) Leading the way amid crisis. *The Dominion Post* Thursday, March 23, p. 3

126   Ibid (Whyte) p. 3

127   McLauchlan, D. (2023) Blowin' in the wind. *The NZ Listener*, February 11, p. 15

128   Gravis, I (2023) Slip, Sliding Away. *The NZ Listener*, May 13, p. 3

129   Wannan, O. (2023) Slash and burn. *The Dominion Post* Tuesday, March 7, p. 18

130   Wannan, 0. (2023) Your future resilient home. *The Forever Project*. March, Issue 13, pp. 10-12

131   Uys, G. (2023) First methane inhibitor, but no application. *The Post*, Tuesday, August 15, p. 20

132   Wannan O. (2023) Pill dramatically reduces cattle's planet-heating burps, says start-up. https://www.stuff.co.nz/environment/climate-news/130932496/pill-dramatically-reduces-cattle's-planet-heating-burps-says-start-up/ p. 3/11

133   Nelson, D. (2021) Feeding Cattle Seaweed Reduces Their Greenhouse Gas Emissions 82 Percent.https://caes.ucdavis.edu/news/feeding-cattle-seaweed-reduces-their-greenhouse-gas-emissions-82-percent#/

134   Cuff, M. (2024) Vaccine could cut cow burp impact. *New Scientist*, 10 August, p. 16

135   Uys, G. (2023) What do farmers want from politicians? *The Post*, Tuesday, August 8 p. 24

136   Griffin, P. (2022) An eye in the sky to detect methane emissions. https://www.rnz.co.nz/national/programmes/ourchangingworld/audio/2018870892/an-eye-in-the-sky-to-detect-methane-emissions/ pp. 1/7; 3/7-5/7

137   Meduna, V. (2024) Track and Trace: New Zealand is a perfect natural laboratory to test the capability of a satellite designed to track methane emissions. *The New Zealand Listener*, March 23, p. 90

138   Cuff, M. (2024) Can machines that suck atmospheric carbon truly help tackle climate change? *New Scientist*, 25 May, p. 12

139   Gates, B. (2022) *How to avoid a climate disaster: The Solutions We Have and The Breakthroughs We Need*. UK-USA: Penguin Random House UK, p. 217

140   Pullar-Strecker, T. (2024) Call for 'climate technology roadmap.' *The Post*, Friday April 12, p. 10

141   Wannan, 0. (2023) Electricity is the cleanest it's been since records began https://www.stuff.co.nz/environment/climate-news/131459073/electricity-is-the-cleanest-its-been-since-records-began pp. 2/5; 4/5

142   Anon. 'Hug pylons, not trees.' *The Economist*, April 8th-14th, 2023, p. 7

143   Ghebreyesus, A., T. (2022) Health and Climate. IN G. Thunberg (created by) *The Climate Book*, UK: Allen Lane an imprint of Penguin Books p. 135

144   Anon (2023) Record rain helps New Zealand emissions fall – but the path to net zero won't be so simple. https://www.theguardian.com/world/2023/aug/05/record-rain-helps-new-zealand-emissions-fall-but-the-path-to-net-zero-wont-be-so-simple#/ p. 3/9

145   Gibson, E. (2022) Think carefully about connecting to natural gas, warns climate boss. *The Dominion Post*, Tuesday 17, May, p. 10

146   https://www.beehive.govt.nz/release/government-refers-solar-energy-projects-fast-track-consenting/ p. 1/3

147   https://www.beehive.govt.nz/release/nearly-two-million-solar-panels-fast-tracked

148   https://www.mysolarquotes.co.nz/about-solar-power/commercial/solar-power-farms/ p. 1/2

149   Rowe, M. (2023) Solar is the future, but growing workforce integral to its success. *The Post*, December 23, p. A10

150   McCarthy, (2023) Edgecumbe farmers say solar farm a waste of elite soil. https://www.nzherald.co.nz/the-country/news/edgecumbe-farmers-say-solar-farm-a-waste-of-elite-soil/ p. 2/4

151   Ibid (Rowe 2023) p. A10

152   Pullar-Strecker, T. (2024) Billions need to be invested in electricity by 2050, MPs told. *The Post*, Friday, February 9, p. 8

153   https://www.windenergy.org.nz/operating-&-under-construction/ p. 1/3

154   https://www.windenergy.org.nz/wind-energy/nz-onshore-wind-farms/ p. 1/3

155   https://www.windenergy.org.nz/20-of-nz-generation-by-2030/ p. 1/2

156   https://www.eeca.govt.nz/insights/energy-role-in-climate-change/the-future-of-energy-in-new-zealand/ p. 1/10

157   https://www.mbie.govt.nz/building-and-energy-and-natural-resources/energy-generation-and-markets/offshore-renewable-energy/ p. 2/3

158   https://www.ea.govt.nz/news/eye-on-electricity/wind-power-sets-new-records/ p. 4/6

159   Steyl, L. (2024) Reliance on radiata is a risk: Forestry expert https://www.co.nz/rural/350193324/reliance-radiata-risk-forestry-expert/ pp. 1/8;6/8

160   Le Page, M (2024) Tree-planting effects overestimated. *New Scientist* 2 March p. 10

161   https://sheffieldwire.co.uk/index.php/2024/03/04/climate-change-planting-forests-is-up-to-a-third-less-effective-at-combating-warming-than-previously-thought/ p. 4/8

162   Ibid (*New Scientist* 2024) Dr Weber, Dr Stephanie Roe and, the independent researcher cited in article. p. 10

163   https://sheffield.co.uk/index.php/2024/03/04/climate-change-planting-forests-is-up-to-a-third-less-effective-at-combating-warming-than-previously-thought/ p. 4/8

164 Cuff, M. (2024) Trees are even better for the climate than we thought. *New Scientist*, 3 August, p. 20

165 Mayron, S. (2024) Our underwater forests are key to fighting climate change, but the kelp needs our help. *Sunday News*, February 11, Sunday p. 7

166 Heeringa, S. (2023) This is climate change, here's what we can do about it. https://www.stuff.co.nz/environment/climate-news/131243406/this-is-climate-change-heres-what-we-can-do-about-it/ p. 4/16

167 Thunberg, G. (created by) (2022) *The Climate Book*, UK: Allen Lane an imprint of Penguin Books. pp. 43;48

168 Renwick, J. (2023) *Under The Weather: A Future Forecast for New Zealand*. New Zealand: HarperCollins Publishers, pp. 268-269

169 https://cdsouthland.nz/media/3a3ixtz3/media-advisory-01-state-of-emergency-declared-for-bluecliffs/ p. 1

170 https://rnz.co.nz/news/national/511174/very-stressed-bluecliffs-residents-unhappy-over-evacuation/

171 Thunberg, G. (2022) created by Greta Thunberg: *The Climate Book*, p. 73

172 Fuller, P. (2024) Dry Wairarapa close to drought. *The Post*, Wednesday March 27, p. 6

173 Corlett, E. (2023) The fast-growing invasive seaweed choking New Zealand's coastline. https://theguardian.com/world/2023/nov/23/gaulerpa-seaweed-new-zealand-invasive-threat/ pp. 1-2

174 Hoggard, A. (2024) Government boost to fight against Caulerpa. https://www.beehive.govt.nz/release/government-boost-fight-against-caulerpa/ p. 1

175 https://www.rnz.co.nz/national/morningreport/audio/20189289877/oversupply-of-units-rendering-ets-ineffective-rod-carr/ p. 1

176 Hood, C. (2024) Ministers should be accountable for policies that affect emissions. *The Post*, Friday June 28th p. 15

177 Anon (2024) Critics of climate policies say emissions targets at risk. *The Guardian Weekly*, 26 July, p. 7

178 McConnell, G. (2024) Genetic engineering 'ban' to be gone by end of 2025. *The Post*, Wednesday, August 14, p. 2

179 Anon (2024) Methane emissions rising at fastest rate in decades. *The Guardian Weekly*, 9 August, p. 9

180 Ibid (Anon, 2024) p. 9

181 Melia, N. (2024) Climate Change is fanning the flames of New Zealand's wildfire future. https://www.1news.co.nz/2024/02/25/analysis-climate-change-is-fanning-the-flames-of-nzs-wildfire-future/ pp. 2/15-4/15

182 Ibid (Melia, 2024) p5/15

183 Nixon, P., & Franks, R. (2024) https://www.nzherald.co.nz/nz/christchurch-port-hills-fire-city-under-local-state-of-emergency/ p. 5/6

184 Milne, J. (2023) Govt backing for Taranaki seabed mining, amid environment debate https://www.bing.com/search?q=newsroom-govt-backing-for-taranaki-seabed-mining-amid-environment-debate/ p. 2/5

185 McDonald, J. (2024) Seabed mining shaping up as early assault on environment laws. *The Post*, Opinion Piece, Thursday, April 4, p. 16.

186 Ibid (McDonald 2024) p. 16

187 Small, V. (2024) Blind Freddy gets a break, as Jones' focus shifts to green minerals. Opinion. *Sunday Star-Times*, May 26, p. 18

188   Vance, A. (2024) Death limit for endangered New Zealand sea lions scrapped. *The Post*, Wednesday, April 10, p. 4

189   Pullar-Strecker, T. (2024) Seven concessions the Government could make. *Sunday Star-Times*, Sunday, May 5, pp. 27;29

190   Puller-Strecker, T. (2024) Upton: Fast-Track regime would lead to 'disasters.' *The Post*, Friday, May 24, p. 13

191   Puller-Strecker, T. (2024) Seven concessions the Government could make. *Sunday Star-Times*, Sunday, May 5, p. 27

192   Anon (2024) UN issues red alert on climate change. *The Post*, Thursday, March 21, P. 19

193   Wilson, S. (2023) Our clean, green image needs help. *The New Zealand Herald*, Tuesday, October 3, p. A7

194   Flannery, T. (2020) *The Climate Cure: Solving the Climate Emergency in the Era of COVID-19*. Melbourne: The Text Publishing Company, pp. 18; 95

195   Ibid (Flannery 2020) p. 9

196   Brown, R. (2023) It never rains but it pours. *The New Zealand Listener*, October 21-27, p. 15

197   Thunberg, G. (created by) The Climate Book, UK: Allen Lane an imprint of Penguin Books p. 48

198   Ibid (Thunberg) p. 429

199   Duval, L. (2024) Nature's gains look set to be lost. *The New Zealand Listener*, March 23, p. 4

200   Cade, O. Weathering the storms: The dire consequences of climate change have become fertile ground for fiction writers. *The NZ Listener* 287, 4319, October 14-20, p. 43

Chapter 8: Conclusions and reflections

1   Malpas, L. (2022) Last political week of a rubbish three years. *The Dominion Post* Saturday, December 10, p. B5

2   https://rnz.co.nz/news/political/483045/chris-hipkins-sworn-in-as-prime-minister

3   https://stuff.co.nz/national/politics/31030608/who-is-new-deputy-prime-minister-carmel-sepuloni

4   https://en.wikipedia.org/wiki/Cyclone-Gabrielle#:-:text=Existing states of emergency in, declared on 14 February 2023/

5   https://www.rmets.org/metmatters/cyclone-gabrielle-causes-national-state-emergency-new-zealand

6   Palmer, R. (2023) https://www.rnz/news/political/503151/timeline-three-way-coalition-government-comes-togethe / p. 3/3

7   Oiley, S.(2023) 'We're out the other side': https://www.stuff.co.nz/national/health/coronavirus/300839129/were-out-the-other-side-sir-ashley-bloomfield-reflects-on-covid-three-years-on

8   Mundasad, S., & Roxby, P. (2023) https://bbc.com/news/health-65499929 pp. 1/7-2/7

9   Schwartz, J., with Riss, S. (2021) *Work Disrupted: Opportunity, Resilience, and Growth in the Accelerated Future of Work*. Hoboken: New Jersey, p. xix

10   Barnes, A., with Jones, J. (2020) *The 4 Day Week: How The Flexible Work Revolution Can Increase Productivity, Profitability and Well-Being, And Create A Sustainable Future*. Britain, Piatkus, p. 11

11   Gawrylewski, A. (2022) Truth under Attack, *Scientific American*, Fall, p. 1

12   Schwanecke, G. (2022) Combo Covid-flu vaccine trial. *The Dominion Post* Wednesday, December 21, p. 1

13   Martin, H. (2022) Only 35% of Covid infections reported, says ministry. *The Dominion Post* Friday November 18, p. 3

14   Mayron, S. (2022) Explainer: How many Covid-19 infections really out there? https://www.stuff.co.nz/national/explained/130538183/explainer-how-many-covid-19-infections-really-are-out-there

15   Macdonald, N. (2022) Should we mind the gap? *The Dominion Post* Friday November 18, p. 16

16   Daly, M. (2022) Second time around. *The Press*, Wednesday, November 9, pp. 18-19

17   Anon (2024) Long Covid linked to cognitive decline, *The Post*, Saturday, March 2, p. B6

18   https://www.beehive.govt.nz/release/new-booster-plan-time-winter pp. 1/4-2/4

19   Witton, B. (2022). Covid inquiry scope 'limited' *The Dominion Post*, Tuesday December 6, p. 1

20   Blakey. T. (2023) We need to talk about pandemics. *The Post*, Wednesday, June 28, p. 25.

21   Moore, R. (2022) Infection experts get ready to fight disease. *The Dominion Post*, Friday November 18, p. 5

22   Bak-Coleman, J., & Bergstrom, C. (2022) A High-Speed Scientific Hive Mind Emerged. *Scientific American*, 326, March, pp. 30-31

23   Glaunsinger, B. (2022) Pandemic-Era Research Paid Off – and Will for Years. *Scientific American*, 326, March, p. 71

24   Geddes, L. (2023) https://www.theguardian.com/science/2023/apr/07/covid-vaccines-golden-era-pandemic-techology-diseases

25   Anon, (2023) Brains behind Covid vaccines win praise for Nobel Prize success. *The NZ Herald*, Wednesday, October 4, pp. A20-A21

26   Sample, I. (2024) Scientists create vaccine with potential to protect against future coronaviruses. https://www.theguardian.com/society/article/2024/may/06/scientists-create-vaccine-potential-protect-against-future-coronviruses/ pp. 1/5-2/5

27   Anon (2024) Why did Covid barely touch some? *The Post*, Friday June 21, p. 16

28   Schwartz, J., with Riss, S. (2021) *Work Disrupted: Opportunity, Resilience, and Growth in the Accelerated Future of Work.* Hoboken: New Jersey, p. xix

29   Blackburn, C., C. (2022) COVID Is Here to Stay: How do we live with it? *Scientific American*, 326, March, p. 75

30   Moodie Kim (2022) Covid 19 Omicron outbreak: Extended restrictions taking toll on public sentiment – psychologist https://www.nzherald.co.nz/nz/covid-19-omicron-outbreak-extended-restrictions-taking-toll-on-public-sentiment- p psychologist p. 2/5.

31   Schwartz, J., with Riss, S. (2021) *Work Disrupted: Opportunity, Resilience, and Growth in the Accelerated Future of Work.* Hoboken: New Jersey, p. xx.

32   Barnes, A. with Jones, S. (2020) *The Four Day Week: How the Flexible Work Revolution Can Increase Productivity, Profitability and Well-Being, and create a sustainable Future.* Britain, Piatkus, p. 11.

33   Schwartz, T., with Gomes, J., & McCarthy, C. (2010) *The Way We're Working Isn't Working: The four Forgotten Needs That Energise Great Performance.* London: Simon & Schuster UK Ltd, p. xii.

34   Hobsbawm, J. (2022) *The Nowhere Office: Reinventing Work and the Workplace of the Future.* London: Basic Books, pp. x; 2-3.

35   Gratton, L. (2022) *Redesigning Work: How to Transform Your Organization & Make Hybrid Work for Everyone.* UK: Penguin Random House UK, p. 1

36   Mednick, S., C. (2022) *The Power of the Downstate: Recharge Your Life Using Your Body's Own Restorative System.* Carlsbad: California, Hay House, pp. 1; 3; 7

37   Schwartz, T., with Gomes, J., & McCarthy, C. (2010) *The Way We Are Working Isn't Working: The four Forgotten Needs That Energise Great Performance.* London: Simon & Schuster UK Ltd, pp. 3-4

38   Barnes, A. with Jones, S. (2020) *The Four Day Week: How the Flexible Work Revolution Can Increase Productivity, Profitability and Well-Being, and create a sustainable Future.* Britain, Piatkus, p. 41

39   Hobsbawm, J. (2022) *The Nowhere Office: Reinventing Work and the Workplace of the Future.* London: Basic Books, pp. ix, x, 3

40   Gratton, L. (2022) *Redesigning Work: How to Transform Your Organization & Make Hybrid Work for Everyone.* UK: Penguin Random House UK, pp. 6,7,8,10,13

41   Barnes, A. with Jones, S. (2020) *The Four Day Week: How the Flexible Work Revolution Can Increase Productivity, Profitability and Well-Being, and create a sustainable Future.* Britain, Piatkus, pp. 23, 5

42   Hobsbawm, J. (2022) *The Nowhere Office: Reinventing Work and the Workplace of the Future.* London: Basic Books, p. 7

43   Walker, R. (2021) Postcovid. *The Dominion Post* Saturday, September 18, p. A12

44   Hobsbawm, J. (2022) *The Nowhere Office: Reinventing Work and the Workplace of the Future.* London: Basic Books, p. xi, 1

45   https://newshub.co.nz/home/lifestyle/2022/6/hybrid-working-is-it-the-future-of-employment/ p. 4/5

46   Happy workers are hybrid workers – news – AUT 22 February 2022 Media contacts (https://news.aut.ac.nz/media-contacts)

47   Griffin, P. (2023) Remote possibilities. *The NZ Listener*, March 25, p. 46

48   Catherall, S. (2022) Remote control. *The NZ Listener*, December 3, p. 16

49   Barnes, A. with Jones, S. (2020) *The Four Day Week: How the Flexible Work Revolution Can Increase Productivity, Profitability and Well-Being, and create a sustainable Future.* Britain, Piatkus, p. 23

50   Hobsbawm, J. (2022) *The Nowhere Office: Reinventing Work and the Workplace of the Future.* London: Basic Books, p. 4

51   Armstrong, C. https://www.iabuk.com/news-article/christine-armstrong-moment-reset-how-we-work p. 4/8

52   Gratton, L. (2022) *Redesigning Work: How to Transform Your Organization & Make Hybrid Work for Everyone.* UK: Penguin Random House, p. 61;217; 13-14

53   Ibid (Gratton (2022) p. 10

54   Ibid (Gratton 2022) p. 10

55   Fallon, V. (2023) Beware the pandemic's newest threat. *The Post,* Thursday, August 24, p. 20

56   Macpherson, W., Tootell, B., Scott, J., & Kobayashi, K. (2022) https://theconversation.com/survey-reveals-two-thirds-of-nz-employees-want-more-life-flexibility-how-should-employers-respond-189879/ p. 2/4

57   Cooper, K., & Moricz, Z. (2023) NZ companies embrace hybrid working trends. *The Post* Tuesday, September 12, p.14 and Read, G. (2023) Kiwis embrace flexi-work-JLL survey *The Post*, Saturday, September 16, p. A16

58   Ibid (Cooper & Moricz) p. 14

59   Williams, S. (2023) NZ tech sector using the office the least as NZ embraces hybrid working. https://itbrief.co.nz/story/nz-tech-sector-using-the-office-the-least-as-nz-embraces-hybrid-working/ p. 2/3

60   Ibid (Cooper & Moricz) p. 14

61   Read, G. (2023) Kiwis embrace flex- work – JLL survey. *The Post,* Saturday, September 16, p. A16

62   Kauntze, R. (2024) *The Guardian:* Promotional Supplement Distributed on behalf of Mediaplanet, which takes sole responsibility for its contents: Future of Work: Why next-generation offices should benefit employees – and local communities.

63   Malpass, L. (2024) https://www.waikatotimes.co.nz/business/350277762/executive-appointment-why-nibs-rob-henin-bullish-about-choice/ p. 6/10

64   Mahon-Heap, J. (2023) Boss sees value in gentle start to week. *The Post,* Saturday, June 3, p. A8

65   Kinnear, C. (2023) The company offering unlimited annual leave to staff. https://www.nzherald.co.nz/business/the-company-offering-unlimited-annual-leave-to-staff/S7GU3KFDOHVE3ETU3TAR5ZJWUQ/ p. 2-3/3

66   Hobsbawm, J. (2022) *The Nowhere Office: Reinventing Work and the Workplace of the Future.* London, Basic Books. p. 15

67   Haar, J (2023) Research finds a third of NZers still working from home. https://www.rnz.co.nz/national/programmes/morningreport/audio/2018911775/research-finds-a-third-of-nzers-still-working-from-home/ p. 1/13

68   Beard, C. (2024) https://www.1news.co.nz/2024/01/18/working-from-home-can-my-boss-make-me-work-from-the-office-instead/ p. 2/13

69   https://www.1news.co.nz/2024/01/18/working-from-home-can-my-boss-make-me-work-from-the-office-instead/ pp. 1/14-5/14

70   Ibid (Hobsbawm) p. 16

71   Cooper, K., & Moricz, Z. (2023) NZ companies embrace hybrid working trends. *The Post* Tuesday, September 12, p. 14

72   Ambrose, T. (2023) SHRINKING DEMAND-The Zoom boom appears to be over. *The Guardian Weekly,* 209, 7, July 4, p. 14

73   Hobsbawm, J. (2022) *The Nowhere Office: Reinventing Work and the Workplace of the Future.* London, Basic Books. p. 18

74   Hunt, T. (2023) $8.32m cost of 23-day occupation. *The Dominion Post* Thursday, March 2, p. 10

75   Miles, D. (2023) The threat of a growing disinformation industry. *The Dominion Post* Monday, February 20, p. 16

76   Gawrylewski, A. (2022) Truth under Attack. *Scientific American,* (Special Collector's Edition) 32 (5) Fall, p. 1

77   Ibid (Gawrylewski) p. 1

78   Lewis, T. (2022) Science Journalism Shifted with New Realities. *Scientific American,* 326 (3) March, p. 34

79   Higgins, K. (2016) Post-truth: a guide for the perplexed. *Nature,* 540, p. 9

80   Cann, G. (2023) AI is 'likely to be used' in election. *The Dominion Post* Friday, March 10, p. 17

81   Manch, T. (2023) Tik Tok app-rehension. *The Dominion Post* Saturday, March 4, p. 1

82   https://www.apa.org/topics/jornalism-facts/psychology-misinformation-guide-journalists/ p. 2/4

83 Ibid (Higgins) p. 9

84 Moyer, M., W. (2022) Why we Believe Conspiracy Theories. *Scientific American* (Special Collector's Edition) 32 (5) Fall p. 93

85 Hunt, T. (2023) ChatGPT: It may be faking it. *The Dominion Post* Saturday, April 1, p. A5

86 Monbiot, G. (2024) The World according to Jason. *The Guardian Weekly*, 10 May, p. 35

87 Ibid (Moyer) p. 93

88 Ibid (apa.org) p. 2/4

89 Schwartz, J., with Riss, S. (2021) *Work Disrupted: Opportunity, Resilience, and Growth in the Accelerated Future of Work.* Hoboken: New Jersey, John Wiley & Sons, Inc. pp. xix, 7

90 Nelson, R. G. (2022) A Microbe Proved That Individualism Is a Myth: Humans evolved to be interdependent, not self-sufficient. *Scientific American,* 326 (3) March, p. 29

91 Martin, H. (2022) Bloomfield signs off with upbeat finale. *The Dominion Post,* Thursday, July 28, p. 7

92 Heeringa, S. (2023) This is climate change, here's what we can do about it. https://www.stuff.co.nz/environment/climate-news/131243406/this-is-climate-change-heres-what-we-can-do-about-it p. 4/16

93 Thunberg, G. (created by) (2022) *The Climate Book,* UK: Allen Lane an imprint of Penguin Books p. 43

94 Renwick J. (2023) *Under The weather: A future Forecast for New Zealand.* New Zealand: HarperCollins Publishers, pp. 268-269

95 Runciman, D. (2024) How Covid changed politics. *The Guardian Weekly,* 15 March, p. 36

96 https://newshub.co.nz/home/politics/2024/05/livestream-outgoing-green-mp-james-shaw-valedictory-speech.html/ p. 11/11

97 Dewe, P., & Cooper, C. (2017) *Work And Stress: A Research Overview.* London: Routledge, Taylor & Francis Group, p. 4. Embedded in this citation are other researchers mentioned and they follow this reference.

98 Ragu-Nathan, T., Tarafdar, M., & Ragu-Nathan, B. (2008). The consequences of technostress for end users in organizations: Conceptual development and empirical validation. *Information Systems Research* 19, pp. 417-433

99 Chiang, I-P., & Su, Y-H. (2012) Measuring and analysing the causes of problematic internet use. *Cyberpsychology, Behavior and Social Networking* 11, pp. 591-596

100 Griffiths, M. D. (1995) Technological Addiction. Clinical Psychology Forum 76, pp. 14-19, **AND** Griffiths, M.D. (2010) Internet abuse and internet addiction. *The Journal of Workplace Learning* 22, pp. 463-472

101 Lim, V. K. G., & Chen, D. J. Q. (2012) Cyberloafing at the workplace: Gain or drain on work. *Behaviour & Information Technology* 31, pp. 343-353

102 Baruch, Y. (2005) Bullying on the net: Adverse Behavior on e-mail and its impact. *Information & Management* 42, p. 361-371

103 Dewe, P., & Cooper, C. (2017) *Work And Stress: A Research Overview.* London: Routledge, Taylor & Francis Group p. 5

104 Gill, M. (2024) Forget connectedness-the internet makes juveniles of us all. *The Guardian Weekly,* 24 May, pp. 45-46

105 Wong, P. T. P. (2011) Positive Psychology 2.0: Towards a balanced Interactive Model of the Good Life. *Canadian Psychology,* 52 (2), p. 77 **AND** Dewe, P., & Cooper, C. (2021) *Work and Stress: A Research Overview.* London: Routledge, Taylor & Francis Group, p. 2

106 Ibid (Wong) p.77.

107   Youssef, C. M. & Luthans, F. (2007) Positive organizational behaviour in the workplace: The impact of hope, optimism, and resilience. *Journal of Management*, 33 pp. 774-800.

108   Ibid (Wong) pp. 77-78

109   Ardern, J. Rt Hon (2019) Opinion: An economics of kindness https://behive.govt.nz/ an-economics-of-kindness/ Originally published by the Financial Times: 22 January 2019. Also see Dewe, P. & Cooper, C. (2021) *Work And Stress: A research Overview.* London: Taylor & Francis Group, p. 11

110   Feehly, C. (2024) The happiness trap. *New Scientist*, 8 June, pp. 36;38

111   Nimmo, K. (2024) The Pollyanna Principle: Are You Too Happy For Your Own Good? *The Post*, Wednesday, June 19, p. 24

112   Ibid (Feehly) pp. 38-39

113   Ibid (Nimmo) p. 24

114   Harris, R., & Aisbett, B. (2013) *The Happiness Trap Pocket Book: An illustrated guide on how to stop struggling and start living.* Wollombi & Auckland: Exisle Publishing Pty Ltd, p. 10

115   Ibid (Feehly) p. 39

116   Schwartz, T., & McCarthy, C. (2007) Manage Your Energy, Not Your Time. *Harvard Business Review* https://hbr.org/2007/10/manage-your-energy-not-your-time pp. 1,2,7

117   Harari, Y. N. (2018) 21 *Lessons for the 21st Century.* London, Jonathan Cape, p. 7

118   Newport, C. (2019) *Digital Minimalism: Choosing a Focused Life in a Noisy World.* UK: Penguin Random House, p. xiv

119   Turkle, S. (2012) *Alone together: Why We Expect More from Technology and Less from Each OTHER.* USA: Basic Books, pp. (subtitle of book, pp. 17; 2)

120   Catherall, S. (2023) Not getting the message. *NZ Listener*, March 18, p. 14

121   Morgan, K. (2023) What does work-life balance mean in a changed work world? https:// www.bbc.com/worklife/article/20230227/what-does-work-life-balance-mean-in-a-changed-work-world pp. 1/5,3/5,4/5

122   Maitland, A., & Thomson, P. (2011) *Future Work: How Businesses Can Adapt and Thrive in the New World of Work.* Houndmills: Basingstoke, p 32

123   Ibid (Maitland & Thomson) p. 152

124   Hillman, H. (2021) *EM-PA-THY: The Human Side of Leadership.* Auckland: Bateman Books, p. 5

125   Turits, M. (2023) How Gen Z are disrupting the definition of 'prestigious' jobs. https:// www.bbc.com/worklife/article/20230426/gen-z-values-entrepreneurship-flexibility-jobs/ p. 3/5

126   Mulcahy, D. (2017) *The Gig Economy: Getting Better Work, Taking More Time Off, and Financing the Life You Want.* New York: AMACOM p. 2

127   Suzman, J. (2020) *Work: A History of How We Spend Our Time.* London: Bloomsbury Circus, p. 10

128   Leong, G., & Ross, M. (2022) *This Working Life: How to Navigate Your Career in Uncertain Times.* Melbourne: Hardie Grant Books, p. 52;62

129   Stolzoff, S. (2023) *The Good Enough Job: What We Gain When We Don't Put Work First.* London: Penguin Random House UK, pp. xxiv; xxiii

130   Ibid (Stolzoff) p. 205

131   Thompson, D. (2019) Workism Is Making Americans Miserable https://theatlantic.com/ ideas/archive/2019/02/religion-workism-making-americans-miserable/583441/ p. 3/13

132   Ibid (Stolzoff) p. 205

133   Ibid (Stolzoff) p. xxvi

134   Reed, K. M., & Allen, J. A. (2022) *Suddenly Hybrid: Managing the Modern Meeting*, Hoboken: New Jersey, John Wiley & Sons Inc, p. xi

135   Baker, M.G et al., (2023) Continued mitigation needed to minimise the high health burden from COVID-19 in Aotearoa New Zealand. *New Zealand Medical Journal,* 136 (1583) October 6, p. 67-72

136   Thomas, R (2023) Deaths from respiratory diseases 'not inevitable' *The Post*, Friday, October 6, p. 3

137   Morton, J. (2023) 'Treat flu like Covid': Experts want new strategy for pandemic's next phase. https://www.nzherald.co.nz/nz/treat-flu-like-covid-experts-want-new-strategy-for-pandemics-next-phase/LUP4K2H5BGVGFDWVKGDYYNGY/ p. 1/3

138   Morton, J. (2024) Tricky new Covid variant on the rise as NZ's sixth wave approaches peak. https://www.nzherald.co.nz/nz/tricky-new-covid-variant-on-the-rise-as-nzs-sixth-wave-approaches-peak/ p. 1/4

139   Matthews, P. (2021) National Portrait: Rod Carr, climate tsar. https://www.stuff.co.nz/environment/climate-news/124292382/national-portrait-rod-carr-climate-tsar p. 5/8

Index

Acknowledgements

This book allowed me to stand on the shoulders of giants whose work enabled me to lay out the debates, discussions and arguments, that followed the journey of the pandemic. I am also grateful to colleagues who read through early drafts of the chapters and my thanks go to Professor of Organizational Behaviour and Human Resource Management, Riccardo Peccei at King's College, University of London, and to Emeritus Professor of Psychology, Michael O'Driscoll at Waikato University, Hamilton, New Zealand, and to the 50th Anniversary Professor of Organizational Psychology & Health Sir Cary Cooper, CBE, Alliance Manchester Business School, University of Manchester. Their constructive comments were invaluable and allowed me to direct my attention to tightening the focus of the book. My grateful thanks go to Dave Taylor, Strategic Thinker and Story Teller at Intelligent Ink for his inciteful comments about the structure of the book which gave the story I was telling a better sense of flow, and expressed more cogently the arguments, opinions, and views that surrounded it. My grateful thanks also go to Elsa Klein, Strategic Thinker and Storyteller at Intelligent Ink who worked tirelessly to ensure the production process flowed smoothly and for her incredible support that accompanied that process. Any flaws of course are mine.

About the author

Philip Dewe is an Emeritus Professor at Birkbeck, University of London. He has written widely on work stress research and coping. He is a fellow of the Academy of Social Sciences, the European Academy of Occupational Health Psychology and Birkbeck, University of London.

www.ingramcontent.com/pod-product-compliance
Lightning Source LLC
Chambersburg PA
CBHW061156240326
R18026500001B/R180265PG41519CBX00018B/29